COVENTRY RECORDS

BIRTHS, MARRIAGES
BAPTISMS AND DEATHS

FROM THE

RECORDS OF THE TOWN AND CHURCHES

IN

COVENTRY, CONNECTICUT

1711–1844

COPIED FROM THE RECORDS

BY

SUSAN WHITNEY DIMOCK

JANAWAY PUBLISHING
Santa Maria, California

Notice

In many older books, foxing (or discoloration) occurs and, in some instances, print lightens with wear and age. Reprinted books, such as this, often duplicate these flaws, notwithstanding efforts to reduce or eliminate them. The pages of this reprint have been digitally enhanced and, where possible, the flaws eliminated in order to provide clarity of content and a pleasant reading experience.

Births, Marriages, Baptisms and Deaths From The Records Of The Town And Churches In Coventry, Connecticut, 1711-1844

Originally published:
New York
1897

Reprinted by

Janaway Publishing, Inc.
732 Kelsey Ct.
Santa Maria, California 93454
(805) 925-1038
www.janawaygenealogy.com

2015

ISBN: 978-1-59641-108-2

Made in the United States of America

TOWN OF COVENTRY, CONN.

Prior to 1675, the Indians used the land of what is now the Town of Coventry, as a hunting ground. It was annually burned over to give fresh feeding place for wild animals, thus furnishing food for the Mohegans. The land in this way was denuded of timber, so that, it is said, when the town was first settled, an ox-cart could be driven over most of the young timber lands, which had sprung up since the yearly fires of the Indians had ceased. In the early part of the year 1676—Joshua, third son of Uncas, chief of the Mohegans, made a will in which he bequeathed to Captain Joseph Fitch, of Windsor, and to fifteen others, all the tract of land which includes the present towns of South Windsor, Bolton, Vernon, Andover, Hebron, Coventry, Mansfield, Hampton, and Chaplin. This donation was approved by the General Assembly.

The legatees conveyed their rights, so far as the town of Coventry was concerned, to William Pitkin, Joseph Talcott, William Whiting, and Richard Lord, to be a committee to lay out the township and settle on the lands. This committee was appointed by the General Assembly on May 9, 1706. On October 11, 1711, this committee was reappointed, and Nathaniel Rust, who had already settled on the lands, was added to the committee, to carry into execution the designs of the former appointment.

At the same session of the General Assembly the township was named Coventry.

Nathaniel Rust and some others settled in the town about the year 1700. In the spring of 1709 there came a number of good householders from Northampton, Essex County, Mass., Hartford, Conn., Reading and Lancaster, Mass., Stonington, Killingworth, Windham, Conn., and some other towns. The region was then a pasture ground for the horses of Hartford. These horses were branded and turned loose into the wilderness to the east. The town was laid off 6 miles square, October 11, 1705. The first survey of land was made April 8, 1708, by Mr. Caleb Stanley, Colony Surveyor. The town was laid off into 78 allotments by the committee above named. The first proprietors, 15 in number, each received 5 allotments, and 3 allotments were reserved for the support of religion and schools.

The town was incorporated at the May session of the General Assembly, in 1712.

The settlement of the town is usually dated from 1709, when, as before said, there arrived quite a number of families from the towns above named. At that time there were but two towns in what is now the County of Tolland, viz., Mansfield, settled in 1703, and Hebron, settled in 1704.

The first house in the town seems to have been built by Samuel Birchard, on the south side of Wangaumbaug Lake—near the house now owned by Henry F. Dimock, formerly occupied by his father, the late Dr. Timothy Dimock. In the valley of the Hop River, near the house known as the Cyril Parker place, there was a village of savages. The religious community was for about 30 years embraced in what is known as " The first Church and Society in Coventry." This is in what is known as South Coventry. Rev. Joseph Meacham, of Enfield, commenced preaching here as early as 1713. The church was formed and he was ordained its pastor October 8, 1714.

The first settler in the Parish of North Coventry was John Bissell, who came from Lebanon, Conn., in 1716. A church was organized in the North Parish October 8, 1745, and the following day the first pastor, Nathan Strong, was ordained. The records of the first church, prior to the year 1766, have either been lost or destroyed.

No records of the Second (North Parish) Church seem to have been kept until about 1800.

It is apparent in going over all these old records, that there have been different spellings of what is evidently the same family name. I have tried to preserve, in most instances, the spelling which has been used in the records.

There are also, what seem to me to be, some mistakes of dates in the records, but I have not undertaken to correct them.

All the following records have been most carefully transcribed by me. They are now published, so that they may be preserved from the further ravages of time.

SUSAN WHITNEY DIMOCK.

South Coventry, June 14, 1897.

CONTENTS

TOWN RECORDS

	PAGE
BIRTHS—1711 TO 1840 .	1
MARRIAGES—1711 TO 1840 .	126
DEATHS—1711 TO 1844 .	172

FIRST CHURCH RECORDS

BAPTISMS—1776 TO 1844	200
DEATHS—1763 TO 1844 .	218
MARRIAGES—1763 TO 1843 .	249
PASTORS—1714 TO 1844	268

SECOND CHURCH RECORDS

DEATHS—1801 TO 1842 .	269
BAPTISMS—1819 TO 1843	281
INDEX .	289

Copy of Births Taken from Town Records, in Coventry, Conn., from 1711 to 1840.

ABBEY.

Children of Eliphilet and Lydia (Brunson) Abbey.

Eliphilet, the father,	b. East Hartford, 1792
Lydia, the mother,	b. Vernon, October 28, 1797

Children.

Amanda,	b. East Hartford, March 11, 1816
Zada,	b. March 29, 1817
Abigail,	b. Andover, February 22, 1819
Edmund,	b. February 24, 1820
Lucretia,	b. March 31, 1821
Walter,	b. May 16, 1823
Eliphilet B.,	b. June 21, 1825
George W.,	b. September 24, 1827
Albert,	b. February 27, 1830
An Infant,	b. October 25, 1831
An Infant,	b. January 15, 1832
An Infant,	b. October 24, 1835
Lydia Maria,	b. June 17, 1837

ABBOT.

Children of Rev. Abiel and Elisabeth Abbot.

Elisabeth,	b. May 22, 1798
Abigail,	b. October 17, 1799
Dorcas,	b. January 22, 1801

ADAMS.

Children of David and Sarah Adams.

Nancy H.,	b. April 7, 1806
Mary C.,	b. November 15, 1809
John H.,	b. December 5, 1812

ALEXANDER.

Children of Ebenezer and Mehitable Alexander.

Mehitable,	b. August 11, 1713
Ebenezer,	b. February 16, 1716
Anna,	b. January 7, 1718-19

ALLIN or ALLEN.

Children of Samuel and Mary Allin.

Mary,	b. January 15, 1715-16
Samuel,	b. May 19, 1717
Hannah,	b. May 3, 1719

Children of George and Naomy (Grover) Allen.

Eunes,	b. October 26, 1738
Mary,	b. December 2, 1739
Ebenezer,	b. January 23, 1745; d. same day

Children of Daniel and Azubah (Lad) Allen.

Daniel,	b. July 28, 1742
Hepsa,	b. August 15, 1744
Rachael,	b. July 21, 1746

ANDREWS and ANDRUS.

Children of Ephraim and Elizabeth Andrus.

Rachael,	b. September 13, 1744
Lydia,	b. April 20, 1746
Hannah,	b. October 19, 1747
Ephraim	b. June 7, 1750; d. same day
Elizabeth,	b. July 10, 1751
Mary,	b. August 2, 1753
Sarah,	b. November 28, 1756
Abigail,	b. January 29, 1758
Ephraim,	b. November 4, 1759
Nathan,	b. March 20, 1762
Zachariah,	b. March 14, 1764

ANDREWS.

Children of —— Andrews and Irena (Cook) Andrews.

Irena,	b. February 26, 1790

ANTISEL.

Children of Simon and Martha (Fuller) Antisel.
Thankfull, b. July 8, 1768
Leah, b. February 5, 1770

ARNOLD.

Children of John and Elisabeth Arnold.
Elisabeth, b. October 10, 1758
Hannah, b. November 6, 1759

ARMSTRONG.

Children of Benjamin and Rachael Armstrong.
Benjamin, Jr., b. June 26, 1820

ATHERTON.

Children of Simon and Mary Atherton.
Simeon, b. November 19, 1735
Peter, b. October 9, 1738
Simon, b. September 15, 1741
Mary, b. October 15, 1744
Sarah, b. September 13, 1746
Peter, b. March 19, 1749
Eunice, b. November 3, 1751
Elijah, b. August 19, 1752

Children of Elijah and Hannah (Hills) Atherton.
Silas, b. March 27, 1776
Polly, b. May 9, 1778
David, b. September 29, 1780
Zenus, b. October 5, 1785

AVERY and AVARY.

Children of Amos, Jr., and Abigail (Loomis) Avery.
Amos, b. April 30, 1783
Irena, b. February 22, 1787
Nabby, b. December 19, 1788
Polly, b. March 3, 1791
Loray, b. October 28, 1793

Hariot, b. August 3, 1797
Ephraim Kingsbury, b. December 18, 1799
Louis, b. February 22, 1802
    Children of Amos and Anne Avary.
Jabez, b. January 3, 1763

BACON

Children of Ebenezer and Betsey Bacon.

Eliza Turner, b. September 13, 1803
Marietta, b. January 17, 1806
Hannah Ugene, b. July 11, 1812
Ezbon Carter, b. July 19, 1815

BADCOCK or BABCOCK.

Children of Jams and Mary Badcock.
Elisabeth, b. July 8, 1716
Jams, b. September 27, 1719
    Children of Daniel and Sarah Badcock.
Josepha, b. August 23, 1718
Joshua, b. April 2, 1723
Sarah, b. January 24, 1725
    Children of John and Marthew Badcock.
Josiah, b. August 14, 1724
John, b. June 22, 1726
Marthew, b. May 10, 1728
    Children of Ebenezer and Mehitable (Burt) Badcock.
William, b. July 17, 1726
Dorothy, b. July 17, 1729
Robert, b. July 5, 1732
Stephen, b. May 25, 1728; d. same day
Abigail, b. February 16, 1734-5
Ebenezer, b. July 18, 1740
Daniel, b. December 30, 1742
    Children of Simeon and Abigail Badcock.
Lediah, b. October 11, 1737
Abigail, b. April 13, 1739
John, b. November 20, 1740

BIRTHS FROM TOWN RECORDS

Lidiah,	b. August 20, 1742
Hudson,	b. July 20, 1744
Ellishur,	b. July 19, 1746
Simeon,	b. February 20, 1748
Abigail,	b. June 1, 1750
Rachael,	b. March 10, 1752

Children of Benjamin and Mary (Long) Badcock.

Ebenezer,	b. January 17, 1730-31
William,	b. May 5, 1732
Sarah,	b. May 7, 1734
Hannah,	b. October 8, 1736
Mary,	b. October 19, 1737

Children of Josiah and Mary Badcock.

John,   b. August 17, 1746

Children of Hutson and Mary Badcock.

Hutson,   b. September 12, 1767

Children of Ebenezer 3d and Elanor (Knight) Babcock.

Levi,	b. February 17, 1773
Permalia	b. October 4, 1774
Elias,	b. January, 1777
Ehelenday (daughter),	b. February, 1779

Children of Amos and Mary (Williams) Badcock.

Elias,	b. August 9, 1779
Timothy,	b. February 17, 1781
Theodamy,	b. April 7, 1783
Evangely,	b. February 7, 1785

Children of John and Lydia Babcock.

Hannah,	b. June 26, 1780
Lydia,	b. March 5, 1782
Diantha,	b. April 12, 1784
John,	b. April 19, 1786
Deodat,	b. June 19, 1790
Betsey,	b. June, 1792

Children of William and Mary (Gates) Badcock.

Ebenezer,	b. May 8, 1751
Daniel,	b. July 29, 1753
Azubah,	b. June 21, 1755

COVENTRY RECORDS

Hannah,	b. April 2, 1757
Rogger,	b. June 9, 1759
Martha,	b. December 10, 1760
Jonathan,	b. Mansfield, December 8, 1762
Susannah,	b. Coventry, November 9, 1764
Molley,	b. November 16, 1766
Sibbel,	b. December 3, 1768
Jerusha,	b. March 8, 1771
Olive,	b. February 13, 1773
Caleb,	b. March 25, 1775

Children of Robert and Jedidah (Turner) Badcock.

Gideon,	b. October 13, 1754
Amos,	b. August 8, 1756
Robart,	b. August 17, 1758
Merabe,	b. June 2, 1760
Mehitabel,	b. July 5, 1762
Ruth,	b. September 11, 1764
Harmoni,	b. December 29, 1767
Abraham,	b. August 12, 1769
Eunice,	b. January 30, 1773

Children of Ebenezer 2d and Hannah (Preston) Badcock.

Beniamon,	b. January 22, 1755
Daniel,	b. October 9, 1756
Joseph,	b. March 7, 1758
Joseph,	b. November 24, 1759
Reodolphus,	b. March 3, 1761
Hannah,	b. March 3, 1763
Nathaniel,	b. March 26, 1765
Ebenezer and Mary (twins),	b. June 3, 1767
Tabothy,	b. March 13, 1770
Elisabeth,	b. April, 1772
Lydia,	b. January 27, 1774
Ester,	b. February 23, 1776

Children of Gideon and Triphene Badcock.

Asa,	b. March 19, 1787
Cyllinda,	b. March 25, 1789
Desire,	b. September 11, 1791
Diadama,	b. November 7, 1793

BIRTHS FROM TOWN RECORDS

David,	b. August 3, 1795
Elijah,	b. December 14, 1798
Lucy,	b. March 29, 1801
Leonard,	b. February 10, 1804
Sophronia,	b. September 7, 1806

Children of Amos and Mary Badcock.

Robert 3d,	b. July 25, 1787
Polly,	b. July 25, 1789
Eunice,	b. June 28, 1791

Children of David and Mary (Barrows) Badcock.

Nancy Delia,	b. November 24, 1822
Wealthy Amanda,	b. November 7, 1824
Sara Ann,	b. August 20, 1828
David Barrows,	b. January 4, 1830

Children of Elijah and Mary Badcock.

Norman Leander,	b. April 27, 1823
Charles,	b. March 13, 1826
Julia Sophronia,	b. February 10, 1828
Austania,	b. October 13, 1833

Children of Elijah and Mary Ann Badcock.

Alonso,	b. February 20, 1838
Francis Le Roy,	b. July 29, 1845

Children of Samuel and Hannah (Dow) Babcock.

Samuel, Jr.,	b. August 9, 1779
Sophia,	b. April 26, 1781

Children of Robert and Hannah (Arnold) Babcock.

Hannah,	b. October 9, 1783

Children of Elihu and Elisabeth (Preston) Babcock.

Ephraim,	b. September 3, 1763
Thripena,	b. January 24, 1764
Elisabeth,	b. December 30, 1765
Timothy,	b. August 9, 1768
Mary,	b. February 12, 1770
Anna,	b. May 4, 1772
Jehiel,	b. May 8, 1774

COVENTRY RECORDS

Children of James and Mary Babcock.

Mary Ann,	b. March 13, 1814
James Stanton,	b. November 7, 1815
Charles Joseph,	b. State of New York, March 25, 1819
Lucy Delight,	b. Coventry, October 7, 1822
Sarah E.,	b. November 11, 1824

BADGER.

Children of Enoch and Mary Badger.

Abner,	b. June 9, 1748
Mary,	b. March 9, 1752
Enoch,	b. July 5, 1750

Children of Enoch, Jr., and Mary (Lamphear) Badger.

Enoch (3rd son),	b. January 5, 1774
Polly,	b. March 20, 1776
Lydia,	b. May 8, 1778
Edmund,	b. April 30, 1780
Tirza,	b. May 12, 1782
Willard,	b. January 12, 1785
Walter,	b. January 18, 1787
Lebra (son),	b. November 3, 1788
Bela (son),	March 26, 1791
Barber (son),	b. June 24, 1793
Louisa,	b. March 27, 1796
Milton,	b. May 6, 1800

Children of Moses and Jerusha (Janes) Badger.

Ariel,	b. July 30, 1776
Timothy,	b. December 18, 1777
Daniel Waldo,	b. October 26, 1779

BALDWIN.

Children of Theophilus and Sarah (Kingsbury) Baldwin.

Irane,	b. October 8, 1746
Elamuel,	b. November 7, 1748

BARKER.

Children of Oliver and Mary (Fowler) Barker.

Alethea,	b. May 6, 1746
Oliver,	b. June 8, 1754
Phebe,	b. August 28, 1758
Eleazer,	b. May 1, 1760
Jarius (?),	b. March 2, 1762
Rhode,	b. June 8, 1764
Daniel,	b. August 29, 1765
Nathan,	b. February 17, 1768

BARNARD.

Children of Benony and Freedom Barnard.

Jasper,	b. April 10, 1713
Freedom (daughter),	b. March 8, 1715
Samuel,	b. September 14, 1718
Joseph,	b. June 11, 1720
Abigail,	b. March 16, 1725
Miriam,	b. February 23, 1726-7
Dan,	b. May 15, 1730

Children of Dan and Lydia Barnard.

Joseph,	b. April 30, 1754
Esther,	b. January 20, 1756
Abigail,	b. September 10, 1757
Dan,	b. September 15, 1759
Rufus,	b. September 12, 1761
Andrew,	b. November 28, 1763
Roger,	b. May, 1766
Lydia,	b. September, 1768
Myriam,	b. March 12, 1771
Freedom,	b. March 21, 1773

Pharoh Barnard, son of Lydia (Brown), b. December 28, 1766

BARSTOW.

Children of Jeremiah and Rebeckah Barstow.

Salome,	b. July 23, 1760
Jeremiah,	b. April 17, 1763

BELDING.
Children of Matthew and Elisabeth Belding.
Matthew,   b. July 31, 1731
John,   b. January 14, 1732-3

BELKNAP.
Children of Ralzamon and Desiah (Dimick) Belknap.
Maria Ann,   b. March 13, 1826
Emma Virginia,   b. Wilmington, Del., February 13, 1837
Roxana Bingham,   b. Coventry, December 25, 1840

BENIT or BENNIT.
Children of Thomas and Anne Benit.
Samuel,   b. September 9, 1721
Children of Christopher and Irene (Baldwin) Benit.
Christopher Baldwin,   b. August 3, 1773
Irene,   b. August 27, 1775
Orenda (son),   b. October 24, 1777
Elemuell,   b. January 6, 1780

BENTON.
Children of Jedediah and Jerusha Benton.
Selah,   b. January 23, 1739-40
Stephen,   b. February 23, 1741-2
Jerusha,   b. December 28, 1744
Martha,   b. April 29, 1747
Eben.,   b. February 19, 1750-51

BESTOR.
Children of Daniel and Dorcas (Hibbard) Bestor.
Hervey (son)   b. March 3, 1783
Orson,   b. September 18, 1784

BILL.
Children of John and Irene Bill.
Ruth,   b. February 13, 1755

BIRTHS FROM TOWN RECORDS

BISSELL.
Children of John and Sary Bissell.

Zeriah,	b. April 21, 1717
Joseph,	b. August 20, 1719
Amis (daughter),	b. September 17, 1725

BLACKMAN.
Children of Benjamon and Sarah Blackman.

Benjamin,	b. February 19, 1733-4
Semian,	b. July 12, 1736
Elijah,	b. February 27, 1740
Aaron,	b. March 24, 1742
Sarah,	b. April 5, 1744
David,	b. June 5, 1747
Jonathan,	b. July 5, 1749

Children of Elijah and Mary Blackman.

Elijah,	b. January 23, 1772 (mistake of the records)
Jabez,	b. March 26, 1772

Children of Benjamin, Jr., and Eunice (Sawyer) Blackman.

Standish,	b. May 11, 1779

Children of David and Mary (House) Blackman.

David,	b. December 30, 1775
Church,	b. September 1, 1779

Children of David and Anna (Ensworth) Blackman.

Anna,	b. December 16, 1792

Children of Aaron and Mary (Upham) Blackman.

Hannah,	b. August 28, 1776
Selden,	b. October 16, 1780
Aaron Justice,	b. March 17, 1782
Clark,	b. December 9, 1784

BOOTH.
Children of Rev. Chauncey and Laura (Farnam) Booth.

Chauncey,	b. September 21, 1816
Laura Farnam,	b. April 6, 1818
Elisabeth,	b. July 6, 1820

Caleb,   b. March 7, 1822
Thomas Fitch,   b. May 30, 1824
Henry Martin,   b. October 2, 1826
Kirtland Farnam,   b. January 10, 1829
William Howard   b. August 15, 1831
Ellen Maria   b. September 2, 1836

BOLS or BOWLES.

Children of William and Caroline Bols.

Polly,   b. February 8, 1776
Tabothy,   b. March 27, 1777

BOYNTON.

Children of Zachariah and Sarah Boynton.

John,   b. October 9, 1718
Hannah,   b. December 30, 1720
Joshua,   b. February 26, 1723
Sarah,   b. April 23, 1724
Mehitabel,   b. March 21, 1726
Abigail,   b. June 17, 1729
Wicom,   b. July 28, 1732

Children of Moses and Abigail Boynton.

Phebe,   b. April 15, 1743
Eunice,   b. April 25, 1745
Oliver,   b. April 30, 1747
Bille,   b. July 27, 1752

Children of Jeremiah and Mary Boynton.

Apphia,   b. July 5, 1737
Moses,   b. October 6, 1739
Hannah,   b. June 6, 1741
Lydia,   b. February 10, 1743
Samuel,   b. December, 1744
Stephen,   b. July, 1749
Joshua,   b. March 5, 1761
Jerome,   b. January 6, 1768

BOYNTON.

Children of John and Tabethy (Daves) Boynton.

Ace,	b. December 22, 1741
Sarah,	b. February 20, 1743
Irena,	b. January 14, 1746-7

Children of Oliver and Mary (Brown) Boynton.

Libernt (?),	b. March 24, 1771
Paul,	b. February 19, 1773
Thaddeus,	b. June 3, 1777
Mary,	b. March 25, 1779

Children of Joshua and Rachael (Carpenter) Boynton.

Phebe,	b. November 23, 1750
Anne,	b. March 24, 1752

BREED.

Children of Joseph and Prisillah Breed.

Presillah,	b. October 14, 1742
Prudence,	b. December 7, 1744-5
Hebe,	b. August 11, 1746

BRIANT.

Children of Ebenezer and Mehitabel (Damman) Briant.

Mehitabel,	b. March 15, 1737

BRIDGMAN.

Children of Isaac and Dorothy Bridgman.

Abigail,	b. August 8, 1712
John,	b. October 10, 1714
Isaac,	8th day (no month), 1718

Children of Isaac and Elisabeth Bridgman.

Cloae,	b. January 12, 1741-2
Elisabeth,	b. October 14, 1744
John,	b. January 26, 1746-7
Anne,	b. March 29, 1749

Olive, b. July 7, 1751
Gideon, b. May 21, 1753
Dorothy, b. February 20, 1755
Isaac, b. April 20, 1757
Abel, b. April 15, 1759
Eunice, b. July 8, 1761
Salomy, b. May 20, 1763
Joseph, b. September 10, 1767

BRIGHAM.

Children of Uriah and Anne (Richardson) Brigham.

Roger, b. October 28, 1755
Bethiah, b. July 14, 1757
Anne, b. October 14, 1759
Norman, b. December 2, 1761
Don Carlos, b. February 21, 1764
Cephas, b. December 7, 1765
Martha, b. January 28, 1770
Lieushe (?), b. November 6, 1771

Children of Paul and Catherine (Turner) Brigham.

Thomas, b. March 7, 1742
Dinah, b. November 14, 1743
Paul, b. January 6, 1746

Children of Paul and Lydia (Sawyer) Brigham.

Thomas, b. March 23, 1769
Mary, b. October 12, 1770
Don Josephus, b. March 24, 1774
Lydia, daughter of Capt. Paul and Lydia, b. October 5, 1778

Children of Asa and Anne Brigham.

Jeremiah, b. June 29, 1767

Children of Thomas and Susannah (Eells) Brigham.

Alexander, b. January 26, 1770
Salinda (daughter), b. April 26, 1772
Orleans (son), b. December 10, 1773
Thomas, b. July 13, 1775
Don Ferdinand, b. September 8, 1777

BIRTHS FROM TOWN RECORDS 15

Royal,	b. September 27, 1779
Eunice,	b. December 17, 1782
Don Carlos Brigham,	b. February 21, 1763
Polly Greenleaf (his wife),	b. January 7, 1764

BROWN.

Children of Ebenezer and Martha Brown.

Martha,	b. July 16, 1734
Mary,	b. May 6, 1736
Ebenezer,	b. April 16, 1738
Mary,	b. April 26, 1741
Sarah,	b. August 4, 1743
Ephraim,	b. March 24, 1748
Timothy,	b. March 21, 1750
Anne,	b. February 5, 1753

Children of Jonathan and Mary (Tarels) Brown.

Febe,	b. June 19, 1741
Eunice,	b. April 22, 1743
Mary,	b. October 16, 1750

Children of Ephraim and Hannah Brown.

Hannah,	b. October 7, 1741

Children of Moses and Ruth (Ingraham) Brown.

Rebeckah,	b. October 4, 1752
Ruth,	b. April 27, 1754
Jeremiah,	b. May 17, 1756
Nehemiah,	b. July 29, 1758

Children of Abraham and Abigail Brown.

Benjamin,	b. September 16, 1740
James,	b. April 25, 1743
Elisha,	b. April 14, 1745
Stephen,	b. March 9, 1749

Children of Nathaniel and Esther Brown.

Nathaniel,	b. May 23, 1783
Bille,	b. October 22, 1785
Polle,	b. October 30, 1788
David,	b. April 12, 1790
Lydia,	b. November 30, 1796

COVENTRY RECORDS

Children of Elijah and Lydia (Gary) Brown.

Elijah,	b. March 28, 1756
Abraham,	b. March 11, 1758
Bethiah,	b. June 3, 1759
Eli,	b. December 8, 1760
James,	b. December 24, 1762
Noah,	b. April 2, 1765
Ephraim,	b. June 20, 1767
Allan,	b. August 29, 1769
Esther,	b. December 31, 1771
Cyrenius,	b. April 30, 1774

Children of Ebenezer 2nd and Lucy Brown.

Mary,	b. February 27, 1747-8
Tabithe,	b. March 22, 1750
Tabithe,	b. May 15, 1752
Margaret,	b. May 14, 1755
Martha,	b. September 23, 1757

Children of Elifilet and Elisabeth Brown.

Hannah,	b. March 11, 1745-6
Daniel,	b. January 22, 1747-8
Daniel 2d,	b. December 28, 1751

Children of John and Ruth Brown.

Ruth,	b. October 24, 1746
Ephraim,	b. July 9, 1748
Ruth,	b. July 16, 1750

Children of Stephen and Jerusha Brown.

Stephen,	b. December 19, 1752

Children of Joshua, Jr., and Prudence (Welch) Brown.

Benjamin,	b. November 5, 1758
Simeon,	b. December 19, 1770

Children of Abraham and Mary (Dean) Brown.

Abigail,	b. July 20, 1755
Anne,	b. July 18, 1761
Mary,	b. April 1, 1763
Susannah,	b. November 18, 1764
Abraham Church,	b. November 18, 1766
Huldah,	b. June 7, 1768

BIRTHS FROM TOWN RECORDS 17

Children of Joseph and the Widow Abigail Lamb Brown.
Joseph, b. February 19, 1758
Olline, b. September 2, 1760
Abigail, b. April 2, 1762
Anne, b. May 20, 1764
Grace, b. December 6, 1766
Jared, b. January 15, 1769
  Children of Timothy and Esther (Chapin) Brown.
Ebenezer, b. February 24, 1776
Timothy, b. December 15, 1777
Francis, b. August 22, 1779
  Children of James and Prudence Brown.
James, b. 24th day (no month), 1787
Prudence, b. April 28, 1794
  Children of Josiah and Mary (Lathrop) Brown
Hannah, b. July 19, 1781
Abigail, b. November 20, 1782
Selah, b. December 11, 1784
Jonathan Clark, b. October 18, 1786
Zolva, b. February 11, 1788
Josiah, Jr., b. June 26, 1790
Oliver, b. September 11, 1792
Polly, b. July 31, 1794
  Children of Jonathan Clark and Sophia Bingham Brown.
Jonathan Clark, Jr., b. October 9, 1808
  Children of Silas and Elizabeth Brown.
Henry, b. July 27, 1825

BUELL.

  Children of Mr. Peter and Hannah (Wells) Buell.
Peter, b. June 10, 1715
Samuell, b. August 20, 1716
Hannah, b. January 15, 1718-19
  Children of Lieut. Peter and Martha Grant Buell.
Peter, b. October 22, 1729
Benjamin, b. June 30, 1732
Abigail, b. February 28, 1733-4
Ruth, b. April 12, 1736
Elias, b. October 8, 173?

Children of Elias and Sarah Turner Buell.
Anne,   b. January 12, 1759
Solomon,   b. April 12, 1760
Jesse,   b. January 4, 1778
   Children of Benjamin and Elisabeth (Gove) Buell.
Peter,   b. October 15, 1757
Beniamon,   b. February 20, 1760
Elisabeth,   b. February 14, 1763

BURNAP.

   Children of John and Susannah Burnap.
Susannah,   b. November 30, 1749
Isaac,   b. January 3, 1750-1
   Children of Abraham and Irene (Wright) Burnap.
Jerijah,   b. November 23, 1754
Daniel,   b. November 1, 1759
Abner,   b. May 23, 1764
Irene,   b. September 22, 1766
   Children of Jerijah and Lois Lyman Burnap.
Lneena (?),   b. January 3, 1783
   Children of Abner and Sarah Bingham Burnap.
Ela (son),   b. December 26, 1784
   Children of Irene Burnap.
Milton,   b. August 25, 1794
   Children of Milton and Martha Burnap.
Daniel Milton,   b. March 30, 1819
Martha Irene,   b. August 5, 1821
   Children of Daniel and Mary Burnap.
Daniel Kingsbury,   b. June 29, 1824
Mary Delia,   b. October 22, 1827
Charlotte Elisabeth,   b. August 9, 1830

BURTON.

   Children of Jacob and Rachael Burton.
Joshua,   b. September 17, 1741
Elisha,   b. November 7, 1743
Jerusha,   b. December 8, 1745
Lucy,   b. March 4, 1748

CADY or CADEY.

Children of James and Thomosine Cady.

Rufus   b. April 16, 1733

Children of Cornelius and Elisabeth (Safford) Cady.

Lucy,   b. May 6, 1760

CARPENTER.

Freedom,	b. June 1, 1692
Amos,	b. November 16, 1693
Beniamon,	b. October 1, 1695
Jedediah,	b. October 1, 1697
Eliphilet,	b. October 16, 1703
Noah,	b. December 4, 1705
Elisabeth,	b. June 15, 1707

Children of Beniamon and Hannah Carpenter.

Ebenezer,	b. November 9, 1709
Rebecca,	b. November 23, 1711

Children of Israel Carpenter.

Eunice,   b. October 22, 1778

Children of Benjamin, Jr., and his wife.

Rhoda,	b. July 9, 1783
Roxa,	b. February 27, 1785
Jeremiah,	b. May 29, 1786
Benjamin,	b. July 1, 1787
Oliver,	b. 2d day (no month), 1789
Asael,	b. March 27, 1792

Children of Charles and Mary (Chappel) Carpenter.

Harmony,	b. January 11, 1791
Horatio G.,	b. July 26, 1794
Josiah 2d,	b. February 4, 1798
Lucius C.,	b. April 20, 1803

Children of Amos and Deborah (Long) Carpenter.

Mary,	b. July 18, 1719
John,	b. February 20, 1721-2

Seth,	b. July 18, 1719
Seth,	b. April 13, 1723
Elisha,	b. April 27, 1725
Timothy,	b. May 5, 1727
Rachael,	b. March 29, 1729
Phebe,	b. May 20, 1731
Joshua,	b. June. 30, 1734
Anna,	b. September 22, 1736
Ephraim,	b. April 1, 1738
Simeon,	b. March 23, 1740
Azubah,	b. September 13, 1744

Stephen Palmer, son of Anna Carpenter, b. June 26, 1757

Children of Benjamin, Jr., and Rebeckah (Smith) Carpenter.

Benjamin,	b. December 21, 1727
Don,	b. July 17, 1730
Elijah,	b. May 3, 1732
Mabel	b. July 29, 1734
Joseph,	b. February 4, 1735-6
Esther,	b. February 8, 1736-7
Mary,	b. August 12, 1739
Comfort,	b. November 4, 1740
Lois,	b. July 14, 1742
Levy (son),	b. September 17, 1744
Ruben,	b. January 3, 1745-6
Jonathan,	b. June 23, 1748

Children of Eliphilet and Elisabeth (Andrus) Carpenter.

Hannah,	b. March 22, 1728
Elisabeth,	b. April 15, 1731
Asahel,	b. January 30, 1733
Lois,	b. May 21, 1735
Abigail,	b. December 6, 1736
Anne,	b. April 9, 1739
Submit,	b. January 27, 1743
Hannah,	b. May 15, 1744
Lois,	b. December 13, 1745
Eliphilet,	b. November 9, 1747

BIRTHS FROM TOWN RECORDS

Children of Noah Carpenter and wife.

Abner,	b. April 24, 1736
Silence,	b. April 25, 1743

Children of Noah and Widow Curtis Elisabeth Carpenter.

Bulah,	b. June 26, 1745
Noah,	b. June 26, 1747
Eunis,	b. November 5, 1749
Ezra,	b. April 5, 1752
Benjamin,	b. February 27, 1756

Children of Ebenezer & Eunes (Thompson) Carpenter.

Asa,	b. December 18, 1739
James,	b. April 4, 1741
William,	b. October 16, 1742
Bridget,	b. February 22, 1743-4
Josiah,	b. April 16, 1745
Catharine,	b. March 24, 1747
Eunice,	b. October 5, 1748
Febee,	b. December 2, 1749
Ebenezer,	b. December 30, 1751
Amos,	b. July 31, 1755

Children of Elisha and Deliverance (Meraugh) Carpenter.

Seth,	b. January 4, 1749
Mary,	b. June 29, 1752
Bethiah,	b. January 20, 1754
Anna,	b. January 18, 1756
Elisha,	b. December 3, 1757
Zebulon,	b. October 20, 1760
Elisabeth,	b. September 9, 1762
Deliverance,	b. September 5, 1763
Phebe,	b. Becket, July 2, 1770

Children of James and Irene (Lad) Carpenter.

James,	b. April 4, 1763
Irene,	b. April 4, 1765
Nathaniel,	b. September 20, 1766
Cephas,	b. July 6, 1770

COVENTRY RECORDS

Jason,	b. August 15, 1772
Eunice,	b. September 14, 1774
Alpheus,	b. August 17, 1776
Eben.,	b. August 8, 1778

Children of Benjamin, Jr., and Widow Catherine Brigham Carpenter.

Alven,	b. April 29, 1752
Mabel,	b. November 14, 1754

Children of Joseph and Phebe (Lad) Carpenter.

Elisabeth,	b. October 2, 1758
Irene,	b. February 12, 1762
Phebe,	b. April 12, 1764
Joseph,	b. May 28, 1766
Hannah,	b. July 20, 1768
Lucretia,	b. August 3, 1770
Stephen,	b. June 17, 1773

Children of Timothy and Miriam (Parker) Carpenter.

Phebe,	b. January 14, 1760 (?)
Lydia,	b. December 31, 1760 (?)
Silas,	b. August 12, 1762
Eunice,	b. October 28, 1764
Solomon,	b. June 8, 1768
Jerusha,	b. April 15, 1770
Jesse,	b. June 17, 1772
Isaac,	b. May 27, 1775.
Elisabeth,	b. June 20, 1776

Children of Elijah and Patience (Bruster) Carpenter.

Benjamin,	b. December 3, 1765
Elijah,	b. April 27, 1767
Patience,	b. August 12, 1769
Mille (or Milly)	b. February 15, 1772
Persis,	b. May 31, 1774 (?)
Sibbel,	b. October 26, 1774 (?)

Children of Daniel and Elisabeth Carpenter.

Maranah,	b. January 24, 1751
Elisabeth,	b. April 5, 1752
Daniell,	b. May 9, 1755

BIRTHS FROM TOWN RECORDS

David,	b. December 25, 1756
John,	b. August 16, 1759
Moses,	b. April 1 (no year)
Abner,	b. July 16, 1764

Children of Levi and Elisabeth (Parker) Carpenter.

Levi,	b. August 30, 1768
Jesse,	b. April 9, 1771

Children of Alvin and Irena Carpenter.

Joseph,	b. May 26, 1779
Irena,	b. November 22, 1780

Children of William and Rachael (Badger) Carpenter.

William,	b. March 6, 1768
Rachael,	b. September 29, 1769

Children of Josiah and Phebe (Porter) Carpenter.

Charles,	b. May 1, 1771
Zebulon,	b. July 28, 1773
Horatio Gates,	b. August 31, 1775
Camilla,	b. March 7, 1778
Martain,	b. January 16, 1781
Phebe,	b. April 4, 1783
Cleanthe	b. December 14, 1785
Fanna,	b. June 4, 1789

Children of Noah, Jr., and Elisabeth Carpenter.

Jonathan,	b. June 13, 1770
Zenas,	b. May 3, 1772
Curtis,	b, June 16, 1774
Sinthy,	b. October 27, 1776
Molle,	b. February 16, 1779

CARY.

Children of Joseph and Phebe Cary.

Mary,	b. December 5, 1751
Jemima,	b. November 21, 1753
Elisabeth,	b. March 10, 1755

CHAMBERLAIN.

Children of James Chamberlain and the Widow Abigail Palmer, daughter of Zachariah Boynton.

Joseph,	b. November 4, 1757
Joseph,	b. November 4, 1758

Children of Joseph and Elisabeth Chamberlain.

Abner, b. November 14, 1751

CHAPPEL.

Children of Simon and Abigail (Sarl) Chappel.

Noah,	b. March 6, 1760
Stephen,	b. April 8, 1762
Sarah,	b. August 7, 1765
Abigail,	b. January 1, 1768
Mary A.,	b. May 23, 1770
Jerusha,	b. August 27, 1773
Betsey,	b. February 9, 1776
Alford,	b. August 17, 1779
Jesse,	b. October 16, 1781
Dyer,	b. October, 1787

CHURCH.

Children of Daniell and Eunice Church.

Gideon,	b. November 22, 1734
Asa,	b. February 29, 1735-6
Eunice,	b. January 29, 1737-8
Samuel,	b. May 21, 1739
Daniell,	b. February 21, 1740-1
Thomas,	b. July 15, 1742
Rachael,	b. July 3, 1744
Triphena and Christiana (twins),	b. September 17, 1745
Deliverance,	b. June 4, 1747
Rebeckah,	b. May 2, 1749

CLARK.

Children of David and the Widow Sarah Badcock Clark.

Barnab and Daniel (twins), b. February, 1736-7 (one died same day; other lived six days).

BIRTHS FROM TOWN RECORDS

Children of Seth and Abigail Badger Clark.

Anwenmoth (daughter),	b. August 30, 1736
Elijah,	b. 25th day (no month), 1737

Children of Joseph and Grace Clark.

Elisabeth,	b. May 20, 1739
Meriah,	b. April 25, 1741
Samuel,	b. March 7, 1743
Daniell,	b. March 20, 1745
Amos,	b. November 24, 1747
Joseph,	b. October 25, 1749

Children of Joseph and Coziah (Hearick) Clark.

Lekins,	b. September 24, 1737
Ezekiel,	b. January 20, 1739-40
Leakins,	b. March 16, 1744
Sarah, daughter of Joseph and Sarah,	b. August 29, 1766

Hannah, daughter of Joseph Clark, b. December 5, 1721

Children of John and Lucy Clark.

Rufus,	b. November 27, 1793
Augustus,	b. April 6, 1796
Maria,	b. April 27, 1799
Eliza,	b. August 11, 1801

Children of Milton and Anna C. Clark.

John Milton, b. January 7, 1809

CLASON.

Children of Nehemiah and Miriam Clason.

Meriam, b. September 27, 1760

COGGESHALL.

Children of Joshua and Mary Coggeshall.

Joshua,	b. July 15, 1726
Peter,	b. June 12, 1728
Joseph and Benjamin (twins),	b. July 1, 1730
Elisabeth,	b. March 29, 1733

Children of Joshua, Jr., and Lucy (Dowe) Coggeshall.

Daniel,	b. March 1, 1749
Rufus,	b. February 6, 1750
Luther,	b. July 28, 1754
Salome,	no date
Mary,	b. April 17, 1767

Children of Beniamon and Seriah (Thompson) Coggeshall.

James,	b. September 29, 1752
Amos,	b. February 19, 1754
Beniamon,	b. August 22, 1755

COGSWELL.

Children of Amos and Rebecca (Chamberlis) Cogswell.

Alice,	b. June 19, 1778
James,	b. December 30, 1779
Amelia,	b. May 5, 1781
Joseph,	b. April 2, 1783
Hannah,	b. July 10, 1784
Betsey,	b. December 11, 1785
Rebecca,	b. February 18, 1787
Sarah,	b. March 2, 1788
Amos,	b. August 22, 1789
Dosha,	b. August 17, 1791
Orpha,	b. March 3, 1793
George,	b. March 23, 1795

Children of Amos and Sally Cogswell.

Serviah,	b. October 15, 1800
Adelina,	b. October 4, 1802

COLE or COWLES.

Children of Timothy and Abigail (Woodworth) Cole.

Daniell,	b. 26th day (no month), 1776
Abner,	b. 29th day (no month), 1777
Amaria (son),	b. May 19, 1780
Luther,	b. February 23, 1782

BIRTHS FROM TOWN RECORDS

Children of Samuel and Abigail Cowles.

Abigail,	b. March 26, 1733
Eunice,	b. December 24, 1734
Samuel,	b. January 27, 1735-6
Ruth,	b. February 20, 1737-8
Lidiah,	b. April 1, 1740
Samuel,	b. March 3, 1742
Eunice,	b. August 2, 1745
Joseph,	b. October 6, 1747

COLLINS.

Children of Abraham and Hannah Collins.

Abraham,	b. February 10, 1746-7
Nathaniel,	b. January 9, 1748-9
Phebe,	b. August 21, 1750
Zerubbe (son),	b. October 26, 1753
Solomon,	b. December 10, 1755
Anna,	b. March 3, 1757
Hannah and Joanna (twins),	b. March 15, 1759
Bette,	b. February 25, 1761
Samuel,	b. February 27, 1765
Justus,	b. March, 1767

Children of Abraham, Jr., and Sarah Collins.

Rheodolphus,	b. February 21, 1770

COLMAN.

Children of Judah and Hepzibah Colman.

Gershom,	b. July 11, 1717
Eleazer,	b. December 16, 1719

Children of Ebenezer and Sarah (Brown) Colman.

Ephraim,	b. June 13, 1739
Ephraim,	b. March 30, 1741
Samuel,	b. March 16, 1743
Sarah,	b. March 4, 1745
Ebenezer,	b. October 20, 1751
Eliphilet,	b. January 1, 1754
Asa,	b. August 31, 1756

COVENTRY RECORDS

Children of Ephraim and Widow Laviniah Curtis Colman.

Bildad,	b. October 23, 1765
Marah,	b. August 6, 1767
John,	b. July 27, 1769
Joseph,	b. July 10, 1771
Jesse,	b. July 15, 1773
Hannah,	b. August 17, 1775
Jesse,	b. November 9, 1778
John,	b. December 27, 1779

Children of Eliezer and Mehitable Colman.

Easter,	b. December 27, 1748
Lemuel,	b. May 10, 1751
Joannah,	b. August 19, 1753
Samuel,	b. April 30, 1755
Phebe,	b. September 1, 1758
Levi,	b. June 1, 1763
Jerusha (still-born),	b. November 23, 1766
Jerusha,	b. June 24, 1768

Children of Gershom and Mercy (Alles) Colman.

Sarah,	b. November 9, 1745
Miriam,	b. August 20, 1747
Nathaniel,	b. March 4, 1753
Nathan,	b. December 27, 1755
Gershom,	b. June 8, 1756
Triphene,	b. March 5, 1759
Mindwell,	b. November 22, 1760
Timothy,	b. March 2, 1764
Phenias,	b. November 25, 1767

Children of Samuel and Esther (Bishop) Colman.

Benjamin,	b. August 6, 1766
Solomon,	b. August 25, 1768

Children of Mr. Asa and Hannah (Badcock) Colman.

Betsey,	b. September 12, 1778
Lydia,	b. February 18, 1780
Martha,	b. March 23, 1781
Hannah,	b. 5th day (no month), 1783

Children of Ebenezer and Phebe (Carpenter) Colman.

Sarah,	b. June 17, 1783
Fanny,	b. November 24, 1784

BIRTHS FROM TOWN RECORDS

Children of Asa, Jr., and Betsey Colman.
Alvin Emelous,   b. Cazenovia, New York State,
                                October 22, 1805
Harlin,   b. Coventry, September 25, 1807
Freeman Rawley,   b. November 13, 1809
Eben Shepard,   b. January 20, 1812

COOK.

Children of Jesse and Submit Cook.
Febe,   b. February 19, 1743-4
Nathan,   b. November 6, 1745
Submit,   b. December 29, 1747
Sarah,   b. October 22, 1749
Elisabeth,   b. May 8, 1752
Mary,   b. November 20, 1754
Silence,   b. February 19, 1758
Jesse,   b. July 18, 1760

Children of Josiah and Lucy (Deman) Cook.
Huldah,   b. April 23, 1765
Lucy,   b. June 23, 1767
Josiah,   b. October 16, 1770

Children of Moses and Eunice (Allin) Cook.
Jemima,   b. October 10, 1760

Children of Moses and Jerusha Cook.
Daniel,   b. November 14, 1772

Children of Nathan and Dorcas (Meacham) Cook.
Hester,   b. September 17, 1776
Hannah,   b. February 15, 1769

Children of Jesse and Priscilla Talcott Cook.
Lovice (daughter),   b. October 31, 1786
Amelia,   b. January 26, 1791
Azel,   b. April 26, 1793

Children of Joseph and Mehitabel (Badcock) Cook.
Asenath,   b. September 8, 1786
Daniel and Luther (twins),   b. April 24, 1788
Narcissus (daughter),   b. February 27, 1790
Anna,   b. February 21, 1792
Robert,   b. July 14, 1794
Jerusha and Mehitabel (twins), b. March 1, 1797

CRANDALL.

Children of Edward and Sarah (Brown) Crandall.

Ethan,	b. August 28, 1785

CRANE.

Children of John and Prudence (Belding) Crane.

Elithame,	b. March 13, 1718
Sibbel,	b. August 1, 1719
Hezekiah,	b. March 31, 1721
Prudence,	b. July 4, 1723
Lemuell,	b. July 12, 1725
Hannah,	b. March 15, 1727
Rhoda,	b. March 28, 1729
Adonijah,	b. May 12, 1731

Children of John and Abigail Crane.

John Crane's child,	b. September 8, 1713
Abigail,	b. October 20, 1714
John,	b. October 25, 1716
Ebenezer,	b. July 4, 1720
Mary,	b. May 22, 1722
Samuel,	b. April 23, 1724
Hezekiah,	b. October 10, 1725
Deborah,	b. August 5, 1727
Daniell,	b. January 29, 1728-9
Ruth,	b. December 22, 1730

CROCKER.

Children of Andrew and Loes Crocker.

Andrew,	b. October 14, 1750
Roswell,	b. February 17, 1754
Samuel,	b. December 27, 1756
Simeon,	b. March 21, 1759
Martha,	b. June 26, 1761

Children of John and Sarah (Baldwin) Crocker.

John,	b. February 20, 1753
Sarah,	d. May 20, 1757 (by register)
Mary,	b. September 24, 1757 (by register)
Ruth,	b. February 20, 1760

Sophia, daughter of Lois Crocker,　　　b. January 7, 1779

CROSS.

Children of Peter and Mary (Fuller) Cross.

Ellither,	b. March 27, 1742
Aaron,	b. September 6, 1743

CROSBY.

Children of Jonathan and Hannah Crosby.

Abijah,　　　　　　　　　　　b. April 26, 1751

CROSSMAN.

Children of Ebenezer and Widow Mehitable (Dow) Crossman.

Orpah,	b. March 3, 1782
Cynthia,	b. July 22, 1783
Eben,	b. July 17, 1785
Ira,	b. April 17, 1787
Almira,	b. May 8, 1789

CUMMINS or COMINS.

Children of John and Elisabeth Comins.

Simeon,	b. August 18, 1764
Willson,	b. October 2, 1767
Elisabeth,	b. July 7, 1769
Jerusha,	b. August 6, 1771

Children of John and Weltha Cummins.

Lorenzo M.,	b. November 21, 1824
William M.,	b. August 9, 1827

CUSHMAN.

Children of Ephraim and Sarah (Colman) Cushman.

Stephen,	b. December 7, 1765
Hannah,	b. September 22, 1767
Asa,	b. August 10, 1769
Ephraim,	b. September 6, 1771
Sarah,	b. September 10, 1773
Ephraim,	b. July 2, 1775
Hannah,	b. February 5, 1778
Luther,	b. February, 1780
Stephen,	b. March 6, 1782
Rebeccah,	b. January 6, 1785

Children of Allerton, Jr., and Harmony (Allen) Cushman.

Minerve (son),	b. November 6, 1762
Timothy,	b. March 6, 1765
Harmony,	b. December 8, 1766
Timothy,	b. March 6, 1768
Joseph,	b. March 8, 1770
Diadata,	b. April 4, 1773

CUTLER.

Children of Daniell and Mary Cutler.

Sarah,	b. Windham, January 30, 1738
Eleazer,	b. November 20, 1739
Daniel,	b. January 22, 1742
Samuel,	b. February 26, 1744
Mary,	b. October 8, 1746
Amos,	b. May 20, 1749
Hannah,	b. Mansfield, March 28, 1751
Eunice,	b. Coventry, March 21, 1755
Nathaniel,	b. June 13, 1757
Sarah,	b. June 13, 1759

CURTIS.

Children of Bildad and Zeriah (Bishop) Curtis.

Abigail,	b. October 1, 1761

BIRTHS FROM TOWN RECORDS

Children of Samuel and Joanna (Dimick) Curtis.

Bildad,	b. August 10, 1765
Samuel,	b. January 15, 1768
Sabrina,	b. March 13, 1771
Joanna,	b. December 22, 1774

CURTICE or CURTIS.

Children of Henry and Silance (Janes) Curtice.

Esther,	b. October 4, 1727
Henry,	b. February 13, 1729
Silance,	b. November 23, 1730
Bildad,	b. September 27, 1733
Anne,	b. June 18, 1736
Rhoda,	no date
Samuell,	no date
Nathaniell,	b. February 9, 1739-40

Children of Henry, Jr., and Elizabeth (Root) Curtis.

Nathaniell,	b. August 11, 1752
Jesse,	b. May, 1754
Lowes,	b. July 30, 1756
Mary,	b. December 29, 1759
Hannah,	b. September 20, 1761
Hannah,	b. September, 1765
Abijah, (son)	b. February 16, 1767
Anne,	b. May 8, 1770

DAGGET or DOGGETT.

Children of Samuel and Anne Dagget.

Asenah,	b. January 25, 1755
Tabothy,	b. April 5, 1757

DAGGETT.

Children of Isaiah and Ester (English) Daggett.

Isaiah, Jr.,	b. August 1, 1785
Chester,	b. September 25, 1786
Anna,	b. November 22, 1791
Betsey,	b. July 13, 1794
Calvin,	b. August 16, 1797
Samuel B.,	b. October 7, 1800

Children of Samuel B. and Amelia Daggett.
Samuel Henry,   b. December 23, 1829
  Children of Isaiah, Jr., and Harriet Daggett.
William Henry Harrison,   b. December 13, 1820
Lucy Harriet Arnold,   b. December 15, 1826
  Children of Chester and Cynthia Daggett.
Chester La Fayette,   b. April 25, 1824

DAMMAN or DAMON.

Children of Samuell, Jr., and Thankfull (Root) Damman.
Abigail,   b. March 4, 1730-31
Steaven,   b. July 5, 1732
Ebenezer,   b. February 4, 1733-34
Ebenezer,   b. December 18, 1739
  Children of John and Elisabeth Daman.
Elisabeth,   b. September 15, 1742
Presilla,   b. November 15, 1744
John,   b. February 7, 1747-8

DARBEY.

Children of John and Mary Darbey.
Nathan,   b. February 15, 1778
Mary,   b. August 25, 1780

DAVENPORT.

Children of Richard and Elies Davenport.
Elisabeth,   b. March 28, 1742
Rachael,   b. March 2, 1745
Anne,   b. January 25, 1746
Hannah,   b. March 12, 1749
Humphrey,   b. March 5, 1751
Abigail,   b. October 15, 1753

Denis Parker, son of Rachael Davenport,   b. April 17, 1772
  Children of Benjamin and Narissa Davenport.
Walter,   b. September 16, 1798
Bishop,   b. November 6, 1800

DAVES or DAVIS.

Children of Thomas and Hannah Daves.

Hannah,	b. December 20, 1706
Joseph,	b. January 18, 1711
Tabethy,	b. May 21, 1720

Children of Joseph and Johannah Daves.

Joseph,	b. August 18, 1727
Irene,	b. May 1, 1728
Loes,	b. November 30, 1729
Thomas,	b. June 7, 1733
Benjamin,	b. December 23, 1734
Ada,	b. September 11, 1739

DANES or DEAMS.

Children of Solomon and Ruth (Neff) Danes.

William,	b. January 22, 1757
Solomon and Levy (twins),	b. October 1, 1758
Ruth,	b. May 26, 1760

Children of Solomon and the Widow Anne Brown Danes.

Mary,	b. April 16, 1771
Asa,	b. February 4, 1774
Levina,	b. June 30, 1775
Palley (?)	b. May 9, 1778

DELANO.

Children of Jonathan, Jr., and Susannah (West) Delano.

Mary,	b. September 18, 1744
Susannah,	b. February 15, 1745
Elisabeth,	b. October 31, 1747

Children of Jonathan and Anne Delano.

Anne,	b. August 10, 1759
Caleb,	b. January 15, 1761

Children of Jabez and Prudence Delano.

Jonathan,	b. November 23, 1735

DUTY or DEUTY.

Children of Matthew and Eunice (Boynton) Duty.

Samuel,	b. January 9, 1772
Abigail,	b. August 14, 1773
Anne,	b. August 21, 1775
Ambrose,	b. July 17, 1777
Mary,	b. August 6, 1779
Nathan,	b. August 31, 1783
Eunice,	b. October 1, 1791

DEWEY.

Children of Moses and Marah Dewey.

Hannah,   b. September 14, 1753

DEXTER.

Children of Nathan and Irene (French) Dexter.

Hannah Gurley,	b. September 29, 1806
Nathan,	b. October 11, 1808
Irene,	b. April 8, 1810

Children of Minerva and Betsey (Wheet) Dexter.

Eliza,   b. July 8, 1808

DIMMICK or DIMICK or DIMOCK.

Children of Timothy and Desire (Dimick) Dimmick.

Desire,	b. January 22, 1751
Eunice,	b. February 9, 1753
Anne,	b. September 15, 1754
Lois,	b. May 12, 1756
Sibel,	b. March 18, 1758
Lucy,	b. May 22, 1760
Timothy,	b. August 22, 1762
Daniel,	b. February 20, 1765
Mason,	b. June 22, 1767
Rhoda,	b. August 10, 1770
Rogger,	b. August 5, 1772

BIRTHS FROM TOWN RECORDS

Children of Lot and Hannah Dimmick.
Rhoda,   b. August 22, 1762
Jonathan,   b. July 25, 1764
Hannah,   b. April 5, 1766

DIMICK or DIMOCK or DIMMICK.

Children of Captain Daniel and Anna (Wright) Dimick.
Anna C.,   b. August 18, 1787
Parthena,   b. April 9, 1789
Lucinda,   b. March 18, 1791
Salle,   b. June 23, 1793
Harty,   b. December 24, 1794
Clara Maria,   b. September 14, 1796
Eliza,   b. May 24, 1798
Timothy, Jr.,   b. April 17, 1799
Desiah,   b. March 31, 1802

DIMICK.

Children of Mason and Anna Dimick.
Mason, Jr.,   b. July 26, 1787
Rufus,   b. March 21, 1789
Clarissa,   b. May 7, 1791
Samuel,   b. September 18, 1793
Desiah,   b. September 26, 1795
Wealthy,   b. March 22, 1798
Chauncey,   b. November 16, 1801
John A.,   b. September 16, 1806

DOAN.

Children of Joseph and Jane Doan.
Polly,   b. July 27, 1795
Dianthe,   b. October 15, 1796
Chauncey,   b. September 18, 1798
Jane,   b. July 15, 1801
Joseph, Jr.,   b. June 13, 1803
Zenus,   b. July 8, 1805
Leonard,   b. March 17, 1808
Marcia,   b. January 11, 1811
Aletia,   b. May 21, 1813

DORMAN.

Children of Amos and Mary Dorman.
Mary, b. April 14, 1746
Stephen, b. April 3, 1749

Children of Dudley and Eunice (Hawkins) Dorman.
Tabitha, b. February 26, 1762
Eunice, b. February 5, 1764

Children of Amos and Keziah (Brown) Dorman.
Daniel, b. September 20, 1761
Susannah, b. October 1, 1762
Hannah, b. August 12, 1764
Amos, Jr., b. September 14, 1770
Selende, b. August 4, 1772
John, b. September 1, 1774
Martha, b. January 14, 1777
Stephen, b. August 19, 1779
Anne, b. November 23, 1781

Children of Joseph and Lucy (Aspenwall) Dorman.
Eunice, b. August 6, 1801
Joseph, b. June 5, 1805
Lucy Aspenwall, b. June 6, 1807
William Augustus, b. April 19, 1810
Anna, b. July 25, 1814
Emily, b. February 9, 1818

Children of William and Lucy Dorman.
Lydia Joanna, b. February 20, 1837

DOWE or DOW.

Children of Ephraim and Elisabeth Dowe.
Humphrey, b. July 3, 1742
Calvin, b. January 10, 1746-7

Children of Pelatiah and Catharine Dowe.
Mabel, b. September 25, 1763
Saford, b. September 18, 1764
John, b. December 16, 1766

BIRTHS FROM TOWN RECORDS

Elisabeth,	b. September 29, 1768
Jane,	b. December 28, 1773
Hannah,	b. September 29, 1775
Margary,	b. November 28, 1777
Clarinda,	b. February 14, 1780

Children of Daniel and Mehitabel (Palmer) Dowe.

Azrah,	b. September 26, 1773
Amasa,	b. March 9, 1775
Tirza,	b. January 20, 1777

Children of Ephraim and Hepsibah (Hawkins) Dowe.

Daniel,	b. November 27, 1752
Jesse,	b. September 8, 1755
Jesse,	b. May 31, 1754
Ephraim,	b. April 19, 1762
Hepsibah (son),	b. March 6, 1767
Joseph, Children of Ephraim and Mary,	b. July 5, 1777
Solomon,	b. December 30, 1778
Daniel Clark Dow,	b. April 8, 1783
Betsy,	b. August 26, 1786

Children of Levi and Phebe Dowe.

Marah,	b. December 26, 1760
Esther,	b. September 3, 1762
Samuel,	b. October 3, 1766
Jeremiah,	b. December 28, 1770
John,	b. March 17, 1773
Sarah,	b. February 7, 1775
Paul and William, twin sons,	b. June 28, 1777
Anson,	b. June 11, 1780
Harvey,	b. August 19, 1782

Children of Lemuel and Anna (Millenton) Dowe.

Susannah,	b. April 10, 1759
Salmon,	b. April 28, 1762
Anne,	b. July 24, 1765
Lemuel,	b. April 25, 1768
Lydia,	b. February, 1771
Abigail,	b. August 1, 1774

Children of John Dow.

Dianthe,	b. September 7, 1800
Almira,	b. August 4, 1802
John N.,	b. February 5, 1805
Silas Newcomb,	b. April 25, 1810

DOW.

Children of Humphry B. Dow and Tabitha (Parker) Dow.

Ulyses,	b. August 4, 1768
Ethelinda,	b. July 22, 1770
Mirza,	b. May 25, 1772
Porelana,	b. April 25, 1774
Lorenzo,	b. October 16, 1777
Tabitha,	b. August 21, 1782

Children of Ulysses and Anna (Tilden) Dow.

Anna, b. July 15, 1789

Children of Solomon and Tirzah Dow.

Simon,	b. August 17, 1798
Cyrus,	b. September 26, 1800
Solomon George,	b. September 9, 1803
Emily,	b. May 3, 1806
Lucy,	b. March 26, 1808
Beverley Abbot,	b. November 26, 1811
Ezra Abbot,	b. September 4, 1814
Frederick Haughton,	b. October 11, 1817

EANSWORTH.

Children of Jeremiah and Sarah Eansworth.

Jeremiah, b. March 14, 1762

EDGERTON.

Children of Jabez and Martha Edgerton.

Martha, b. January 8, 1755

Children of Hezekiah Jr. and Marisa Edgerton.

Ward, b. July 12, 1803

Children of Justin and Mary Edgerton.

Leonard Pember, b. January 31, 1833

EDWARDS.

Children of Ebenezer and Mary Edwards.

Sary,	b. April 29, 1716
Mary,	b. September 17, 1718
Thankful,	b. February 25, 1721-2
Ebenezer,	b. August 26, 1724
Loes,	b. October 5, 1728

Children of Thomas and Mary Edwards.

Rachael,	b. October 31, 1736
Catharine,	b. April 17, 1738
Ephraim,	b. September 15, 1740
Elisabeth,	b. November 2, 1742
Simeon,	b. June 16, 1744
Oliver,	b. September 8, 1745
Mary,	b. May 27, 1747
Thomas,	b. August 22, 1749
William,	b. January 20, 1751

EDWARDS.

Children of Joseph and Mary (French) Edwards.

Joseph,	b. November, 1722
Samuell,	b. July 11, 1732
Eunice,	b. November 12, 1734

Children of Jabez and Triphene Edwards.

Jabez,	b. June 8, 1763
William,	b. February 6, 1765
Bette,	b. October 21, 1769
Eleazer,	b. September 28, 1771

Children of Samuel and Mary Edwards.

Samuel,	b. December 16, 1760
Abiel,	b. May 9, 1763

Children of William and Temperance Edwards.

Benajah,	b. May 26, 1772

Children of Daniel, Jr., and Hannah Edwards.

Lucy,	b. March 7, 1726
Elijah,	b. September 12, 1727
Joseph,	b. September 22, 1729
Beniah,	b. March 14, 1731
Lurany,	b. May 7, 1733
Samuel,	b. July 27, 1738
Jobe,	b. September 4, 1740
Adonijah,	b. August 28, 1742
Thomas,	b. July 13, 1746
Daniel,	b. April 21, 1748

Children of Adonijah and Mary (Sarls) Edwards.

Reodolphus,	b. January 26, 1766
Ralph,	b. May 27, 1768

Children of Joseph and Anne (Porter) Edwards.

Anne,	b. February 23, 1760

Children of William and Jane (Harris) Edwards.

Jerusha,	b. May 4, 1729
Anne,	b. December 3, 1730
William,	b. August 12, 1732
Jane,	b. September 13, 1733
Elifilet,	b. May 21, 1735
Joshua,	b. November 16, 1737
Waram,	b. November 6, 1742
John,	b. February 27, 1744-5
James,	b. July 2, 1747

Children of Joshua and Dorkas Edwards.

William,	b. September 28, 1759
Gideon,	b. September 4, 1761
Dorcas,	b. March 14, 1764
Wearham,	b. April 21, 1766
Lorenda,	b. April 28, 1768
William,	b. May 7, 1770
Joshua,	b. March 20, 1772
Sarah,	b. October 2, 1774
Gideon,	b. October 22, 1777
John,	b. October 26, 1781

EELLS.

Children of John and Susannah Eells.

Freelove,	b. Rocksbery, March 17, 1748
Abigail,	b. Coventry, July 20, 1750
Moses,	b. May 22, 1752
Eunice,	b. August 13, 1755
Oliver,	b. July 24, 1758
Loyes,	b. March 21, 1763

Children of John and Lois Eells.

Sinthia,	b. March 16, 1777
Lois,	b. March 4, 1778
Moses,	b. March 2, 1780

FITCH.

Children of Jeremiah and Mary (Porter) Fitch.

Lucy,	b. September 12, 1730
Mary,	b. January 18, 1732-3
Hannah,	b. June 12, 1735
John,	b. September 13, 1742

Children of Jeremiah and Widow Martha Gifford Fitch.

Marcy,	b. June 7, 1746
Jeremiah,	b. January 4, 1748
Mary and John (twins),	b. December 20, 1754 (Mary still-born).

Children of Jeremiah and Sybil Fitch.

Mariah,	b. February 23, 1777
Jeremiah 3d,	b. November 22, 1778

Children of Abner and Ruth (Rose) Fitch.

Jeremiah,	b. March 29, 1737
Jephthah,	b. March 22, 1740
Bettee,	b. September 11, 1743
Ruth,	b. October 13, 1744
Abner,	b. November 18, 1749
Jephthah,	b. September, 1752

Children of James and Febe (-Meraugh) Fitch.
Febe, b. December 23, 1738
Rachael, b. July 31, 1742
Phebe, b. March 4, 1748
Jesse, b. March 11, 1752
Children of Elisha and Prissillah (Patten) Fitch.
Daborah, b. July 5, 1736
Elemuel, b. July 6, 1739
Deborah, b. July 24, 1742
Joseph, b. August 5, 1743
Josiah, b. March 18, 1746
Nathaniel, b. May 5, 1748
Deborah, b. February 12, 1752
Elijah, b. January 31, 1754

Marth Fitch, illegitimate child of Rebeckah (House),
b. July 1, 1788
Children of Jephthah and Ursula (Root) Fitch.
Diadamia, b. November 23, 1777
Ephraim, b. December 9, 1778
Apollos, b. March 10, 1780
Phebe, b. December 31, 1781

Chauncey Fitch, b. May 31, 1791
His wife Mary, b. September 30, 1795
Children of Chauncey and Mary Fitch.
Joseph Addison, b. May 10, 1816
James Monroe, b. June 7, 1818
Jeremiah Jones Chauncey, b. November 30, 1820
Children of Jasper and Eunice Fitch.
Fanny G., b. August 3, 1808
Henry H., b. May 23, 1810
Mary T., b. May 16, 1812
William A., b. May 20, 1814
Lucy P., b. May 1, 1816
Alfred H., b. July 15, 1819
Caroline, b. February 14, 1824

BIRTHS FROM TOWN RECORDS

Children of Apollos and Sybil (Edgerton) Fitch.

George Edgerton,	b. August 18, 1802
Lucy Eliza,	b. May 6, 1804
Ursula Root,	b. November 2, 1805
Ephraim Alson,	b. October 1, 1807
Newton,	b. November 14, 1809
Lucretia,	b. October 9, 1811
Jephtha (son),	b. June 29, 1813
Phebe,	b. May 29, 1815
Sibel,	b. November 16, 1817

FLINT.

Children of Talcott and Prudence Flint.

Minerva,	b. October 6, 1804
Leonard Foster,	b. November 14, 1807

Children of Ralph and Esther L. Flint.

Leonard,	b. June 18, 1835
Lucy Mariah,	b. September 28, 1837
Sidney Pitkin,	b. December 31, 1839

FOWLER.

Children of Jonathan and Hannah Fowler.

Mary,	b. October 30, 1727
Daniel,	b. June 3, 1729
Ichabod,	b. January 28, 1730-31
Gurden,	b. March 8, 1733
Elizabeth,	b. November 12, 1735
Israel,	b. June 3, 1736
Gurden,	b. April 28, 1738

Children of John and Dorythy Fowler.

Jerusha,	b. July 26, 1732
Thomas,	b. December 17, 1733
Mary,	b. January 9, 1735-6
Sarah,	b. February 11, 1737-8
Abraham,	b. November 1, 1745
Hannah,	b. May 26, 1749

COVENTRY RECORDS

Children of Jonathan, Jr., and Abigail (Bissell) Fowler.
Sarah,   b. July 24, 1741
Tabitha,   b. September 6, 1743
Joseph Bissell,   b. September 28, 1749
Sarah,   b. June 9, 1753

Children of John and Mehitable Fowler.
Mary,   b. March 11, 1741
Sarah,   b. May (no date)

Children of Joseph Bissell and Sarah (Baldwin) Fowler.
Lavinia,   b. August 18, 1772
Silas Bissell,   b. May 18, 1774

Children of Ichabod and Ruth (Grover) Fowler.
Bette,   b. November 2, 1754
Hannah,   b. October 20, 1757
Ruth;   b. February 9, 1761
Anna,   b. April 9, 1764
Jemima,   b. August 30, 1766
Jesse (son),   b. August 31, 1768
Asel,   b. September 9, 1771

Children of Israel and Eunice (Bissell) Fowler.
Abigail,   b. September 17, 1758
Esther,   b. August 22, 1760
Eunice,   b. September 25, 1762
Joel,   b. May 18, 1764

FREEMAN.

Children of Otis and Ruth Freeman.
James,   b. September 29, 1772
Jonathan,   b. October 15, 1774

FRENCH.

Children of John and Mehitable (Root) French.
Sarah,   b. May 3, 1737
Sarah,   b. April 6, 1739
Selah,   b. August 30, 1741
Stephen,   b. July 12, 1743
Samuel,   b. November 8, 1746
John,   b. September 27, 1748
Ichabod,   b. November 27, 1750

BIRTHS FROM TOWN RECORDS

Children of Ebenezer and the Widow Rachael Boynton French.

Mary,	b. June 22, 1755
Ebenezer,	b. April 5, 1759
Nathan,	b. February 3, 1760

Children of Joseph and Lucy French.

Trifeny,	b. May 30, 1739

Mr. Aaron French,	b. February 28, 1756
Miss Abigail Brown (his wife),	b. July 20, 1758

Children of Mr. Aaron and Abigail (Brown) French.

Irene,	b. May 16, 1776
Stephen,	b. August 3, 1778
John,	b. January 16, 1781
Eleazer,	b. February 20, 1783
Selah,	b. March 13, 1785
Oliver,	b. December 9, 1787
Jonathan,	b. May 10, 1790
Aaron,	b. November 7, 1792
Oliver,	b. May 18, 1795
Nabby,	b. December 6, 1797

FULLER.

Children of David and Constant Fuller.

Christian,	b. October 23, 1721
Mary,	b. July 30, 1723
Elijah,	b. September 24, 1724
Hepzibah,	b. April 27, 1726
Josiah,	b. August 24, 1728

Children of Josiah and Margaret Fuller.

Josiah,	b. December 14, 1753
Esther,	b. April 25, 1755
Hannah,	No date.
Ruth,	b. January 2, 1758
Margaret,	b. June 13, 1759
Catherine,	b. January 13, 1761
Hepzebah,	b. October 6, 1762
Eunice,	b. July 20, 1764

Huley,	b. September 18, 1766
Bettie,	No date.
Anne,	b. December 26, 1770
Joel,	b. April 24, 1773

Children of Shubael and Sarah (Scott) Fuller.

Hannah,	b. June 4, 172;
Benjamin,	b. January 27, 1729
Patiance,	b. June 1, 1731
Asa,	b. February 2, 1733-4

Children of Peleg and Bette Fuller.

Mary,	b. September 19, 1731
Keziah,	b. August 1, 1739

Children of Elijah and Mary (Millinton) Fuller.

Nathaniel,	b. March 26, 1748
Hosea,	b. August 17, 1749
Martha,	b. February 8, 1750-51
Mary,	b. December, 1752
Elijah,	b. November 6, 1754
Solomon,	b. March 19, 1757
Cloe,	b. January 16, 1759
John,	b. December 26, 1760
Abial,	b. December 29, 1763
Samuel,	b. March 31, 1766
Mehitable,	b. February 15, 1768
Mehitable,	b. May 22, 1769

GAGER.

Children of Simon and Anna (Porter) Gager.

Luther P.,	b. September 13, 1821

GEER.

Children of Jedediah and Sarah (Dodge) Geer.

Benaiah,	b. December 5, 1755
Jedediah,	b. December 8, 1757
Sibbel,	b. November 9, 1759

GILBERT.

Children of Nathaniel and Mary Gilbert.
Nathaniel,	b. October 3, 1725
Lois,	b. October 8, 1727
Thomas,	b. September 25, 1731
Ebenezer,	b. August 3, 1733
Elisha,	b. May 25, 1736

Children of Nathaniel, Jr., and Hannah Fowler Gilbert.
Eunice,	b. April 7, 1748
Hannah,	b. November 23, 1751
Isaac,	b. January 4, 1753
Mary,	b. September 3, 1755
Elisabeth,	b. September 25, 1757
Anne,	b. April 29, 1761

Children of Thomas and Rachael Gilbert.
Salla,	b. August 16, 175-
Susannah,	b. May 24, 1761
Irene,	b. August 16, 1763

Children of Samuel, Jr., and Abigail Gilbert.
Ann,	b. October 7 (date gone)

GILLIT.

Children of Eleazer and Sarah Gillit.
Eleazer,	b. November 8, 1752

GOODRIDGE.

Children of Edmund Goodridge and wife.
Sally,	b. October 31, 1801
Alfred,	b. July 10, 1804

GOODWIN.

Children of Abel and Clarissa (Hunt) Goodwin.
Clarissa Hunt,	b. February 19, 1811

GRANDY.

Children of Robert and Bethiah Grandy.
Bazaleel,	b. April 3, 1754
Rachael,	b. June 11, 1755
Lydia,	b. December 2, 1756

GREEN.

Children of Ebenezer and Susannah Green.

Joseph,	b. April 27, 1740
Jerusha,	b. August 5, 1742
Lucresha,	b. June 15, 1744
Ebenezer,	b. August 6, 1746

Children of Joseph and Sarah Green.

Alline,	b. February 18, 1771
Joseph,	b. March 17, 1773
Ebenezer,	b. August 26, 1775

Children of Joseph and Deborah Green.

John Manley,	b. October 12, 1787
William Manley,	b. August, 1789
Hannah,	b. August 13, 1793
Harlin,	b. December 19, 1797

GRISWOLD.

Children of John and Margery (Doggitt) Griswold.

Eunice,	January 30, 1754
Joseph,	b. September 15, 1755
Lavinia,	b. February 15, 1757
John,	b. May 16, 1760
Frederick,	b. November 29, 1762
Frederick,	b. April 23, 1766
Bille,	b. July 8, 1767

GROVER.

Children of Matthew and Naomi Grover.

Elisabeth,	b. July 23, 1719
Ebenezer,	b. April 22, 1721
Mary,	b. May 4, 1723

Children of Matthew, Jr., and Lideah Grover.

Hembery,	b. December 25, 1726
Matthew,	b. June 5, 1728
Lidia,	b. June 23, 1730
Simon,	b. October 4, 1732

BIRTHS FROM TOWN RECORDS 51

Children of Ebenezer and Zariah (Larrabe) Grover.
Joseph, b. January 16, 1743-4
Daniel, b. October 3, 1745
Jerusha, b. October 9, 1747
Anne, b. December 28, 1748
Jabez, b. January 15, 1751-2
Eben, b. March 13, 1754

Children of Benjamin and Mary (Shailler) Grover.
Mary, b. April 26, 1729
Susannah (still-born), April 2, 1732
Naomy, b. March 3, 1733
Sarah, b. July 1, 1735
Elisabeth, b. November 14, 1737
Sible, b. May 6, 1741

Children of Benjamin and Mary Grover (2d wife).
Benjamin, b. September 22, 1750

Children of Ephraim and Tabothy (Manley) Grover.
Anna, b. March 17, 1774

Children of Edmund and Elisabeth (Thomas) Grover.
Hosea, b. June 13, 1743
Josiah, b. April 21, 1745
Phenias, b. October 16, 1747
Aaron, b. July 7, 1749
Edmund, b. April 6, 1751

Children of Leonard and Sarah Acley Grover.
Sarah, b. October 10, 1739
Micah, b. March 13, 1742
Nathan, b. July 21, 1743
Leonard, b. March 18, 1745
Lydia, b. May 20, 1747
Matthew, b. July 31, 1749
Eunice, b. July 20, 17
Amisiah, b. August 2, 1753
Mariah, b. December 23, 1755

Children of Matthew, Jr., and Lidiah Grover.
Abigail, b. November 28, 1739

Children of Simon and Phebe Grover.
Isaiah, b. January 4, 1756
Phebe, b. November 8, 1757

Children of John and Elisabeth (Miller) Grover.

Ruth,	b. May 2, 1733
Phebe,	b. October 5, 1735

Children of John and Sarah (Chapen) Grover.

John,	b. June 9, 1739
Ephraim,	b. February 25, 1741-2
Chloe,	b. October 15, 1745
Elijah,	b. May 6, 1755

Children of John, Jr., and Abigail (Flint) Grover.

Daniel,	b. October 17, 1763
Sarah,	b. October 4, 1765
Elijah,	b. February 17, 1768
Hester,	b. June 29, 1770
Gaal,	b. April 15, 1772
Ebenezer,	b. September 15, 1774
Abigail,	b. May 13, 1777
Oliver,	b. September 22, 1779
Eleazer,	b. June 1, 1782
Asenath,	b. April 10, 1788

Children of Benjamin and Lois Grover.

Joseph,	b. March 10, 1772

Children of Joseph and Sarah (Thompson) Grover.

Amasa,	b. September 22, 1794
Dida,	b. July 4, 1745 (correct by Town records)
Ashbel,	b. April 21, 1797
Anson,	b. April 20, 1799
Delia,	b. September 24, 1802
Wm. Thompson,	b. November 2, 1804
George,	b. October 23, 1806
Nelson,	b. September 28, 1808
Chauncy,	b. September 17, 1810

Children of Benjamin and Theodora (House) Grover.

Lois,	b. November 7, 1784
Lucy,	b. May 23, 1786
Anne,	b. June 14, 1787
Abel,	b. July 6, 1790
David,	b. May 18, 1792

Mary,	b. November 17, 1793
Chester,	b. June 13, 1795
Mabel,	b. February 25, 1797

Children of Hembrey and Abigail (Simon) Grover.

Daniel,	b. September 15, 1769
Abigail,	b. July 29, 1771
Ezekiel,	b. August 9, 1774
Sarah,	b. November 9, 1776
Mary,	b. November 2, 1779
Sophia and Eunice (twins),	b. January 30, 1782

GURLEY.

Children of Samuel and Experience Gurley.

Esther,	b. February 24, 1713

Children of Titus and Patty Gurley.

Royal Coladine,	b. June 30, 1810

HABART.

Children of Jonathan and Hannah Habart.

Hannah,	b. April 7, 1717

HALE.

Children of Richard and Elisabeth (Strong) Hale.

Samuel,	b. May 25, 1747
John,	b. October 21, 1748
Joseph,	b. March 12, 1750
Elisabeth,	b. January 1, 1751-2
Enoch,	b. October 28, 1753
Nathan Hale,	b. June 6, 1755
Richard,	b. February 20, 1757
Bille,	b. April 23, 1759
David and Jonathan (twins),	b. December 15, 1761
Joanna,	b. March 19, 1764
Susannah,	b. February, 1766

Children of John Hale and Sarah Adams Hale.

Still-born child (daughter),	b. August 19, 1786

Children of Lieut. Joseph and Rebeccah (Harris) Hale.

Elisabeth,	b. September 29, 1779
Rebeccah,	b. January 9, 1781
Mary,	b. November 23, 1782
Sarah,	b. November 27, 1783

Children of Billy and Hannah (Barker) Hale.

Billy,	b. January 15, 1786

Children of Richard, Jr., and Mary (Wright) Hale.

Mary,	b. July 6, 1787
Laura,	b. August 29, 1789
Polly,	b. January 25, 1792

HALL.

Children of Theodora and Mary Hall.

Mary Jane,	b. July 9, 1827
Mariah,	b. July 13, 1829
Theodore Whiting,	b. November 30, 1832
William,	b. July 18, 1834

Children of Adrastus and Lucretia Hall.

Sarah Ann,	b. in East Windsor, April 30, 1839
Adelaide D.,	b. in Coventry, May 1, 1841

HAMLIN.

Children of Timothy and Lucinda (Brown) Hamlin.

Laura,	b. December 15, 1800

HAMMOND or HAMMON.

Children of Elijah and Mary (Kingsbury) Hammond.

Nathaniel,	b. September 11, 1733
Hannah,	b. April 7, 1736
Presilla,	b. August 8, 1741

Children of Zephaniah and Mary (Badcock) Hammon.

Edmister,	b. August 20, 1770
Mary,	b. August 27, 1772
Mehitable,	b. November 2, 1774
Elisabeth,	b. April 17, 1779

HARRIS
Children of Isaac and Prisilla Harris.
Almira,	b. October 3, 1796
Barris (?),	b. September 10, 1798

HATCH.
Children of Joseph and Mercy Hatch.
Amy,	b. October 11, 1713
Mercy,	b. August 23, 1717

Children of Benjamin and Sarah Hatch.
Jonathan,	b. August 16, 1750
Sarah,	b. December 3, 1752

Children of Ephraim and Sophia Hatch.
Seabury Manning,	b. December 3, 1809
William Dana,	b. March 26, 1812
Ralph Lathrop,	b. March 25, 1814
George,	b. April 9, 1816
Olive Sophia,	b. April 6, 1822

Children of Roswell Hatch and Wife.
Jesse West,	b. July 19, 1809
Amelia Sophia,	b. October 26, 1814

HAWKINS or HALKINS or HOLCKINS.
Children of Joseph and Sarah (Southworth) Haukins.
Sarah,	b. January 21, 1753
Mary,	b. May 11, 1754
Zebulon,	b. May 16, 1756
Rebeckah,	b. March 30, 1758
Elisabeth,	b. February 6, 1760
Martha,	b. August 5, 1761
Joseph,	b. March 22, 1763
Ebenezer,	b. October 30, 1764
Olive,	b. April 23, 1766
Roger,	b. June 4, 1768
Lavinia,	b. November 28, 1769
Susannah,	b. October 1, 1771
Jonathan,	b. January 9, 1774

Children of Ozias and Anne (Rose) Hawkins.
Jerusha,   b. May 2, 1757
Reodilfus,   b. May 2, 1759
Daniel,   b. June 10, 1764
Children of James and Phebe (Dimick) Hawkins.
Leurethe (?), (dau.)   b. January 13, 1758
James and Phebe (twins),   b. August 11, 1759
Salome,   b. February 2, 1764
Bershabe,   b. April 26, 1765
Christiany,   b. October 31, 1770
Children of John and Naony (Shipman) Hawkins.
Abel,   b. September 19, 1757
Amariah (son),   b. January 30, 1758
John,   b. November 28, 1741 (died)
Trifene,   b. June 15, 1743
Tabethe,   b. March 30, 1745
John, Jr.,   b. May 18, 1747
George,   b. May 5, 1749
Samuel,   b. February 12, 1751
Hannah,   b. February 1, 1754
Children of George and Hannah Hawkins.
Martha Day,   b. April 23, 1770
George, Jr.,   b. 26th day (no month), 1775
Jesse,   b. January 11, 1778
Mary,   b. September 10 1780
Hepsibah,   b. December 22, 1783
Hannah,   b. August 20, 1785
Nathan,   b. July 7, 1788
Children of Joseph and Zerviah (Howard) Hawkins.
Zerviah,   b. June 26, 1778
Lucy,   b. April 1, 1780
Joseph,   b. November 14, 1781
Rufus,   b. April 3, 1785
Gordon,   b. July 9, 1786

HEARICK.

Children of Daniel and Elizabeth (Rust) Hearick.
Samuel,   b. April 27, 1732
Sylva,   b. February 12, 1734

Tyrean, b. April 3, 1737
Margaret, b. April 6, 1740
    Children of Steven and Mary Hearick.
Steven, b. August 9, 1728
    Children of Joseph and Lydia (Rust) Hearick.
Bial and Mehitable (twins), b. October 24, 1738
Ledia, b. September 28, 1739
Hebe, b. January 6, 1741
Joseph, b. September 25, 1743
Ann, b. March 1, 1746
Ledia, b. June 22, 1749
Abigail, b. November 11, 1755

HEATH.

    Children of Isaac and Rachael Heath.
Joseph, b. July 20, 1723
    Children of Ebenezer and Lidia Heath.
Lydia, b. January 26, 1729
Solomon, b. March 31, 1741
Joshua, b. March 17, 1743

HENDEE.

    Children of Jonathan and Martha (Millinton) Hendee.
Rachael, b. October 29, 1741
Jonathan, b. March 27, 1743
Richard, b. June 14, 1744
Caleb, b. August 30, 1745
Solomon, b. November 14, 1746
    Children of Joshua Hendee and wife.
Joshua, b. June 2, 1739
    Children of Asa and Mary Hendee.
Asa, b. December 8, 1739
Asa, b. January 19, 1740-1
Lydia, b. July 14, 1746
Eunice, b. November 24, 1748
Mary, b. January 14, 1751
Abner, b. May 22, 1753
Esther, b. May 29, 1757

HENDEY.

Children of Eliphilet and Mary Hendey.

Mary,	b. June 3, 1780
Eliphilet, Jr.,	b. July 25, 1783
Justin,	b. July 2, 1785

HIBBARD or Hibberd.

Children of Selah and Esther (Loomis) Hibbard.

Selah,	b. June 2, 1793
Chauncey,	b. December 31, 1794
Clarissa,	b. November 11, 1796
Arabella,	b. March 8, 1800
Dorcas,	b. March 27, 1802

Children of Selah and Roxana (Sweetland) Hibbard.

Chauncey,	b. June 25, 1817
Munroe,	b. December 17, 1818

Children of Henry and Sally Hibbard.

Henry Edgbert,	b. November 5, 1815

HOCKINGS or HOLCKINS.

Children of George, Jr., and Hepsibah (Janes) Hockings.

Hannah,	b. April 7, 1730
Hepsibah,	b. December 17, 1731
Phebe,	b. January 4, 1734
Ozias,	b. August 1, 1736
Dorkis,	b. April 22, 1738
Eunis,	b. February 26, 1739-40
Ann,	b. September 23, 1741
Deborah,	b. February 8, 1743-4
George,	b. April 13, 1746

Children of James and Sarah Holckings.

Joseph,	b. February 6, 1730-31
James,	b. November 24, 1733

HOUSE.

Children of Samuel and Mary House.

Samuel,	b. September 13, 1745
Lydia,	b. May 6, 1750

Joseph,	b. November 18, 1752
Mary,	b. May 6, 1755
Benjamin,	b. August 27, 1757

Children of Jonathan and Ruth House.

Theodora,	b. in Lebanon, March 16, 1754
Rebeckah (daughter),	b. in Coventry, August 8, 1757
Asel,	b. July 3, 1759
Rebeckah,	b. April 15, 1762
Abiel and Mabel (twins),	b. May 2, 1765
Betty,	b. May 23, 1767

Children of Samuel, Jr., and Hannah (Perry) House.

Samuel ye 3d,	b. May 15, 1771
James,	b. December 7, 1773

HOWARD.

Children of Dr. Nathan and Joanna (Hale) Howard.

John,	b. November 10, 1784
Joanna,	b. December 10, 1787
Anne,	b. August 29, 1789
Chauncey,	b. December 18, 1791
Nathan,	b. March 20, 1795
Elisabeth,	b. July 21, 1797 (died next day)
Rufus,	b. July 22, 1799
Richard Hale,	b. February 17, 1802

A son, born March 7, 1804, lived one hour.

Children of John and Lucy (Ripley) Howard.

John Ripley,	b. February 18, 1810
Chauncey,	b. April 1, 1812

HUBBARD.

Children of Jonathan and Hannah Hubbard.

Rachael,	b. September 30, 1719

HUNT.

Children of William and Rachael Hunt.

Ebenezer (still-born),	May 12, 1760

Children of William and Mary (Crosby) Hunt.

Oliver,	b. May 10, 1763
Rachael,	b. March 8, 1765

Children of Eliphaz and Hannah Hunt.

Ebenezer,	b. July 2, 1766
Eliphaz,	b. April 18, 1772
Hannah,	b. September 30, 1774
Ruth,	b. July 2, 1779
Eleazer (son of Capt. Eliphaz and Hannah),	b. December 28, 1786

Children of Gad and Elisabeth (Woodward) Hunt.

Gad,	b. April 14, 1773
Horace,	b. January 7, 1788
Clarissa,	b. November 27, 1799

Children of Gad, Jr., and Molly (Bissell) Hunt.

Polly Bissell,	b. March 28, 1803
Clarissa Harlowe,	b. January 3, 1805
Sanford Myrtillo (son),	b. November 23, 1807
Lucius Abbot,	July 3, 1813

Children of Doctor Ebenezer and Anne Hunt.

Ebenezer Jr.,	b. June 14, 1794

Children of Elijah and Mehitabel (Dexter) Hunt.

Hannah Haul,	b. March 23, 1805

Children of Eliphaz, Jr., and Anna (Phelps) Hunt.

Trumbull,	b. March 25, 1805
Mary Eliza,	b. May 3, 1806
Emily,	b. March 29, 1809

Children of Dr. Eleazer and Sybil Hunt.

Ebenezer,	b. August 26, 1810
Eleazer Pomroy,	b. June 21, 1814
Mary Elisabeth,	b. May 10, 1816
Ruth Francis,	b. July 20, 1830

HUNTINGTON.

Children of Joseph, Jr., and Mirza (Dow) Huntington.

Flavius Josephus,	b. May 13, 1789
Eduard Guy,	b. Washington, Ga., October 22, 1792

Children of Septimus G. and Mary (Tyler Morse) Huntington.

Mary Elisabeth, b. May 16, 1811

HUTCHINSON.

Children of Ephraim and Elizabeth (Jones) Hutchinson.

Warren,	b. November 17, 1779
Levina,	b. April 23, 1782
Polly,	b. October 2, 1784
Betsey,	b. January 5, 1787
Luther,	b. November 28, 1791

Children of Willard and Sophia (Kingsbury) Hutchinson.

Caroline Sophia,	b. August 9, 1812
Joseph Willard,	b. November 11, 1814
Ruth Elisa,	b. October 7, 1816
Henry Willard,	b. October 6, 1819
Mary Kingsbury,	b. May 26, 1826

HIBBARD.

Children of Henry and Sally Hibbard.

Henry Edgbert, b. November 5, 1815

ISHAM.

Children of Oliver H. and Minerva Isham.

James Edgar,	b. August 17, 1823
Lucius Dwight,	b. August 23, 1824

JACSON.

Children of James and Mary Jacson.

Caleb, b. February 11, 1749-50

JANES.

Children of Seth and Sarah (Larrabe) Janes.

Iraney,	b. February 11, 1740-1
Lucy,	b. June 19, 1742
Elijah,	b. April 19, 1744
Eunice,	b. March 10, 1748
Samuel,	b. March 9, 1750
Elias,	b. March 6, 1752
Oliver,	b. November 12, 1754
Seth,	b. July 8, 1756
Solomon,	b. February 6, 1758
Timothy,	b. March 9, 1764

Children of Elisha and Widow Mary Dimock Janes.

Elisha,	b. June 30, 1741
Bethshale,	b. February 10, 1742-3
Mary,	b. February 10, 1744-5

Children of Elijah and Anne (Hawkins) Janes.

Heman,	b. June 9, 1765

Children of Elisha and Mary Janes.

Samuel and Daniel (twins),	b. February 1, 1747

One lived seven days, the other eight days.

Benjamin,	b. March 3, 1748
Daniel,	b. March 17, 1750
Triphena,	b. January 3, 1755
Tabothy,	b. February 22, 1757
Jerushe,	b. July 27, 1752

Children of Elisha, Jr., and Elizabeth (Davenport) Janes.

Elisabeth,	b. May 30, 1764

Children of Elisha, Jr., and Desire (Thompson) Janes.

Roger,	b. August 7, 1767
Esther,	b. January 6, 1769
Daniel,	b. August 12, 1770
Eliphama,	b. January 21, 1772
Mary,	b. June 10, 1774
Nathaniel,	b. September 21, 1777
Jessie,	b. June 24, 1779
Livinia,	b. June 26, 1781
David,	b. January 17, 1783

Children of Samuel and Abigail Janes.

Eunice,	b. January 17, 1774
Betheny,	b. March 2, 1775
Lucy,	May 22, 1777
Abigail,	b. July 19, 1779
Royal,	b. October 7, 1781
Joseph,	b. May 13, 1784
James,	b. July 3, 1786
Infant child,	b. October 11, 1791 (died same day)

BIRTHS FROM TOWN RECORDS

Children of Samuel and Rebeckah (House) Janes.
Samuel, b. September 17, 1792
Children of Oliver and Judith (Rollo) Janes.
Sarah, b. January 31, 1776
Children of Elias, Jr., and Susannah (Robertson) Janes.
Elias, Jr., b. August 19, 1775
Children of Solomon and Susanna (Trapp) Janes.
Henry, b. October 11, 1796
Sally, b. April 20, 1798
Wealthy, b. November 15, 1799
Children of Elias and Hannah Janes.
Oliver, b. April 29, 1789
Polly, b. September 2, 1790
Sterling, b. December 24, 1792
Chauncey, b. June 11, 1795
Harmony, b. November 8, 1797
Clarissa, b. June 9, 1801

JEWETT.

Children of Ichabod and Mary (Carpenter) Jewett.
Anna, b. April 12, 1762
Ichabod, b. September 19, 1763
Benjamin, b. April 23, 1765
Children of Elam and Eunice (Richardson) Jewett.
Jemima, b. July 6, 1769
Elam, b. November 19, 1770
Jared, b. January 26, 1771
Jeremiah, b. December 7, 1773
Othnial, b. April 1, 1775

JOHNSON.

Children of Seth and Hannah Johnson.
David and Jonathan (twins), b. February 14, 1752
Samuel, b. October 11, 1753
Hannah, b. August 8, 1755

JONES.

Children of Benjamin and Hannah Jones.
Seth, b. August 31, 1715

COVENTRY RECORDS

Children of Benjamin and 2d wife, Patience Jones.

Ebenezer,	b. April 8, 1718
Ester,	b. May 1, 1720
Jonathan,	b. June 21, 1722
Noah,	b. May 15, 1724
Benjamin,	b. September 15, 1726
Huldah,	b. June 25, 1729
Asael,	b. July 7, 1731
Sybil,	b. April 22, 1735
Dina,	b. March 29, 1739

Children of Benjamin, Jr., and Mehitabel (Teril) Jones.

Benjamin 3d,	b. January 21, 1757
Huldah,	b. December 31, 1759
Silas,	b. September 1, 1764
Daniel,	b. April 23, 1767

Children of Jonathan and Abijah (Strong) Jones.

Sibel,	b. November 30, 1747
Levy,	b. September 26, 1749
Simeon,	b. November 14, 1751

Children of Noah and Dinah (Hichcock) Jones.

Asael,	b. March 30, 1746
Remembrance,	b. April 13, 1748
Elisha,	b. April 13, 175-
Elisabeth,	b. October 18, 1758
Patience,	b. April 27, 1760
Eliakim,	b. October 1, 1764
Hannah,	b. July 21, 1767

Children of Ebenezer and Zeruiah (Loomis) Jones.

Abigail,	b. February 24, 1747
Adonijah,	b. August, 1748
Dinah,	b. October 11, 1750
Ebenezer, Jr.,	b. April 19, 1752
Israel,	b. October 24, 1753
Abigail,	b. February 2, 1756
Esther,	b. April 24, 1758
Benona,	b. November 5, 1759
Eber,	b. June 4, 1761
Silas,	b. July 28, 1764

BIRTHS FROM TOWN RECORDS

Children of Asael and Eunice (Hende) Jones.

Marting,	b. April 12, 1774
Wharton,	b. September 27, 1777
Millender,	b. November 28, 1779

Children of Adonijah and Sarah (Lyman) Jones.

Sarah, b. April 26, 1771

Children of Eliakim and Rebecca (Webster) Jones.

Rebecka,	b. November 26, 1786
Eliakim, Jr.,	b. January 27, 1788
Gardner,	b. March 25, 1793

Children of Noah, Jr., and Dolla (Hiltham) Jones.

—— (daughter),	b. June 21, 1786
Sabrah,	b. April 27, 1788

Children of Amasa 2d and Lavinia Jones.

Lucy Maria, b. December 30, 1832

Children of John Jones and Wife.

George, b. January 29, 1797

JUDD.

Children of Thomas and Julianna Judd.

Julianna,	b. in Lebanon, June 8, 1752
Elizabeth,	b. in Coventry, August 7, 1754
Thomas,	b. October 8, 1756
Solomon,	b. September 21, 1758
Elias,	b. December 15, 1760
Hannah,	b. April 20, 1764
Lois,	b. May 30, 1766
John,	b. May 25, 1768

Children of Solomon and Anna (Carpenter) Judd.

James Harvey,	b. January 2, 1794
Anna Carpenter,	b. November 15, 1795
John Flavel,	b. September 6, 1798
William Gurley,	b. August 2, 1804

Araunah (son), b. August 9, 1806
Esther Baker, b. March 29, 1812
   Children of William G. and Livia H. Judd.
William Franklin, b. August 23, 1836
Mary Anne, b. August 27, 1838
   Children of Elias and Beulah Judd.
Enoch, b. in Coventry, October 28, 1784
Polly, b. in Pittsfield. Mass., August 18, 1786
Elias G., b. January 8, 1788
Samuel, b. February 11, 1790
Thomas C., b. October 10, 1793
Chauncey, b. in Coventry, January 5, 1796
Elisabeth Larrabe, b. March 19, 1798
Rufus, b. December 25, 1800

KEACH.

Asa Keach, b. in Mansfield, Ct., December 5, 1782
Betsey Cogswell, his wife,
      b. in Coventry, Ct., December 11, 1785
   Children of Asa and Betsey (Cogswell) Keach.
Benjamin Franklin, b. in Vernon, August 26, 1809
Jason Corning, b. in Coventry, October 28, 1810
Horatio Nelson, b. in Coventry, May 29, 1812

KENDAL.

   Children of Peter and Bely Kendal.
Lyman, b. June 7, 1779

KENDRICK.

   Children of Nathaniel and Judah Kendrick.
Samuel, b. January 6, 1746-7
Thomas, b. February 3, 1749
Abigail, b. March 3, 1751
Samuel, b. March 25, 1753
Ruth, b. March 6, 1755
Daniel, b. November 2, 1757
Lydia, b. March, 1763

KIDDER.

Children of Ephraim and Freedom (Barnard) Kidder.

Easther,	b. July 17, 1739
Anne,	b. January 22, 1740-1
Febe,	b. October 2, 1742
Oliver,	b. December 19, 1743
Abel,	b. February 3, 1744-5
Cloe,	b. May 11, 1747
Abigail,	b. July 29, 1748
Sarah,	b. September 19, 1749

KING.

Children of Jonathan and Martha (Woodward) King.

Stephen,	b. December 24, 1743
Silas,	b. February 17, 1745-6
Jonathan,	b. June 13, 1748
Hannah, daughter of Jonathan,	(no date)

KINGSBURY.

Children of Nathaniel and Hannah Kingsbury.

John,	b. April 25, 1710
Nathaniel,	b. September 8, 1711
Mary,	b. November 5, 1713
Simon,	b. July 25, 1715
Jabez,	b. June 21, 1717
Hannah,	b. January 23, 1719
Priscilla,	b. March 22, 1720
Joseph,	b. March 27, 1721
Denison,	b. June 7, 1723
Lemuel, or Samuel,	b. August 23, 1725
Jeremiah,	b. December 2, 1726
Sarah,	b. January 13, 1727-8
Phineas,	b. May 9, 1731
Ruth,	b. May 26, 1737

Children of John and Deborah Kingsbury.

John,	b. September 28, 1704
Irena,	b. July 24, 1731
Eunes,	b. February 17, 1733-4
Lydia,	b. October 10, 1737

Children of Ebenezer and Priscilla Kingsbury.

Ebenezer,	b. August 28, 1744
Mary,	b. March 31, 1746
Ebenezer,	b. January 27, 1749-50
Priscilla,	b. December 26, 1751
Joseph,	b. April 19, 1753
Priscilla,	b. January 21, 1756
Martha Edgerton,	b. July 16, 1758
Ebenezer,	b. August 30, 1762

Children of Thomas and Anne Kingsbury.

Samuel,	b. February 5, 1745-6
Hannah,	b. August 30, 1748
Anne,	b. September 29, 1749
Sarah,	b. April 15, 1752
Thomas,	b. September 1, 1754

Children of Eleazer and Freelove (Rust) Kingsbury.

Freelove,	b. April 22, 1743
Ann,	b. May 18, 1745
Sarah,	b. February 1, 1746-7
Eleazer,	b. February 14, 1749-50
Samuel Rust,	b. February 27, 1754

Children of Simon and Deliverance Kingsbury.

Deliverance,	b. November 18, 1742

Children of Absolom and Rebeckah (Rust) Kingsbury.

Asa,	b. October 10, 1752
Ebenezer,	b. March 2, 1755
Ephraim,	b. September 2, 1759
Margaret,	b. June 13, 1761
Obadiah,	b. May 3, 1763
Elisha,	b. February 2, 1770

Children of Jabez and Mary (Phelps) Kingsbury.

Nathaniel,	b. October 4, 1751
Ruth,	b. May 27, 1753
Joseph,	b. February, 1755
Jabez,	b. May 20, 1758
Jeremiah,	b. March 5, 1757
Mary,	b. October 26, 1760

BIRTHS FROM TOWN RECORDS

Ameliah,　　　　　　　　　　b. January 15, 1764
Anne,　　　　　　　　　　　b. April 20, 1766

Children of Nathaniel and Asenath (Daggett) Kingsbury.

Allen,　　　　　　　　　　　b. February 9, 1779
Wealthy,　　　　　　　　　　b. October 24, 1783
Asenath,　　　　　　　　　　b. October 7, 1785
Jabez,　　　　　　　　　　　b. October 9, 1788

Olive Kingsbury, the wife of Samuel Kingsbury,
　　　　b. in Norwalk, March 7, 1749 (O. S.)

Children of Samuel and Olive Kingsbury.

Josiah,　　　　　　　　　　b. September 7, 1772
Olive,　　　　　　　　　　　b. December 24, 1775
Iza,　　　　　　　　　　　　b. May 31, 1777

Children of Ephraim and Phebe Kingsbury.

Oliver,　　　　　　　　　　b. June 13, 1761
William,　　　　　　　　　b. February 9, 1764
Phebe,　　　　　　　　　　b. March 22, 1766
Jabez,　　　　　　　　　　b. October 22, 1769
Ephraim,　　　　　　　　　b. June 18, 1775

Children of Jabez and Fanny (Davenport) Kingsbury.

Samuel Newel,　　　　　　b. December 12, 1815
Henry Dwight,　　　　　　b. October 18, 1817
Samuel Newel,　　　　　　b. October 8, 1819

Children of Harvey and Polly (Wright) Kingsbury.

Elisabeth Wright,　　　　　b. December 31, 1824
Mary Jeffers,　　　　　　　b. December 31, 1826

Children of Capt. Joseph and Ruth (Benton) Kingsbury.

Sophia,　　　　　　　　　　b. July 27, 1784
Betsey,　　　　　　　　　　b. February 16, 1786
Polly,　　　　　　　　　　　b. November 16, 1787
William,　　　　　　　　　b. August 13, 1789
Joseph,　　　　　　　　　　b. July 19, 1791
Harvey,　　　　　　　　　b. December 17, 1794
Royal,　　　　　　　　　　b. July 4, 1798

Children of Joseph and Lois (Porter) Kingsbury.

Lois,	b. January 14, 1781
Oliver,	b. June 24, 1782
Eunice Barker,	b. November 14, 1784
Ward,	b. January 10, 1787
Roxane,	b. August 5, 1791
Ruth,	b. April 24, 1798
Addison,	b. July 5, 1800

Children of Jabez and Freelove Kingsbury.

Anna,	b. July 12, 1790
Elisha,	b. October 12, 1793
Ameniah,	b. March 10, 1796
Ephraim,	b. July 20, 1799
Alven,	b. March 9, 1803
Backus,	b. September 25, 1805
Nelson,	b. April 3, 1808
Phebe,	b. June 9, 1810
Erastus,	b. April 29, 1812

Harriet Newel, daughter of Jabez and Chloe, b. May 25, 1825

Children of Joseph, Jr., and Wife.

Lucius,	b. September 20, 1828

Children of Nathaniel and Elisabeth Kingsbury.

Elisabeth,	b. November 14, 1778
Clarissa,	b. August 20, 1780
Ebenezer,	b. November 26, 1782
Nathaniel,	b. February 1, 1785
Lora,	b. September 17, 1787
Daniel,	b. July 22, 1790; d. same day

Children of John and Dolly Kingsbury.

Dorothy Leavens,	b. December 9, 1799
John,	b. May 26, 1801
Ezra,	b. January 26, 1804

Children of Ezra and Eunice Kingsbury.

Dorothy Jane,	b. December 7, 1827

BIRTHS FROM TOWN RECORDS

KINNE or KEENEY.

Children of Benjamin and Thankful Kenne.
Elizabeth, b. February 12, 1750-1
Children of George and Lydia (Robertson) Keeney.
Wealthy, b. January 19, 1793

KIMPTON.

Martin Kimpton, b. in Uxbridge, Mass., May 19, 1800
Olive Hoxie, his wife, b. in Voluntown, Conn., June 15, 1804
Children of Martin and Olive (Hoxie) Kimpton.
Joseph M., b. in Smithfield, October 9, 1824
Luther M., b. in Griswauld, October 30, 1826
Huldah M., b. in Coventry, June 4, 1828
William A., b. May 30, 1830
Phebe, b. December 25, 1832
Susan, b. March 19, 1834
Elvira E., b. June 4, 1836
Martin D., b. August 3, 1837
Julia Ann, b. January 4, 1839
Sally, b. August 3, 1840

LAD or LADD.

Children of Timothy and Easter (Parker) Lad.
Anne, b. October 31, 1734
Rachael, b. May 8, 1736
Timothy, b. July 13, 1738
Phenias, b. January 8, 1741-2
Zebulon, b. May 22, 1743
Nathaniel, b. July 15, 1745
Children of Henry and Abigail (Liley) Lad.
Jerusha, b. June 26, 1741
Henry, b. January 25, 1742-3
Nathaniel, b. January 7, 1749-50
Abigail, b. October 5, 1752
Amasa, b. October 18, 1762
Children of Samuel and Anne (Woodward) Ladd.
Nathaniel, b. October 4, 1751
Samuel, b. July 16, 1753

Dorias,	b. October 19, 1756
Ashbel,	b. January 15, 1759
Oliver,	b. October 1, 1760
Anna,	b. November 17, 1762
Frederick,	b. October 9, 1765
Phebe,	b. June 15, 1767

Children of Nathaniel, Jr., and Elisabeth (Rust) Lad.

Febe,	b. January 3, 1741-2
Irane,	b. May 20, 1744

Children of Moses and Keziah (Killeen) Lad.

Oliver,	b. July 30, 1769

Children of Samuel, Jr., and Elizabeth (Remington) Lad.

Ason,	b. March 2, 1776
Wealthy,	b. March 14, 1778

Children of John and Prudence (Shepard) Ladd.

Palmer,	b. March 6, 1765
John,	b. February 24, 1767
Hannah,	b. January 13, 1763 (?)
Prudence,	b. March 3, 1768
Susannah,	b. September 11, 1772

Children of Nathaniel, Jr., and Rachael (Tilden) Ladd.

Nathaniel,	b. January 16, 1774
Lois,	b. February 13, 1776
Jason,	b. April 7, 1778

Children of Dr. Henry, Jr., and Abial (Richardson) Ladd.

Jerusha,	b. February 15, 1767
Henry 3d,	b. August 8, 1768
Herman,	b. February 6, 1770
Jerusha,	b. April 11, 1772
Peregrine,	b. January 1, 1774
Lorin,	b. June 8, 1775
Hiram,	b. October 16, 1776
Benoni,	b. July 24, 1778

Children of Samuel and Hannah Ladd.

Moses,	b. June 24, 1745
Mary,	b. November 16, 1746
Ruth,	b. January 22, 1749-50

Children of Dr. Henry & Mary (Hendee) Ladd.
Silenda, b. February 10, 1772
Children of Palmer Ladd.
Rachael, b. December 23, 1794
Children of Ashbel and Irene (Babcock) Ladd.
Ashbel, b. October 4, 1782
Children of Philip N. and Betsey (Davenport) Ladd.
Miranda, b. September 1, 1795
Lyman Lathrop, b. April 1, 1797

LAMB.

Children of Ebenezer and Abigail (Larrabe) Lamb.
Ebenezer, b. October 21, 1753
Children of Benjamin and Abigail (Sims) Lamb.
Zerviah, b. January 8, 1756
Benjamin, b. August 17, 1758

LAMPHEAR.

Children of Isaac and Marah (Edwards) Lamphear.
Marah, b. September 13, 1755
Isaac, b. August 3, 1757
Children of Isaac and Sarah (Hamilton) Lamphear, 2d wife.
Salem, b. February 5, 1763
John, b. August 14, 1764
Sarah, b. April 6, 1766
Ebenezer, b. March 7, 1768
David, b. April, 1770
Lydia, b. August 12, 1772
Children of Isaac Edward and Lois (Johnes) Lamphear.
Polly, b. September 8, 1779
Children of William and Abigail (Simon) Lamphear.
William, b. June 24, 1765
Abigail Simon, afterward wife to Hembrey Grover.

LARRABE.

Children of Joseph and Judith Larrabe.
Seth, b. April 22, 1729
Jabez, b. July 11, 1734

Enoch, b. October 23, 1736
Ebenezer and Richard (twins), b. February 26, 1738-9
Abigail, b. February 9, 1732-3
    Children of Richard and Martha (Webster) Larrabe.
Ebenezer, b. October 24, 1760
Richard, b. June 26, 1762
Martha b. August 18, 1764
Elias, b. June 2, 1766
    Children of Enoch and Mary (Gera) Larrabe.
Beulah, b. November 7, 1757
Enoch, b. February 27, 1760
Joseph, b. June 30, 1762
Mary, b. November 24, 1765
John, b. September 25, 1767
Justus, b. March 27, 1770
    Children of Seth and Hannah Larrabe.
Jerusha, b. September 4, 1752

LATHROP.

    Children of Roger and Alice Lathrop.
Francis, b. June 24, 1800
Joel, b. November 7, 1802
Albert, b. March 29, 1805
Lucy, b. October 9, 1808
Mary, b. July 26, 1812
Mary, b. January 14, 1815

LAWRENCE.

    Children of Henry and Sarah Lawrence.
Jonathan, b. October 7, 1784
Benjamin Fairbanks, b. April 16, 1787

LEE.

Jedediah Lee, b. February 1, 1696
Lydya Lee, b. April 21, 1699
David Lee, b. June 26, 1705
Josiah Lee. b. October 6, 1707
    Children of Jedediah and Lucy (Dodge) Lee.
Elias, b. July 26, 1723
Jerusha, b. October 20, 1728

BIRTHS FROM TOWN RECORDS

Lydia, (illegible)
Zebulon, b. December 7, 1730
   Children of David and Lydy Lee.
Abigail, b. (no month) 1713
Jonathan, b. July 10, 1718
   Children of David, Jr., and Mary Lee.
David, b. January 11, 1739

LEONARD.

   Children of Abial Leonard.
George, son of Abial Leonard, b. October 7, 1799

LEWES or LUIS.

   Children of Samuel and Rebeckah Lewes.
Mary, b. September 24, 1713
Samuell, b. April 23, 1715
John, b. June 29, 1718
Rebeckah, b. August 2, 1721
Jabez, b. June 7, 1724
   Children of John and Margerit Luis.
Dorety, b. September 11, 1742

LILLY or LILLEY.

   Children of Samuel and Abigail (Lad) Lilly.
Eunice, b. August 20, 1742
Abigail, b. June 28, 1744
Hannah, b. January 5, 1747
   Children of Samuel, Jr., and Elisabeth (Ferry) Lilly.
Eunice, b. September 5, 1777
Ira, b. July 1, 1781
Duthan, b. June 3, 1786
   Children of Samuel and Mehitable Lilly.
Jonathan, b. April 20, 1728

LONG.

   Children of Joseph and Sarah Long.
Jerusha, b. April 13, 1717
Sarah, b. December 8, 1719
Abigail, b. May 30, 1721

Jonathan,   b. May 12, 1723
Martha,   b. April 3, 1725
Samuel,   b. July 12, 1727
Simeon,   b. July 14, 1729
Stephen,   b. July 20, 1732

    Children of Jonathan and Azubah (Cooley) Long.

Luman,   b. February 2, 1745-6
Abigail,   b. October 19, 1747
Lucy,   b. November 26, 1750
Jeremiah,   b. March 28, 1753
Noah Cooley,   b. December 11, 1755
Louise,   b. May 16, 1758
Benony,   b. August 11, 1760
Rhoda,   b. July 15, 1763
Noah Cooley,   b. April 17, 1765

    Children of Silas and Lidia (Euets) Long.

Josiah,   b. February 9, 1730-1
Azubah,   b. June 10, 1733
Ruth,   b. April 21, 1735
Silas,   b. September 26, 1737
Mehitable,   b. October 28, 1739
Sarah,   b. March 25, 1743

    Children of William and Mary Long.

Lidia,   b. February 23, 1697
Mary,   b. April 26, 1703

    Children of Lemuel and Martha (Bristor) Long.

Lemuel,   b. December 28, 1751
Martha,   b. February 6, 1753
Joseph,   b. September 14, 1754
Rufus,   b. April 6, 1756
Levi,   b. July 23, 1758
Jesse,   b. August 22, 1760
Diadema,   b. January 14, 1763
Stephen,   b. March 8, 1765
Reuben,   b. March 29, 1767

    Children of Zelotes and Sophia Long.

Zelotes Clark,   b. October 15, 1815

LOOMIS.

Children of Nathaniel and Sarah (Riley) Loomis.

Sarah,	b. December 2, 1743
Jabez,	b. September 28, 1745
Nathaniel,	b. August 28, 1747
Eunes,	b. October 2, 1749
Abigail,	b. October 19, 1751
Jonathan,	b. December 16, 1753
Ebenezer,	b. May 2, 1756

Children of Jonathan and Margaret Loomis.

John,	b. July 12, 1745
Lydia,	b. May 8, 1749
Rhoda,	b. October 3, 1752

Children of Bennony and Mary Loomis.

Easter,	b. July 16, 1748

Children of Elijah and Rebeckah Loomis.

Joseph,	b. August 24, 1771

Children of Zachariah and Huldah (Jones) Loomis.

Lydia,	b. December 29, 1751
Israel,	b. December 26, 1754
Huldah,	b. January 1, 1756
Hannah,	b. October 1, 1758
Lois and Eunice (twins),	b. February 23, 1761
Ebenezer,	b. October 14, 1763
Zachariah,	b. April 28, 1770
Abigail,	No date

Children of Reuel and Roxsalana Loomis.

John,	b. November 21, 1812
Roxsalana,	b. May 24, 1814
Mary Emma,	b. March 4, 1817
Walter Adams,	b. May 24, 1823

Children of Eleazar 2d and Olive (Palmer) Loomis.

Marshall Ney,	b. July 10, 1816

Children of Daniel Loomis, Jr., and Polly (Hibbard) Loomis.

Eunice,	b. August 29, 1788

Daniel 3d, b. September 18, 1789
Eleazer, b. June 8, 1792
Polly, b. August 25, 1794

    Children of Israel, Jr., and Sarah (Addams) Loomis.

Israel, Jr., b. June 26, 1779
John, b. January 26, 1781
Buel, b. March 27, 1783
Sarah, b. June 8, 1785
Daniel, b. April 1, 1787
David, b. September 5, 1789
Nancy, b. October 20, 1794
Huldah, b. November 26, 1796
Walter Adams, b. September 4, 1802

    Children of Eleazer and Lucretia (Porter) Loomis.

Tirzah Porter, b. March 27, 1804
Lucretia, b. February 10, 1806
Francis, b. July 23, 1808
George Nelson, b. June 6, 1811
Emily, b. September 20, 1813
Joseph Porter, b. February 24, 1816

    Children of Walter and Diantha Loomis.

Caroline, b. October 16, 1808
Sophrona, b. September 10, 1810
Maria, b. September 18, 1812
Lydia Olive, b. December 1, 1814
Walter, Jr., b. August 11, 1817
Oliver Porter, b. January 20, 1820
Milo, b. March 18, 1823
Catharin, b. October 13, 1826

    Children of Levi and Violette (Metcalf) Loomis.

Jabez Metcalf, b. June 13, 1795
Emilia, b. August 5, 1797
Maria, b. July 24, 1800
Peleg Thomas, b. February 24, 1803
Martha Thares, b. March 9, 1806

    Children of William and Matilda Loomis.

Louisa, b. October 3, 1832

BIRTHS FROM TOWN RECORDS

Children of Daniel and Mary Loomis.

Esther,	b. July 3, 1763
Daniel,	b. March 9, 1765
Zenus,	b. June 15, 1767
Mary,	b. September 22, 1769
Gemaliel,	b. November 20, 1771
Silas,	b. December 19, 1773
Faith,	b. February 23, 1776
Pamela,	b. March 12, 1778
Walter,	b. May 6, 1780
Lydia,	b. October 4, 1782
Selah,	b. April 23, 1785

Children of Ebenezer and Eunice (Bourn) Loomis.

Eunice,	b. November 16, 1787
Susannah,	b. December 4, 1790
Ebenezer,	b. March 9, 1794
Mariah,	b. May 1, 1796
Sophia,	b. March 13, 1798
Maria,	b. October 28, 1800
Lucy Matilda,	b. March 3, 1809

LORD.

Children of Solomon and Miriam (Colman) Lord.

Betty,	b. May 16, 1767

LYMAN or LIMAN.

Children of Samuel and Elizabeth Liman.

Ichabod,	b. January 4, 1724-5
Jeams,	b. June 3, 1727
Elizabeth,	b. April 29, 1730
Eunes,	b. September 4, 1733
Desiah,	b. August 17, 1735
Dorcas,	b. June 3, 1739

Children of Jacob and Mehitable Lyman.

Jacob,	b. May 6, 1746
Mehitabel,	b. June 22, 1748
Sarah,	b. June 9, 1750
Ireny,	b. May 3, 1752
Josiah,	b. October 14, 1755

Abiathar,	b. January 16, 1758
Hannah,	b. March 28, 1760
Silas,	b. December 20, 1762
Anna,	b. January 31, 1766
Submit,	b. September 14, 1771

Children of Abiathar and Joanna (Loomis) Lyman.

Josiah,	b. December 21, 1783
Nathan,	b. October 25, 1785
Dellia,	b. May 19, 1787
Joanne,	b. December 1, 1789
Eli,	b. December 28, 1793
Cyrus,	b. May 16, 1796

Children of Asa and Mary Lyman.

Martin,	b. December 27, 1782

Children of Elijah and Patty Lyman.

Elijah,	b. November 14, 1767

Children of Silas and Lydia (Hutchinson) Lyman.

Lydia,	b. August 1, 1791
Laura,	b. August 25, 1794
Sheborn,	b. September 24, 1798
Flavel,	b. December 23, 1807
Levina,	b. January 12, 1800
Harvey,	b. July 3, 1810

Children of Ozias and Ruth (Brown) Lyman.

Jephtha,	b. September 18, 1776
Persis,	b. September 11, 1778
William,	b. August 21, 1780
Jesse,	b. November 4, 1782
Edney,	b. April 11, 1785
Jemima,	b. March 18, 1788

MALBONE.

Children of Godfrey and Dorcas (Edwards) Malbone.

Francis,	b. January 17, 1791
Mary Ann,	b. October 6, 1792
Sally Brewer,	b. January 19, 1794

BIRTHS FROM TOWN RECORDS 81

Fanny, b. April 13, 1796
Horatio Nelson, b. October 2, 1798
Wealthy, b. May 1, 1801

MANLY or MANLEY.

Children of George and Elisabeth (Turner) Manley.

Anne, b. October 28, 1734
Ace, b. February 23, 1735-6
Elisabeth, b. March 13, 1743

Children of Lazarus and Hannah (Clark) Manley.

Elisabeth, b. December, 1741
Joseph, b. December 8, 1743
Bulah, b. October 31, 1746
John, b. November 27, 1748
Tabothy, b. September 28, 1753

Children of Asa and Eunice Manly.

Daniel, b. December 9, 1780
Chloe, b. April 15, 1783
Cornelia, b. January 11, 1787

Children of Joseph and Deborough (Green) Manly.

John, b. October 12, 1787
William, b. August 6, 1789
Hannah, b. August 13, 1793
Harlin, b. December 19, 1797

MANNING.

Children of Calvin and Lydia (Robertson) Manning.

Betsey, b. March 12, 1775
Royal, b. October 4, 1776
Calvin, b. October 4, 1778
Mary, b. June 12, 1783
Lydia, b. March 26, 1785
Lucy, b. March 26, 1785
Hezekiah, b. April 23, 1787
Anna, b. August 17, 1789
James, b. April 3, 1792
Elizabeth, b. January 23, 1799

MARAUGH.

Children of Denis and Abigail Maraugh.

Sarah,	b. October 14, 1719
Martha,	b. June 25, 1722
Abigail,	b. February 3, 1725
Rachael,	b. September 16, 1727

Children of Richard and Deliverance Maraugh.

Mary, b. January 29, 1725-6

MARSH.

Children of Mathias and Priscilla (Bridgham) Marsh.

Elizabeth,	b. October 1, 1727
Matthias,	b. December 28, 1729
William,	b. January 10, 1738
Bethiah,	b. November 2, 1743

MEACHEM.

Children of Rev. Mr. Joseph and Mrs. Esther Meachem.

Eunice,	b. May 25, 1716
Joseph,	b. August 30, 1718
John,	b. September 20, 1720
Jerusha,	b. January 4, 1721-2
Katharine	b. January 1, 1723-4
Esther,	b. July 19, 1725
Sybil,	b. September 10, 1727
Joseph,	b. December 24, 1729
Sybil,	b. August 29, 1734

MEAD.

Children of John and Mary Mead.

John, b. February 24, 1741-2

Children of John and Elizabeth (Manley) Mead.

Mary,	b. March 21, 1766
Hannah,	b. March 4, 1768
Annah,	b. October 28, 1770
John,	b. November 5, 1773
John, Jr.,	b. November 5, 1773

MILLENTON.

Children of John and Martha Millenton.

Sarah,	b. March, 1703-4
Martha,	b. March, 1706-7
John,	b. August, middle of the month, 1711
Solomon,	b. April 17, 1718

MILLER.

Children of Gideon and Sarah Miller.

Gideon, b. July 31, 1743

MINOR.

Children of Andrew and Priscilla Minor.

Lydia, b. November 13, 1757

MORGAN.

Children of Mason and Chloe Morgan.

James Sanford,	b. December 2, 1818
Miles Chandler,	b. June 14, 1826

MOREY.

Children of Isaac and Lucretia Morey.

Elisha, b. March 17, 1803

MURDOCK.

Children of Jonathan and Sarah Murdock.

Submit, b. April 7, 1776

Children of Jonathan and Hannah (Wallbridge) Murdock.

Hannah,	b. January 7, 1778
Polly,	b. May 7, 1779
Dan,	b. November 3, 1781
Roxa,	b. August 10, 1783
Licindia,	b. June 7, 1785
Samuel,	b. March 13, 1787
Betsey,	b. December 20, 1789

NICHOLLS.

Children of Nathaniel and Mary Nicholls.

Nicholas, b. January 12, 1720

NOBLE.

Children of Mr. Oliver and Lucy Noble.

Habijah,	b. February 8, 1761
Lucy,	b. October 7, 1762

ORMSBY.

Children of Nathan and Silance Ormsby.

Abner,	b. March 3, 1769
Rhoda,	b. September 21, 1771

PAGE.

Children of Thomas and Mary Page.

Sarah,	b. March 14, 1746
Abigail,	b. February 3, 1747-8
Thomas,	b. February 1, 1749-50

Children of Thomas and Azubah (Strong) Page.

Elias,	b. December 28, 1751
Mary,	b. September 14, 1753
Phineas,	b. December 25, 1755
Levi,	b. April 10, 1758
John,	b. May 15, 1759
Azubah,	b. September 19, 1760
Elias,	b. October 22, 1761
Gad,	b. March 5, 1764
Samuel,	b. December 14, 1766
Levi,	b. February 3, 1772

Children of Phinias, Jr., and Serviah (Lamb) Page.

Phinias 3d,	b. February 23, 1778

Children of Elias and Ester (Kingsbury) Page.

Alvira,	b. November 24, 1786
Joseph,	b. August 3, 1788
Elias and Ester (twins),	b. November 5, 1790
David,	b. January 3, 1795
Oziah,	b. May 5, 1797
Daniell,	b. September 26, 1799

BIRTHS FROM TOWN RECORDS

Children of Gad and Abigail (Loomis) Page.

Almeria,	b. September 30, 1789
Harlan,	b. July 28, 1791

PALMER.

Children of Benjamin and Rebeckah Palmer.

Gershom,	b. February 13, 1717
Ann,	b. February 5, 1720
Nathan,	b. November 27, 1723
John,	b. February 14, 1725-6

Children of Benjamin and Ruth (Bidwell) Palmer.

Benjamin,	b. October 10, 1729
Ruth,	b. February 20, 1733-4
Rebeckah,	b. February 20, 1737-8

Children of Stephen and Elizabeth Palmer.

Joshua,	b. April 14, 1731
Elizabeth,	b. February 13, 1733
Anna,	b. April 28, 1735
Stephen,	b. June 12, 1737
James,	b. August 2, 1739
Nathan,	b. August 10, 1741
Nathan,	b. in Lebanon, August 2, 1742
Nathaniel,	b. November 4, 1744
William,	b. August 5, 1746

Children of George and Hannah (Marsh) Palmer.

Mary,	b. April 19, 1743

Children of Nathan and Grace Palmer.

Grace,	b. May 4, 1747
Ann,	b. November 15, 1749

Children of Gershom and Mehitable (Badger) Palmer.

Gershom,	b. December 5, 1738
Abigail,	b. April 20, 1742
Elias,	b. January 15, 1744
Rebeckah,	b. March 27, 1747
Amos,	b. February 15, 1749
Beniamon,	b. January 7, 1755
Abel,	b. August 12, 1757
Mehitable,	b. August 10, 1758

Children of Gershom and Elizabeth Palmer.
Sarah, b. April 28, 1767

Children of Gershom, Jr., and Lucy (Feald) Palmer.
Elizabeth, b. April 19, 1761

Children of John and Abigail (Boynton) Palmer.
Hannah, b. May 21, 1749
John, b. June 22, 1751
Mehitable, b. July 13, 1753
Abigail, b. July 22, 1755

Children of Aaron and Mary (Chapen) Palmer.
Cloe, b. July 17, 1749
Nathan, b. September 4, 1751
Elijah, b. May 7, 1754
Mary, b. July 28, 1759

Children of Elias and Elizabeth (Stow) Palmer.
Mary, b. June 10, 1768
Martha, b. May 27, 1770
Elias, Jr., b. July 23, 1772
John, b. December 25, 1778
Elizabeth, b. February 17, 1779
Eunice, b. January 6, 1779 (?)

Children of Nathaniel and Martha Palmer.
Horatio, b. September 6, 1785

Children of Nathaniel and Silence Palmer.
Olive, b. August 14, 1796

PARKER.

Children of Harry and Anna Peck Parker.
Lois Bourn, b. May 26, 1820
Lucy Young, b. April 15, 1823

Children of Deacon Samuel and Mary Parker.
John, b. July 21, 1714
Ester, b. May 28, 1716
Pheniaz, b. February 12, 1719
Joseph, b. November 2, 1723

BIRTHS FROM TOWN RECORDS

Children of Samuel, Jr., and Experience Parker.

Ephraim,	b. March 3, 1727
Hannah,	b. April 20, 1728

Children of Jeams and Tabytha (Strong) Parker.

Elijah,	b. November 13, 1730

Children of Jeams and second wife, Elizabeth (Skinner) Palmer.

Jeams,	b. August 10, 1734
Cardee,	b. February 22, 1736-7
Elizabeth,	b. May 26, 1739
Tabitha,	b. June 25, 1741
Mary,	b. October 19, 1743
Ann,	b. July 16, 1749
Tabithy,	b. March 23, 1747

Children of Phineas and Martha (Meraugh) Parker.

Denis,	b. January 12, 1742-3
Phineas,	b. January 8, 1744-5
Febe,	b. April 12, 1746
Rachael,	b. January 10, 1747-8
Samuel,	b. February 14, 1749-50
Timothy,	b. February 17, 1753
Martha,	b. August 3, 1755
Asa,	b. October 7, 1757
Esther,	b. March 29, 1760
Mary,	b. September 20, 1762

Children of Samuel 2d and Sarah (Badcock) Parker.

Marah,	b. February 21, 1754
William,	b. June 8, 1755
Sarah,	b. March 4, 1757
Samuel,	b. April 14, 1759
Hannah,	b. October 21, 1761
Bettie,	b. December 17, 1763
Elias,	b. May 13, 1765
David,	b. December 5, 1767
Triphene,	b. December 14, 1769
Phebe,	b. August 29, 1771
Eli,	b. July 11, 1774

Children of Joseph and Rachael Parker.

Eunice,	b. September 7, 1747
Rachael,	b. May 3, 1749
Elizabeth,	b. May 3, 1751
Joseph,	b. March 19, 1753
Solomon,	b. September 9, 1755
Amos,	b. October 30, 1757
Rachael,	b. February 24, 1760
James,	b. April 9, 1763
Joannah,	b. April 19, 1765
David,	b. February 26, 1768
Jonathan,	b. May 28, 1770

Children of Elijah and Martha Parker.

Martha,	b. October 19, 1753
Roxana,	b. May 9, 1755
Jerusha,	b. April 23, 1757

Children of Nathan Parker and wife.

Manley,	b. January 25, 1813

Children of Solomon and Lusina Parker.

Eleazer,	b. January 9, 1782
Lusina,	b. September 8, 1783
Horace,	b. September 27, 1785
Elisabeth,	b. October 12, 1787
Sally,	b. September 30, 1790
Polly,	b. August 23, 1793
Solomon,	b. February 15, 1795
Hannah,	b. September 3, 1797
Pamela,	b. March 31, 1799

PAYN.

Children of John and Jemima (Huthenson) Payn.

Jemima,	b. February 1, 1747-8
John,	b. April 13, 1751
Lemuel,	b. March 28, 1755

Children of Stephen and Rebeckah (Bushnal) Payn.

Sarah,	b. May 20, 1758
Rebeckah,	b. May 20, 1760
Ebenezer,	b. September 27, 1762
Allin,	b. March 31, 1765
Tilla,	b. November 1, 1767

PECK.

Children of John and Rebeckah Peck.
Joseph, b. June 10, 1765

PERKINS.

Children of Samuel and Mary Perkins.
John, b. July 21, 1714
Esther, b. May 28, 1716

PHELPS.

Children of Benjamin and Joanna Phelps.
Eunice, b. April 1, 1744
Joseph, b. August 14, 1749
Lydia, b. June 22, 1752

PHILLIPS.

Children of William and Phila Phillips.
Maria Theresa, b. August 13, 1820
Albigence Stone (son), b. May 5, 1823

PIK.

Children of James and Hannah Pik.
James, b. May 18, 1711

PINGREY.

Children of Moses and Abijah Pingrey.
Moses, b. March 27, 1727
Abijah (daughter), b. April 2, 1729
Ann, b. March 27, 1732
John, b. October 8, 1734
Sillramus (?), b. May 22, 1737
James, b. May 30, 1739
George, b. May 2, 1741
David, b. November 2, 1744
Stephen, b. June 9, 1747

Children of Sylvanus and Mary Sawyer Pingrey.

Fillaretta (?),	b. October 13, 1763
James,	b. March 5, 1765

PETTY or PITY.

Children of Joseph and Sary Pity.

Hester,	b. July 23, 1711
Anna,	b. August 9, 1713
Ruth.	b. March 19, 1717

POMROY.

Children of Daniel, Jr., and Eunice (Grant) Pomroy.

Esther,	b. January 7, 1773
Eunice,	b. March 2, 1775
Daniel Starling,	b. December 31, 1776

Children of Eleazer and Sybil (Kingsbury) Pomroy.

Clarry,	b. December 19, 1773
Sybil,	b. November 26, 1775; d. same day
Eleazer, Jr.,	b. October 4, 1776
Widthy (son) (?),	b. October 14, 1778
Daniel Starling,	b. February 18, 1781
Adosha,	b. January 10, 1783
Polly, daughter of Eleazer and Priscilla,	b. April 13, 1787
Sybil,	b. March 2, 1789
Newton,	b. March 25, 1791
Ebenezer,	b. January 17, 1794
Betsey,	b. March 22, 1796
Chauncy,	b. December 6, 1799

Children of Eleazer, Jr., and Ruth (Hunt) Pomroy.

Alexander Hamilton,	b. November 17, 1804
Henry,	b. March 6, 1814
Eleazer, Jr.,	b. January 6, 1817
George,	b. March 3, 1819
Daniel,	b. January 23, 1822

POOL.

Children of Elijah and Mary (Dodge) Pool.

Chester	b. May 16, 1805

PORTER.

Children of Thomas and Thankfull Porter.

Mercy,	b. October 10, 1708
Mary,	b. November 16, 1710
Jonathan,	b. March 20, 1713
Noah,	b. August 24, 1715

Children of Jonathan, Jr., and Lois (Richardson) Porter.

Lois,	b. April 14, 1759
Mercy,	b. May 22, 1760
Rachael,	b. May 28, 1761
Persis,	b. July 10, 1762
Amaziah,	b. December 2, 1763
Irene,	b. March 6, 1765
Jonathan,	b. April 5, 1766

Children of Jonathan, Jr., and Widow Lydia Abel Porter.

Elijah,	b. August 20, 1770
John,	b. June 14, 1772
Reuber,	b. August 20, 1774
William,	b. March 31, 1777
Bette,	b. July 28, 1779

Children of Jonathan and Sarah (Lad) Porter.

Thomas,	b. March 16, 1735
Sarah,	b. September 28, 1736; d. in 2 hours
Jonathan,	b. September 17, 1737
Isaiah,	b. August 21, 1739
Noah,	b. October 6, 1742
Sarah,	b. December 6, 1744
Mary,	b. January 27, 1747-8
Phebe,	b. March 11, 1750
Irene,	b. December 8, 1756

Children of Samuel and Sarah (Skinner) Porter.

Chloe,	b. October 22, 1737
Samuel,	b. April, 1736
Anne,	b. August 26, 1739

Children of Daniel, Jr., and Esther (King) Porter.

Nichles,	b. April 15, 1740
Daniel,	b. December 11, 1741
Sarah,	b. October 26, 1742
Nickles,	b. April 15, 1748

Children of Thomas and Zilpah (Lyman) Porter.

Erastus,	b. July 16, 1763
Eunice,	b. November 24, 1767

Children of Thomas 3d and Ann Porter.

Luther,	b. January 21, 1751-2
Eleazer,	b. February 11, 1754
Elizabeth,	b. June 22, 1756
Thomas,	b. March 19, 1759

Children of William and Esther Porter.

Rebeckah,	b. October 30, 1758
William,	b. November 7, 1760
Esther,	b. August 16, 1762
Lois,	b. March 26, 1764
Vine,	b. December 25, 1765
Joseph,	b. August 6, 1770
Benjamin,	b. 30th day (no month), 1772

Children of Noah 2d and Submit (Cook) Porter.

Asenath,	b. July 8, 1766
Submit,	b. February 12, 1768
Noah 3d,	b. February 20, 1769
Submit,	b. January 13, 1771 (stillborn)
Submit,	b. April 27, 1773
Zelotes,	b. April 28, 1775
Lucretia,	b. April 9, 1777
Ebenezer,	b. April 9, 1780
Anne,	b. June 3, 1782
Joseph,	b. May 5, 1785

Children of Isaiah and Jedida (Cubbusch) Porter.

Abner,	b. June 10, 1788
George W.,	b. October 10, 1792

BIRTHS FROM TOWN RECORDS

Children of Erastus and Hannah (Denton) Porter.
William,   b. June 23, 1789
Eunice,   b. December 27, 1790
Mary,   b. October 27, 1792

Children of William and Sarah Maria Porter.
William Denton,   b. April 4, 1819
Mary Jackson,   b. January 10, 1821
Elisabeth Hannah,   b. November 22, 1822
Henry Cheney,   b. March 29, 1825
Erastus Henry,   b. March 28, 1827
Sarah Maria,   b. October 9, 1828
Thomas Ely,   b. August 28, 1830
Charles Winslow,   b. March 3, 1833
Ellen Adell,   b. October 16, 1836

Children of Noah and Polly (Loomis) Porter.
Polly,   b. January 23, 1795
Oliver,   b. July 23, 1797
Cynthia (daughter of Lieut. Noah),   b. August 3, 1799
Pamelia (daughter of Captain Noah),   b. October 11, 1806
Faith Marilla (daughter of Noah and Faith), b. June 10, 1810
Emma Maria,   b. December 27, 1812
Noah Loomis (son of Col. Noah and Faith), b. January 7, 1816
Phebe Woodruff,   b. August 15, 1821

Children of Ebenezer and Eunice (Kingsbury) Porter.
Sophrone,   b. September 26, 1803

POWELL.

Children of —— and Elizabeth Powell.
Elizabeth,   b. February 18, 1727-8

PRESTON.

Children of Joseph and Elizabeth Preston.
Abigail,   b. April 15, 1744
Marah,   b. November 23, 1746

PRICE.

Children of Rufus and Martha (Grant) Price.
Rufus,   b. August 5, 1751
Abigail,   b. June 2, 1753

Elijah,   b. March 25, 1755
Abigail,   b. August 29, 1757
Martha,   b. August 19, 1760
Elizabeth,   b. February 26, 1763 or 5
Solomon Grant,   b. November, 1766

REED.

Children of Josiah and Silviah (Herick) Reed.

Josiah,   b. October 1, 1756
Sipian,   b. July 30, 1758
Daniel,   b. May 26, 1760

RENALLS.

Children of John and Mary Renalls.

Sarah,   b. December 6, 1720
Hannah,   b. April 2, 1723

RICHARDSON.

Children of Amos and Rachael Richardson.

Nathan,   b. March 20, 1725
Samuel,   b. September 19, 1726
Amos,   b. March 5, 1728
Rachael,   b. May 16, 1729
Jonathan,   b. January 24, 1731
Stephen,   b. July 14 (no year)
Ann,   b. January 4, 1734
Zebulon,   b. March 7, 1735
Humphry,   b. March 19 (no year)
Abigail,   b. July 23, 1739
Lowes,   b. July 18, 1741
Justus,   b. September 30, 1743
Eunis,   b. August 7, 1746
Abigail,   b. March 18, 1749-50

Children of Lemuel and Anna (Rust) Richardson.

Mercy,   b. January 7, 1747-8
Samuell,   b. March 25, 1749
Nathaniell,   b. April 5, 1750
Zebulon,   b. July 31, 1751
Lemuel,   b. December 13, 1752
Mabel,   b. October 13, 1754

BIRTHS FROM TOWN RECORDS

Richard,	b. September 29, 1755
—— Richardson,	b. February 17, 1757
—— (daughter),	b. December 26, 175-
Stephen,	b. May 25, 1760
Anne,	b. October 19, 1761
Stephen,	b. March 27, 1763
Dan,	b. October 21, 1764
Muriel (son),	b. October 18, 1764 (?)
Humphrey,	b. February 22, 1767

RICHARDSON or RITCHARDSON.

Children of Amos, Jr., and Ruth (Stiles) Richardson.

Anne,	b. March 26, 1752
Hezekiah,	b. January 25, 1754
Zebulon,	b. February 10, 1757

Children of Nathan and Phebe (Crocker) Richardson.

Rosamond,	b. July 9, 1749
Andrew,	b. December 13, 1750
Lucy,	b. October 3, 1752
Amos,	b. November 26, 1754
John,	b. November 16, 1756
Esther,	b. October 26, 1758
Nathan,	b. October 27, 1760
Hette,	b. November 6, 1762
Sarah,	b. March 10, 1765
Elizabeth,	b. February 26, 1768
Wells,	b. February 14, 1770
Lois,	b. in Lebanon, October 13, 1772

Children of Andrew and Martha Richardson.

John Closson,	b. September 1, 1776
Rosamon,	b. September 17, 1778

Children of Hezekiah and Olive (Thomson) Richardson.

Nancy,	b. August 6, 1774
Ruth,	b. January 9, 1779
Hannah,	b. October 13, 1780

Children of Justus and Submit (Throop) Richardson.

James,	b. November 17, 1770
Irene,	b. December 8, 1772
Russell,	b. November 16, 1774

Children of Lemuel, Jr., and Rachael (Lothrop) Richardson.

Lothrop,	b. December 19, 1776

Children of Nathaniel Richardson and his wife.

Philena,	b. June 24, 1783

Children of Stephen and Mabel (Marsh) Richardson.

Jane,	b. December 24, 1763
Jennet,	b. November 1, 1765
Lucretia,	b. February 11, 1768
Abigail,	b. March 9, 1770
Alexander,	b. June 17, 1772
Phipps,	b. September 7, 1774
Mabel,	b. March 8, 1778
Daniel,	b. January 8, 1781
Polly,	b. October 12, 1785

RIPLEY.

Children of Elijah and Alice (Adams) Ripley.

Elijah, Jr.,	b. August, 1774

ROBINSON or ROBISON.

Children of Daniel and Lydy Robinson.

Ephraim,	b. April 5, 1720
Daniel,	b. October 1, 1721

Children of Ephraim and Esther (Rose) Robertson.

Daniel,	b. November 9, 1749
Lidiah,	b. October 12, 1744
Ephraim,	b. April 29, 1746
Esther,	b. December 14, 1747
Ashbel,	b. October 20, 1752

Children of Elijah and Lydia Robinson.

Charles,	b. August 28, 1761
Zelotes,	b. May 3, 1764

ROBERTSON.

Children of David and Susannah Robertson.

Theodory,	b. February 6, 1758
Susannah,	b. August 12, 1759
Daniel,	b. June 6, 1761
Emelia,	b. September 23, 1763
Hannah,	b. December 27, 1766

Children of Samuel and Martha (Badcock) Robertson.

(Name illegible) (son),	b. January 3, 1746-7
Daniel,	no date

Children of Samuel and (second wife) Mary (Hindsdel) Robertson.

Martha,	b. December 12, 1750
Lydia,	b. February 12, 1753
Solomon,	b. June 8, 1755
Hannah,	b. March 8, 1757

Children of John 3d and Eunice (Phelps) Robertson.

Ralph,	b. August 20, 1765
John,	b. June 2, 1767
Eunice,	b. April 20, 1769
Lydia,	b. November 11, 1771
Joanna,	b. April 1, 1774
John,	b. October 28, 1782
Benjamin,	b. October 28, 1785

Children of Captain Samuel, Jr., and Mercy Robertson.

Neal,	b. June 16, 1784
Sarah Anne,	b. October 17, 1786

Children of Samuel and Anna (Curtis) Robertson.

Mary,	b. July 5, 1760
Selome,	b. September 22, 1761
Phebe,	b. November 13, 1763

Children of Daniel and Susannah Robertson.

Betty,	b. July 20, 1768
Daniel and Betty (twins),	b. July 22, 1775

COVENTRY RECORDS

Children of Daniel, Jr., and Triphena (Janes) Robertson.

Lydia,	b. August 21, 1775
Ester,	b. December 14, 1776
Guy,	b. April 24, 1778
Charles,	b. January 28, 1780
Polly,	b. November 18, 1781
Salome,	b. May 16, 1783
Hariot,	b. March 3, 1785
Ashbel,	b. February 8, 1787
Daniel,	b. November 1, 1789
Triphena,	b. December 2, 1790
Ephraim,	b. February 15, 1793

Children of Solomon and Martha Robertson.

Patte, b. March 20, 1785

Children of Ephraim Clark and Lavinia Robertson.

Warren,	b. in Weathersfield, May 14, 1803
John Clark,	b. in Weathersfield, May 18, 1805
Julia Ann,	b. in Glastonbury, January 17, 1809
Robert,	b. in Coventry, May 24, 1813

ROCKWELL.

Children of Amariah and Martha (Noble) Rockwell.

Daniel,	b. July 27, 1753
Martha,	b. August 8, 1755
Irenah Kingsbury,	b. July 2, 1758
Jabez,	b. June 4, 1760
Amariah,	b. November 22, 1762
Amariah,	b. June 10, 1765
Daniel,	b. March 8, 1768
Tabothy,	b. November 6, 1771

Children of Martha Rockwell.

William Willson, b. October 9, 1777

ROOT.

Thomas,	b. July 29, 1692
Ebenezer,	b. November 15, 1693
Eliakim,	b. December 28, 1695
Abigail,	b. March 16, 1698

BIRTHS FROM TOWN RECORDS

Thankfull,	b. August 4, 1700
Mindwell,	b. October 4, 1701
Experience,	b. January 18, 1703
Samuel,	b. October 17, 1705
Miriam,	b. September 24, 1707

"What is above written was taken out of the Records from Northampton."

Ephraim Root,	b. December 6, 1709

Children of Thomas, Jr., and Elizabeth (Lee) Root.

Steaven,	b. March 2, 1720-1

Children of Thomas, Jr., and 2d wife Widow Hannah Hindsdale Root.

Elizabeth,	b. January 19, 1731-2
John,	b. June 9, 1732
Lowes,	b. September 3, 1734
Thomas,	b. January 26, 1735-6
Isaac,	b. January 13, 1740

Children of Thomas and Thankfull Root.

Mehitable,	b. February 11, 1713

Children of Ebenezer and Sary Root.

Sarah,	b. December 21, 1719
Hannah,	b. January 19, 1720-1
Submit,	b. March 19, 1721-2
Silence,	b. January 18, 1723-4
Ephraim,	b. November 6, 1725
Hannah,	b. October 24, 1727
Ephraim,	b. November 6, 1728
Sybil,	b. April 26, 1729
Ebenezer,	b. March 9, 1732
Jesse,	b. December 28, 1736

Children of Joseph and Silence (Curtis) Root.

Jerusha,	b. September 26, 1754
Bille,	b. July 1, 1756
Naomi,	b. February 20, 1758
Elijah,	b. March 25, 1760

COVENTRY RECORDS

Children of Ebenezer, Jr., and Phebe (Halkins or Hawkins) Root.

Elizabeth,	b. November 20, 1753
Ursula,	b. March 31, 1755
Nathaniel,	b. March 25, 1757

Children of Eliakim and Mercy Root.

Asahel,	b. April 13, 1726
Eliakim,	b. March 10, 1728

Children of Eleakim and Jemima (Elles) Root.

Joseph,	b. July 13, 1732
Medad,	b. December 29, 1735
Jonathan,	b. January 11, 1737-8
Mariam,	b. November 2, 1739
Jonathan,	b. June 18, 1742
Jemima,	b. January 3, 1746

Children of Ephraim and Elizabeth (Carpenter) Root.

Asal,	b. December 24, 1750

Children of Samuell and Mercy Parker Root.

Samuell,	b. August 26, 1729
Mary,	b. February 10, 1731
Josiah,	b. September 17, 1733
Phebe,	b. July 31, 1735
Rufus,	b. August 30, 1737
Zeruiah,	b. April 7, 1740
Nathan,	b. June 13, 1742
Lemuel,	b. May 6, 1744
Tabitha,	b. March 7, 1747
Ezra,	b. April 27, 1749
Lois,	b. May 27, 1751
Elias,	b. March 23, 1754
Triphene,	b. in Willington, July 20, 1756

Children of Mr. Jesse and Mary (Banks) Root.

Mary,	b. September 27, 1759
Ebenezer,	b. February 14, 1761
Ephraim,	b. October 6, 1762
Sophia,	b. July 19, 1764
Jesse,	b. April 13, 1766

BIRTHS FROM TOWN RECORDS

Children of John and Deborah (Hawkins) Root.

Lois,	b. October 26, 1760
Deborah,	b. October 4, 1762
Phebe,	b. October 28, 1764
Susanna,	b. June 9, 1768
Charles,	b. February 14, 1770
Asenath,	b. November 20, 1771
Lucy,	b. December 27, 1773
John,	b. December 14, 1775
Stephen,	b. August 4, 1777
Amalia,	b. November 15, 1779
Mary,	b. September 22, 1781
Lyde,	b. December 28, 1783

Children of Thomas, Jr., and Elizabeth (Field) Root.

Bete,	b. August 24, 1762
Eleazer,	b. July 2, 1764
Thomas,	b. July 22, 1766
Hannah,	b. Coventry, no date
Molly,	b. Coventry, no date
Zenas,	b. Coventry, no date

Children of Jonathan and Azubah (Brown) Root.

Mary,	b. March 12, 1767
Mary,	b. April 2, 1768
Eli,	b. July 6, 1769
Elipha,	b. December 4, 1770
Lucy,	b. October 13, 1772
Anne,	b. May 2, 1774
Hannah,	b. November 26, 1775
Lydia,	b. May 17, 1777
Azubah,	b. December 23, 1778

Children of Medad and Rhoda (Curtis) Root.

Benjamin,	b. December 17, 1763
Jonathan,	b. January 11, 1765 (died same day)
Simeon,	b. January 12, 1766
Medad, Jr.,	b. December 24, 1767
Rhoda,	b. June 16, 1770

Children of Nathaniel and Candace Root.

Daniel,	b. February 20, 1793
Lemuel,	b. October 14, 1794
Manton,	b. December 17, 1795
Nancy,	b. January 14, 1797
Elijah Hammond,	b. September 16, 1800
Marvin,	b. October 7, 1802
Caroline,	b. November 21, 1804

Children of Joseph and Hannah Root.

Louma, son,	b. July 28, 1788

Children of Ephraim and Phebe Root.

Elisabeth,	b. February 13, 1786
Armina,	b. April 14, 1787
Ephraim Colbourn,	b. March 8, 1789

ROSE.

Children of Daniel and Judah Rose.

Margaret,	b. February 28, 1734
Daniel,	b. January 1, 1737
Catharine,	b. January 2, 1739
Nathaniel,	b. December, 1742 (last Monday in the year)

Children of Dr. Josiah and Eunice Rose.

Josiah,	b. July 5, 1739
John,	b. May 2, 1741
Eunice,	b. October 7, 1742
Joseph Meacham,	b. May 13, 1744
Lidia,	b. June 15, 1746
Samuel,	b. March 17, 1748
John,	b. February 25, 1749-50
Elizabeth,	b. July 28, 1751
Esther,	b. March 12, 1753
John,	b. February 3, 1755
Frederick,	b. November 3, 1757

Children of Joseph and Desire (Dimock) Rose.

Eunice,	b. February 22, 1770

Children of Samuel and Elizabeth (Hale) Rose.

Joseph,	b. September 17, 1774

BIRTHS FROM TOWN RECORDS 103

Nathan Hale, b. November 18, 1776
Fannie, b. January 4, 1779
    Children of Joseph and Millie Rose.
Fanny, b. September 3, 1800
Elizabeth Hale, b. June 28, 1804
Fanny Mary, b. September 24, 1815
    Children of Nathan H. and Eunice (Talcott) Rose.
Eunice Talcott, b. August 26, 1803
Samuel Polydore, b. February 28, 1807
Levi Perkins, b. September 8, 1809
Richard Hale, b. February 3, 1812
Lucy F., b. September 18, 1814
    Children of William and Irene (Loomis) Rose.
Irene, b. November 22, 1798
John Loomis, b. October 9, 1800
Almena, b. October 4, 1802
Ansello, b. August 15, 1804
Angelina, b. April 19, 1806

ROWLER.
    Children of Samuel and Miriam Rowler.
Samuel, b. January 21, 1750-1

RUST.
    Children of Nathaniel and Mary or Mercy Rust.
Daniel, b. February 18, 1711
Elizabeth, b. June 11, 1713
Lydy, b. May 9, 1716
    Children of Daniel and Mary (Parker) Rust.
Mary, b. November 5, 1762
Cynthia, b. December 17, 1764
Clement, b. July 22, 1767
Daniell, b. August 6, 1769
Anne, b. July 31, 1775
Elizabeth, b. March 6, 1777
    Children of Gershom and Mary Rust.
Justen, b. April 23, 1764

Children of Joseph and Tabitha (Kingsbury) Rust.

Nathaniel,	b. May 13, 1765
Joseph,	b. November 30, 1766
Elizabeth Scripture, daughter of Cloe Rust,	
	b. November 23, 1768

Children of Nathaniel, Jr., and Hannah (Hatch) Rust.

Simeon,	b. September 24, 1717
Elizabeth,	b. July 9, 1720
Margaret,	b. December 31, 1722
Malitiah,	b. July 4, 1724
Matthias,	b. April 2, 1726
Abyal (son),	b. January 13, 1728
Johial (son),	b. July 27, 1730
Hannah,	b. March 25, 1732
Rebeckah,	b. July 28, 1733
Nathaniel,	b. October 31, 1735
Joseph,	b. March 26, 1736-7
Nathaniel,	b. August 21, 1739

Children of Ensign Samuel and Sarah Rust.

Anne,	b. May 17, 1720
Freelove,	b. May 25, 1724
Samuel,	b. February 23, 1727-8
Sarah,	b. June 4, 1732
Nathaniel,	b. May 15, 1735
Zebulon,	b. July 12, 1737
Cloah,	b. May 14, 1742

Children of Noah and Keziah (Strong) Rust.

Dille (daughter),	b. July 11, 1729
Noah,	b. January 28, 1731
Ammeziah,	b. June 4, 1733
Keziah,	b. August 16, 1735
Chloah,	b. December 19, 1737
Elijah,	b. April 10, 1740
Cloa,	b. June 23, 1747

Children of Simeon and Sarah Rust.

Christiana,	b. July 31, 1743
Jerusha,	b. June 22, 1746
Levi,	b. September 28, 1750

BIRTHS FROM TOWN RECORDS

Children of Malthias and Lucy (Fitch) Rust.

Mary,	b. May 1, 1750
Rebeckah,	b. December 15, 1751
Lemuel,	b. Hartford, March 15, 176-
Matthias,	b. Hartford, May 8, 1770

Children of Daniell and Anna (White) Rust.

Marcy,	b. June 11, 1732
Daniel,	b. April 16, 1734
Anne,	b. September 26, 1736
Lemuel,	b. February 11, 1740-1
Zebulon,	b. January 5, 1742-3
Marcy,	b. December 27, 1744
Anna,	b. March 14, 1747

Children of Daniell and the Widow Mary (Mead) Rust.

Nathaniel Willson,	b. April 16, 1750

Children of Amaziah and Mary (Marsh) Rust.

Amaziah,	b. April 7, 1754
Phebe Persis,	b. December 28, 1755
Mary,	b. January 3, 1758
Mary,	b. December 30, 1761
Chauncy,	b. May 23, 1773

Children of Nathaniel W. and Rachel (Babcock) Rust.

·Rubia,	b. January 10, 1782
Samuel,	b. November 9, 1783
Ephraim,	b. October 1, 1785
Mary,	b. December 20, 1787
Lore,	b. May 18, 1790
John,	b. November 7, 1792

SARLE or SEARLS.

Children of John and Margaret (Cook) Sarle.

Gideon,	b. November 13, 1742

Children of Ebenezer and Truelove (Brown) Sarle.

Son,	b. March 6, 1743

Children of Elisha and Mary (Acly) Searls.

Abigail,	b. June 15, 1741
Mary,	b. July 28, 1744

Elisha,	b. December 29, 1746
Marthew (daughter),	b. April 2, 1750
Phebe,	b. September 17, 1752
Elisha,	b. July 12, 1754
Lydia,	b. Mansfield, January 13, 1757

SCOTT.

Children of Benjamin and Sarah Scott.

Benjamin,	b. May 6, 1741
Abraham,	b. March 27, 1743
Sarah,	b. January 28, 1744-5

Children of Peter and Hannah (Edwards) Scott.

Zebediah,	b. November 22, 1741

SCRIBNER.

Children of Samuel and Olive Scribner.

Josiah,	b. September 7, 1772
Oliver,	b. December 24, 1775
Ira,	b. May 31, 1777

SCRIPTURE.

Children of Simeon and Ann (Slater) Scripture.

Simeor	b. June 19, 1739
Ann,	b. April 23, 1741
Lidea,	b. April 21, 1744
Jeremiah,	b. August 8, 1746
Loes,	b. November 28, 1748
Irane,	b. November 10, 1750
Abigail,	b. November 21, 1752
Triphena (daughter),	b. February 3, 1757

Children of John and Abigail (Utley) Scripture.

Elizabeth,	b. April, 1714
John,	b. December 11, 1716
Patiance,	b. December 30, 1720
Abigail,	b. May 1, 1722
Jemima,	b. March 10, 1724
Sarah,	b. December 1, 1726
Mary,	b. July 15, 1728

BIRTHS FROM TOWN RECORDS

Children of John and Widow Mary (Slater) Scripture (second wife).

Mary,	b. September 2, 1730
Anna,	b. June 26, 1732
Daniel,	b. February 27, 1736

SEAGRAVE.

Children of Silvanus F. and Caroline Seagrave.

Bezaliel, b. November 14, 1836

SHAW.

Children of Beniamon and Elizabeth (Edwards) Shaw.

Abigail, b. August, 1737

SHEPARD.

Children of Jonathan and Loue (Palmer) Shepard.

Prudence,	b. June 25, 1738
Jonathan,	b. January 6, 1739-40
Olive,	b. December 9, 1742
Nathaniel,	b. October 8, 1744
Amos,	b. January 2, 1746-7
Anne,	b. June 26, 1750
Simeon,	b. January 23, 1751-2
Joshua,	b. December 31, 1753
Rozel,	b. September 9, 1756
Louc,	b. October 10, 1758

Children of Noah and Margaret Shepard.

Noah,	b. in Western, September 8, 1742
Lydia,	b. March 8, 1744

Children of Noah and Abigail (Glason) Shepard (second wife).

Margaret,	b. February 6, 1748
Mary,	b. April 14, 1749
Jacob,	b. October 4, 1750
Eunice,	b. October 8, 1755

SIMONS.

Children of Joshua and Anne Simons.

Anne,	b. March 13, 1755
Elijah,	b. July 12, 1757

Elijah, b. October 22, 1760
Anne, b. March 30, 1763
Eleazer, b. September 24, 1765

SKINNER.

Children of Noah and Patience (Dunham) Skinner.
Sarah, b. October 27, 1737
Children of Noah and (second wife) Mary (Scott) Skinner.
Patience, b. May 2, 1740
Patience, b. December 15, 1741-2
Mary, b. June 12, 1743
Ezekel, b. April 3, 1745
Noah, b. May 5, 1746
Submit and Abigail (twins) (Abigail still-born),
b. September 26, 1747
Anne, b. December 8, 1748
Ebenezer, b. February 12, 1749-50
Joel, b. May 11, 1751
Abiram, b. October 8, 1752
Abigail, b. December, 1753
Triphene, b. April 4, 1756

SMITH.

Children of Francis and Hannah Smith.
Francis (son), b. February 29, 1716
Children of Benjamin and Mary (Roberson) Smith.
Joseph, b. December 6, 1738
Mary, b. April 24, 1740
Rhode, b. December 6, 1741
Benjamin, b. July 12, 1743
Children of Deacon Recompense and Elizabeth (Kinney) Smith.
Roxa, b. November 6, 1788
Daniel, b. December 14, 1790
Children of Daniel and Anna Smith.
Daniel Kingsbury, b. August 22, 1818
Children of Joseph and Eunice Smith.
Emily, b. September 29, 1813

SOUTHWARD.
Children of Gideon and Mary Southward.
Andria, b. July 27, 1751

SPRAGUE.
Children of Samuel and Jerusha Sprague.
Samuel, b. December 24, 1758
Elizabeth, b. August 2, 1760
Eliakim, b. June 5, 1762

Children of Joseph and Hannah (Swetland) Sprague.
Joseph, b. August 18, 1756

Bela Sprague, b. February 23, 1778

Esther Parker, his wife, b. April 24, 1785

Children of Bela and Esther (Parker) Sprague.
Ralph, b. November 9, 1807
Willard, b. June 7, 1809
Sally, b. May 5, 1811
Tilden, (?) b. September 2, 1813
Betsey, b. July 8, 1815
Electa, b. May 27, 1817
Almira, b. September 6, 1819
Louisa, b. April 24, 1822

STACK.
Children of Joseph and Mercy Stack.
Joseph, b. September 12, 1715

STANLEY.
Children of John and Lucy (Edwards) Stanley.
John, b. June 15, 1750
Jerusha, b. March 3, 1753
Elizabeth, b. March 8, 1755
Hannah, b. April 29, 1758
Leurethe (daughter), b. April 4, 1760

Children of Moses and Eunice (Strong) Stanley.
Ashbel, b. September 25, 1769
Eunice, b. April 25, 1773

Children of John and Mary (Fuller) Stanley.
Lucy,   b. November 10, 1774
Elijah,   b. February 10, 1777
  Children of Caleb, Jr., and Martha Stanley.
Caleb,   b. February 11, 1773
Isaac,   b. May 1, 1775
Mary,   b. October 7, 1779
Joseph,   b. January 12, 1784
Hannah,   b. May 22, 1787

STAR.

Children of Thomas and Hannah (Edwards) Star.
Mary,   b. January 10, 1730-31

STEDMAN.

Children of John and Mary (Merrill) Stedman.
Judee Leah,   b. November 1, 1759
Louis,   b. November 4, 1761

STILES.

Children of Ebenezer and Sarah Stiles.
Stephen,   b. August 18, 1741

STRONG.

Children of Phinias, Esq., and Mary (Parker) Strong.
Phinias,   b. November 9, 1725
Mary,   b. March 11, 1727
Sarah,   b. April 2, 1729
Azubah,   .b. October 11, 1731
Ozias,   b. September 30, 1734
Jerusha,   b. February 21, 1737-8
Iranah,   b. January 27, 1741-2
Elisha and Elijah (twins),   b. August 15, 1743
Beulah,   b. March 7, 1746
Hannah,   b. March 16, 1748
  Children of Noah and Deborah Strong.
Esther (still-born),   b. December 17, 1729
Lemoran (son),   b. March 4, 1731
Deborah,   b. March 25, 1737
Noah,   b. August 16, 1738

BIRTHS FROM TOWN RECORDS

Children of Noah and Widow Lidiah (Pers) (second wife) Strong.

Lidiah,	b. March 20, 1742
Adonijah,	b. July 5, 1743
Ann,	b. April 2, 1745

Children of Moses and Sarah (Long) Strong.

Moses,	b. January 4, 1731-2
Sarah,	b. August 28, 1743

Children of Deacon Joseph, Jr., and Elizabeth Strong.

Joseph,	b. April 13, 1726
Elizabeth,	b. February 2, 1727-8
Joseph,	b. March 19, 1728-9
Bille,	b. May 2, 1733
Asa,	b. March 12, 1735
Tabitha,	b. April 3, 1736
Alnathan,	b. September 23, 1736 (?)
Abial,	b. January 19, 1738-9
Benajah,	b. October 13, 1740
Eunice,	b. April 11, 1743
Martha and Mary (twins),	b. July 30, 1745

Children of Thomas and Mary Strong.

Mary,	b. March 11, 1727

Children of Aaron and Rachâel Strong.

Rachael,	b. December 20, 1732
Aaron,	b. March 24, 1734-5
Sarah,	b. April 9, 1737
Oliver,	b. July 7, 1739
Dameris,	b. March 25, 1742
Cloe,	b. June 22, 1744
Cloe,	b. August 15, 1745
John,	b. January 26, 1748-9
Rachael	b. March 1, 1751
Asel,	b. January 28, 1753

Children of Phineas, Jr., and Tabithy (Bruster) Strong.

Phineas,	b. June 30, 1750
Abiel,	b. January 9, 1751-2
Tabithy,	b. December 17, 1753

Daniell,	b. December 14, 1755
Israel,	b. January 14, 1758
Mary,	b. March 5, 1760

Children of Asa and Sarah (Moody) Strong.

Hannah Tappin,	b. April 25, 1765
Elizabeth,	b. April 17, 1766
Tabothy,	b. November 18, 1767
Jane,	b. March 24, 1769

Children of Rev. Mr. Nathan and Hester (Meacham) Strong.

Nathan,	b. July 26, 1747; d. same day
Nathan,	b. October 5, 1748
Esther,	b. April 28, 1750
Joseph,	b. September 21, 1753

Children of Enoch and Sarah (Meraugh) Strong.

Joel,	b. August 14, 1743
Sibbel,	b. February 20, 1746
Abigail,	b. June 5, 1748
Tabitha,	b. September 24, 1750
Phebe,	b. December 12, 1752
John,	b. April 10, 1755

Children of Stephen and Elizabeth Strong.

Lidiah,	b. April 13, 1748
Stephen,	b. December 17, 1749
Sarah,	b. July 27, 1755
Elizabeth,	b. June 23, 1756

Children of Benaiah and Lucy (Bishop) Strong.

Joseph,	b. March 10, 1770
Harissa,	b. November 6, 1771
Roger,	b. October 5, 1773
Billy,	b. August 5, 1775
Lucy,	b. June 9, 1778
Martha and Mary (twins),	b. April 25, 1780
Billy,	b. March 2, 1782
Benajah,	b. January 26, 1783
Sally,	b. July 3, 1788

BIRTHS FROM TOWN RECORDS

Children of Ozias and Susanna (West) Strong.

Oresta,	b. May 16, 1758
Beulah,	b. July 24, 1759
Roxselana,	b. June 9, 1761

SWETLAND.

Children of Joseph and Hannah Swetland.

Hebe,   b. October 8, 1745

Children of Ebenezer and Sarah (Leach) Swetland.

Jude,	b. January 30, 1750
Anne,	b. July 8, 1752
Ebenezer Leach,	b. July 13, 1753
Triphene,	b. June 4, 1756
Samuel,	b. November 4, 1758
Anne,	b. January 11, 1761

Children of Ebenezer and Widow Abigail (Bliss) (second wife) Swetland

Sarah,	b. May 2, 1764 (mistake of records)
Seth,	b. November 13, 1765
Abigail,	b. October 23, 1767
Abner,	b. October 17, 1769

Children of Israel and Dorias (Dewey) Swetland.

Theophais,   b. January 17, 1757

Children of Levi and Ruth (Richardson) Swetland.

Mille,	b. November 28, 1782
Anne,	b. April 26, 1785
Polly,	b. January 17, 1787
Levi,	b. June 2, 1789
Ruth,	b. March 30, 1791
Rosca (daughter),	b. March 21, 1797

Children of Levi, Jr., and Electa (Kingsbury) Swetland.

Mary Ann,   b. July 18, 1811

TALCOTT.

Children of Joseph and Eunice Talcott.

Eunice,	b. January 19, 1759
Esther,	b. February 14, 1762
Prisilla,	b. April 21, 1764

COVENTRY RECORDS

Children of Deacon Joseph, Jr., and Rebeckah Talcott.

Joseph 3d,	b. June 28, 1778
Arad,	b. September 2, 1780
Eunice,	b. April 23, 1783
Son,	b. June 19, 1785; died in 10 hours
William,	b. December 30, 1786
Eleazer,	b. June 7, 1789
Harvey,	b. January 6, 1791
Lymon (son of Captain), Joseph, Jr.,	b. January 25, 1793
Ester,	b. May 25, 1795
Erastus,	b. April 28, 1797
Chester,	b. April 29, 1799

Children of Arad and Anna (Tracy) Talcott.

George Huntington,	b. November 2, 1807
Charles Trumbull,	b. June 16, 1809
Julia Anna,	b. September 6, 1812

Children of Lyman and Harriet Talcott.

Samuel Lyman,	b. July 19, 1817

TAYLOR.

Children of Stephen and Deliverance (Rust) Taylor.

Elisha,	b. June 16, 1747
Elisha,	b. May 19, 1748
Dolle,	b. May 28, 1750
Keziah,	b. April 23, 1753
Noah and Sarah (twins),	b. June 14, 1758
Alvin and Rocksellano (twins, son and daughter),	b. June 11, 1760
Esther,	b. January 19, 1762
Anne,	b. January 9, 1765
Susannah,	b. January 20, 1767
Alwin,	b. April 26, 1769
Octava (daughter),	b. July 29, 1771

Children of William and Jane Taylor.

John,	b. January 3, 1742-3
Humphrey,	b. January 22, 1744-5
Hannah,	b. October 13, 1747
James,	b. March 13, 1750

BIRTHS FROM TOWN RECORDS

Thomas,	b. April 13, 1753
Daniel,	b. August 29, 1755
Triphene,	b. May 18, 1758
Aldad and Medad (twins),	b. August 18, 1761

Children of Mr. John and Elizabeth (Rose) Taylor.

Betsey,	b. July 26, 1785
David,	b. July 1, 1789

TERRILL.

Children of Luis and Ann Terrill.

Josiah,	b. August 23, 1750 (?)
Arad,	b. August 28, 1750
Luis,	b. October 8, 1752
Anne,	b. November 10, 1754
Hannah,	b. Windsor, June 27, 1758
Eunice Simon,	b. January 9, 1762

Children of Thomas and Alathea (Crocker) Terrill.

Lewis,	b. August 31, 1770
Alathea,	b. January 26, 1773

Children of Thomas and Triphena Terrill.

John,	b. November 19, 1756

THAYER.

Children of Elisha and Lucy Thayer.

Harriet,	b. April 18, 1835

THOMPSON or THOMSON.

Children of Nathan and Hannah (Dodge) Thompson.

Jerusha,	b. August 25, 1745
Desier,	b. February 29 (no year)
Hannah,	b. in Coventry (no date)
Chearbrook,	b. in Coventry (no date)
Dorothy,	b. in Coventry (no date)
Nathaniel,	b. March 15, 1752
Olive,	b. in Coventry (no date)
Robert,	b. in Coventry (no date)
Amos,	b. in Coventry (no date)
Nathan,	b. in Coventry (no date)

Children of John and Phebe Thomson.
Esther, b. September 21, 1760
John, b. May 16, 1762
Children of Amos and Irene (Dodge) Thompson.
Amos, b. November 7, 1751
Children of Augustus and Adaline L. Thompson.
Adaline C., b. May 27, 1830
Henry A., b. March 16, 1832

TIFFANY.

Children of Edmund P. and Levinia A. Tiffany.
Salem Judson, b. April 21, 1836
Mary Amelia, b. September 18, 1838

TILDEN.

Children of Joseph and Sarah Tilden.
Joseph, b. December 31, 1746
Sarah, b. November 24, 1748
Elisabeth, b. March 29, 1750
Elisha, b. August 12, 1751
Charles, b. September 9, 1754
Sybil, b. February 25, 1755

TOWNSEND.

Children of John and Tibitha Townsend.
Mary, b. March 29, 1737
Children of Daniel and Irene Townsend.
David, b. June 13, 1756
John, b. December 22, 1758
Nathaniel and Mary (twins), b. December 16, 1760

TRAPP.

Children of Samuel and Alice (Metcalf) Trapp.
Aurelia, b. May 22, 1809
Anne, b. August 8, 1810
Sally, b. March 27, 1813
William B., b. in Mansfield, March 18, 1820
Lewis L., b. in Coventry, April 9, 1822

TROWBRIDGE.

Children of Ira and Cynthia (Crossman) Trowbridge.

Ira Edwin, b. May 18, 1809

TUPPER.

Children of Elisha and Jerusha Tupper.

Elisha, b. February 14, 1754
Miner, b. September 3, 1756

TURNER.

Children of Habakkak and Anne Turner.

John, b. October 25, 1735
Sarah, b. September 25, 1737
Habbakuk, b. September 17, 1739
Samuel, b. January 9, 1743

Children of John, Jr., and Mary Wright Turner.

John, b. February 21, 1766
Mary, b. January 31, 1768
Anne b. February 3, 1770
Sarah b. February 9, 1772

Children of Jethro and Sarah (Badcock) Turner.

Jerusha, b. December 28, 1744
Jedediah, b. May 25, 1746
Lidia, b. April 14, 1748
Daniel, b. July 28, 1750
Caleb, b. November 21, 1752
Sarah, b. April 21, 1755
Meriah, b. March 31, 1758
Mary, b. July 8, 1760
Deborah, b. April 12, 1763
Amos, b. May 15, 1765
Anne, b. January 30, 1768

Children of Joseph 2d and Elizabeth (Bridgman) Turner.

Sarah, b. March 24, 1762
Elizabeth, b. April 24, 1765

Children of Amos and Hannah (Dorman) Turner.

Joseph, b. December 17, 1790
Anne, b. September 4, 1792

Clara, b. January 18, 1794
Hannah, b. May 19, 1796

Children of Stephen and Lois Turner.

Dan, b. July 1, 1779
Mason, b. December 24, 1780
Lucy, b. November 16, 1782
Mary, b. October 20, 1784
Dollie, b. August 24, 1786

TYLER.

Children of Rev. Royal and Lydia Tyler.

Samuel Lockwood, b. November 16, 1794
Royall Wells, b. July 25, 1796
George Washington, b. June 27, 1798
Abigail, b. November 2, 1800
Nathan, b. July 14, 1803

UTLEY.

Children of Vine and Rebecca Utley.

Lydia Mary, b. December 17, 1801

VORRA.

Children of Martin and Abigail (Rust) Vorra.

John, b. January 30, 1784
Elisabeth, b. February 26, 1786
Samuel, b. December 29, 1787
Abigail, b. June 7, 1790
Catharine, b. August 12, 1792

WADSWORTH.

Children of Samuel and Mary (Granger) Wadsworth.

Mary, b. March 16, 1734
Clemence, b. June 30, 1736
Amylias, b. June 7, 1738
Samuell, b. May 20, 1740

WALDO.

Children of John and Lucy (Wordworth) Waldo.

Lyman, b. July 8, 1774
John, b. January 27, 1776
Horatio, b. March 5, 1778

Erastus,   b. November 11, 1782
Orson,   b. November 18, 1784

WALLBRIDGE.
Children of John and Hannah Wallbridge.
Isaac,   b. June 18, 1745
Hannah,   b. May 29, 1748
Henry,   b. January 21, 1751
Lemuel   b. April 15, 1754
Abigail,   b. December 20, 1757
Children of Samuel and Sarah (Page) Wallbridge.
Samuel,   b. October 19, 1768
Sarah,   b. December 1, 1773
Amanda,   b. March 26, 1781
Children of Henry and Sarah (Fowler) Wallbridge.
Sarah,   b. November 15, 1773 (?)

WASHBURN.
Children of Timothy and Kezia Washburn.
Ephraim,   b. May 7, 1748
Son of Elizabeth Washburn.
Phillip N. Ladd,   b. June 16, 1772

WATERS.
Children of Jacob and Mary (Edwards) Waters.
Isaac,   b. October 16, 1750
Jacob,   b. August 25, 1752
Israel,   b. October 13, 1753

WEBSTER.
Children of Beniah and Eunice Webster.
Cloe (son),   b. April 11, 1742
Eunice,   b. August 15, 1743
Samuell,   b. February 21, 1744-5
Cyrenus,   b. July 18, 1747
Justus,   b. December 16, 1747
Abial,   b. January 3, 1749-50

WELLER.

Children of Isaak and Sarah Weller.

Gideon,	b. February 20, 1740-1
Dorkes,	b. February 15, 1741-2

Gideon (son of Gideon and Sarah), b. July 31, 1743

WEST.

Children of Christopher and Anna West.

Louis (daughter),	b. August 5, 1745
Lydia,	b. November 24, 1747

WESTON.

Children of Jonathan and Elizabeth Weston.

Ezra, b. January 13, 1752

WHALEY.

Children of Humphrey Whaley and wife.

Erastus, b. in Columbia, January 8, 1798

WHELDIN.

Children of Jonathan and Anne (Lyman) Wheldin.

Anna,	b. September 30, 1787
Lucina,	b. May 26, 1789
Salmon,	b. February 15, 1792
Filenda,	b. October 12, 1795

WHITE.

Children of James and Abigail White.

Abigail,	b. January 15, 1731-2
Mary,	b. April 25, 1734

Children of Daniel and Sarah White.

Daniel, b. July 14, 1774

Children of Abner and Jerusha (Thompson) White.

John,	b. September 8, 1766
Bettie,	b. February 28, 1768
Dorothy,	b. December 14, 1769

Children of Samuel and Widow Rachael (Tilden) White.

Samuel, b. November 5, 1757

Lemuel,	b. December 30, 1758
Experience,	b. April 2, 1760
Timothy,	b. March 8, 1764

Children of Joel, Jr., and Ann White.

Jabez Loomis,	b. December 29, 1763

Children of Thomas and Hannah White.

Johel,	b. October 20, 1750

Children of Montgomery and Sally (Coleman) White.

Sally,	b. May 14, 1814
Frederick,	b. March 11, 1815
Maria,	b. May 18, 1818
Laura,	b. January 25, 1821
Wealthy,	b. October 24, 1822
Henry K.,	b. September 12, 1825
Lewis,	b. August 15, 1828
Nathan Coleman,	b. March 23, 1832

Children of Capt. Daniel and Sarah White.

Daniel,	b. July 14, 1773
Sarah,	b. February 20, 1775
Samuel,	b. February 23, 1777
Jerusha,	b. January 27, 1779
Fanny,	b. February 5, 1781
Electa,	b. February 20, 1783
Calvin,	b. March 16, 1786

WHITTEMORE.

Children of Almira Whittemore.

Sheldon,	b. April 18, 1813

Children of Shuball Whittemore and wife.

Almira,	b. September 22, 1794

WILLIAMS.

Children of Richard and Rachael Williams.

Palmer,	b. October 24, 1813

WILLSON.

Children of John Willson and wife.

Abigail,	b. August 10, 1738
Joseph,	b. March 31, 1745

COVENTRY RECORDS

Children of William and Sarah (Rust) Willson.

Jacob,	b. 1750
Dorothy,	b. December 17, 1751
William and Sarah (twins),	b. July 1, 1754
Abigail,	b. February 25, 1757
John,	b. April 24, 1760
Sarah,	b. January 24, 1763
Abigail,	b. January 1, 1765
Zebulon,	b. February 26, 1767

Children of Jacob and Hannah Willson.

Hannah,	b. July 31, 1772
Rachael,	b. January 8, 1778

Children of Francis and Abigail (Fellows) Willson.

Anne,	b. January 1, 1758
Abigail,	b. July 1, 1759
Ruth,	b. April 3, 1761
Stephen,	b. November 14, 1764
Submit,	b. February 12, 1767

Children of Jacob and Hannah Willson.

Hannah,	b. July 13, 1772
Rachael,	b. January 8, 1778
Jacob,	b. June 6, 1784
Desire,	b. May 23, 1796

Children of Samuel and Almira (Dow) Willson.

John,	b. March 23, 1832
Jane Catharine,	b. October 7, 1833
Lorenzo Dow,	b. October 19, 1840

WINCHESTER.

Children of Daniel and Ruth (Palmer) Winchester.

John, b. May 29, 1752 (died same day)

WINTWORTH.

Children of Ebenezer, Jr., and Sarah (French) Wintworth.

Sarah,	b. September 16, 1763
Bildad,	b. April 10, 1765
Mehitable,	b. April 15, 1767
Sarah,	b. March 14, 1769

Mary,	b. March 20, 1771
Gad,	b. May 9, 1773
Ichabod French,	b. October 19, 1776

WISE.

Children of John and Catharine Wise.

Elizabeth,	b. June 18, 1766
Benjamin,	b. July 28, 1771

WOOD.

Scipio (son of Robert and Judah Wood) (servant of Peter Buell).
b. January, 1732-3

WOODWARD.

Children of Nathaniel, Jr., and Elizabeth Woodward.

Moses,	b. March 30, 1745
Elisabeth,	b. August 24, 1747

Children of Henry Woodward and wife.

Henry,	b. June 4, 1745
Rachael,	b. October 16, 1747
Oliver,	b. October 1, 1749
Eleazer,	b. October 9, 1752
Elihu,	b. June 25, 1754
Eunice,	b. August 29, 1756

Children of Aaron and Ellener (Benton) Woodward.

Dorias,	b. August 19, 1759
Aaron,	b. October 15, 1760

Children of Nathaniel, Jr., and Surviah (Ensworth) Woodward.

Nathaniel 3d,	b. February 5, 1784
John,	b. April 5, 1786
Hannah,	b. January 31, 1788
Anna,	b. February 7, 1792 (?)
Fanna,	b. April 13, 1792
Daniel,	b. December 10, 1793
Sally,	b. May 10, 1796
Wealthy,	b. May 15, 1798

Children of Daniel and Lydia (Edgerton) Woodward.

George Edgerton,	b. October 15, 1820

WOODWORTH.

Children of Joseph and Rebeckah Woodworth.
Anne,   b. November 6, 1756

Children of Spencer and Amanda (Clark) Woodworth.
Harriet Amanda,   b. September 10, 1809
Lucy Clark,   b. November 14, 1810
John Spencer,   b. September 25, 1813

Children of Joshua and Esther Woodworth.
Harry,   b. June 23, 1797

Children of Simeon, Jr., and Maria Woodworth.
Maria Lord,   b. September 25, 1822
Sarah Howe,   b. November 27, 1829
James Dorman (son of Simeon, Jr., and Lucy),
                                    b. September 16, 1835

WOOLCOTT.

Children of Josiah and Widow Lucy (French) Woolcott.
Lucy,   b. January 19, 1741-2
Anne,   b. March 19, 1744 (lived one week)
Anne,   b. April 29, 1745 (lived 7 weeks)
Theodore,   b. November 4, 1746
Anna,   b. January 15, 1748-9

Children of Thomas and Susannah (Porter) Woolcott.
John,   b. October 24, 1740

WRIGHT.

Children of Nathaniel and Irene Wright.
Marcy,   b. February 18, 1744-5
Joel,   b. November 25, 1742
Nathaniel,   b. March 29, 1747
Samuel,   b. October 13, 1749
Irene,   b. February 5, 1752
Asher,   b. April 28, 1754
Mary,   b. September 24, 1756
Rebeckah,   b. July 6, 1759

Children of Elijah and Temperance Wright.
Eleazer, b. February 3, 1764
Children of Roswell and Mary (Jeffray) Wright.
Son, b. March 14 (died same day) (?)
Polly and Betsey (twins), b. June 3, 1787
Children of Elijah and Jane (Richardson) Wright.
John, b. February 2, 1787
James, b. June 11, 1789
James, b. June 12, 1793
Emily, b. July 25, 1795
Hearvey, b. July 17, 1797

Copy of Marriages from Town Records of Coventry, Conn., from 1711 to 1840.

ABBEY.
Eliphilet Abbey and Lydia Brenson,
m. at Andover, Ct., May 10, 1815

ABBOT.
Rev. Abiel Abbot and Elisabeth Abbot, of Andover, Mass.,
m. May 19, 1796

ALEXANDER.
James Alexander and Triphena Kinne, both of Coventry,
m. September 16, 1822

ALLIN or ALLEN.
Nehemiah Allin and Mary, m. July 2, 1719
Daniel Allen and Azubah Lad, m. October 6, 1741
George Allen and Naomy Grover, m. December 15, 1737
Mr. Levi Allen, of Mansfield, and Miss Maria Brigham, of Coventry, m. July 4, 1821

ANTISEL.
Simon Antisel and Martha Fuller, m. October 28, 1767

ANTRAM.
Mr. Jeremiah Antram, of East Windsor, and Ruth Ann Standly, of Windham, m. October 23, 1838

ATHERTON.
Elijah Atherton and Hannah Hills, of Glassbury,
m. April 12, 1775

AUSTEN.
Benoni H. Austin, of West Greenwich, and Laura Eells, of Coventry, m. August 24, 1835

AVERY.
Amos Avery, Jr., and Abigail Loomis, both of Coventry,
m. October 24, 1782

MARRIAGES FROM TOWN RECORDS

Horatio Avery and Irene Andrus, m. April 25, 1822
William R. Avery, of Windham, and Rhoda C. Avery, of Coventry, m. April 1, 1832

BADCOCK or BABCOCK.

Ebenezer Badcock 2d, and Hannah Preston,
m. August 26, 1754
Robert Badcock and Jedediah Turner, m. November 15, 1753
William Badcock and Mary Gates, m. November 9, 1748
Amos Badcock and Mary Williams, both of Coventry,
m. September 24, 1777
John Badcock, son of Josiah and Mary, and Hannah, daughter of Ephraim and Hannah Brown, m. December, 1773
John Babcock and Lydia Woodward, daughter of Nathaniel and Elisabeth Woodward, m. October 7, 1779
Josiah Badcock and Mary Meraugh, m. February 27, 1745-6
Simeon Badcock and Abigail Hintson, m. October 5, 1736
Ebenezer Badcock and Mehitable Burt, m. September, 1725
Robert Badcock, Jr., and Hannah Arnold,
m. December 5, 1782
Daniel Badcock and Sarah Ensworth, both of Coventry,
m. September 29, 1786
John Babcock and Lydia Woodward, m. October 12, 1779
Elihu Babcock and Elisabeth Preston, m. July 3, 1763
Gideon Badcock and Triphena Badcock,
m. November 11, 1793
David Badcock, of Coventry, and Mary Barrows, of Mansfield,
m. November 11, 1821
Elijah Badcock, of Coventry, and Mary Strong,
m. March 26, 1822
William Babcock and Esther Loomis, m. January 19, 1839
Benjamin Badcock and Mary Long, m. February 10, 1729-30
Ebenezer Badcock 3d, of Coventry, and Eleanor Knight, of Norwich, m. June 11, 1772
William Babcock and Mary Loomis, both of Coventry,
m. in Andover, May 31, 1837
Mr. Leonard D. Babcock and Miss Juliaett Strong,
m. March 22, 1827

BADGER.

Moses Badger and Jerusha Janes, both of Coventry,
	m. June 1, 1775
Daniel Badger, Jr., and Mary Weld,	m. April 19, 1735
Enoch Badger, Jr., and Mary Lamphear, both of Coventry,
	m. February 11, 1773
Daniel W. Badger and Ruth Tarbox,	m. November 20, 1827

BALDWIN.

Theopilus Baldwin and Sarah Kingsbury,
	m. January 18, 1745-6

BALUM.

Lucious Balum and Susan Fields, both of Windham,
	m. February 18, 1838

BARKER.

Oliver Barker and Mary Fowler,	m. July 12, 1753

BARNARD.

Dan Barnard and Lydia Dodge,	m. July 12, 1755
Benony Barnard and Freedom,	m. June 13, 1712

BARROWS.

Elmer Barrows, of Mansfield, and Saripta Brigham, of Coventry,	m. September 4, 1822
Amasa Barrows, of Mansfield, and Wealthy Colman, of Coventry,	m. October 20, 1823
Mr. Alphonso P. Barrows and Miss Betsy Kinney, both of Coventry,	m. in Bolton, September 18, 1839
Thomas A. Barrows, of Mansfield, and Olive K. White, of Coventry,	m. October 4, 1827
Deacon Lemuel Barrows, of Trenton, New York, and Widow Sally Fitch, of Coventry,	m. September 20, 1830
Washington Barrows, of Mansfield, and Sare Ann Root, of Coventry,	m. December 19, 1831

MARRIAGES FROM TOWN RECORDS 129

Joseph Barrows and Mary P. Brown, m. May 11, 1840
Reuben Barrows, of Norwich, and Lydia Edgerton, of Coventry, m. March 16, 1841

BELKNAP.

Ralzamon Belknap, of Ellington, and Desiah Dimick, of Coventry, m. October 14, 1824

BENETT or BENNIT.

James Benett, of Franklin, N. Y., and Laura Andrus, of Coventry, m. March 11, 1830
Christopher Bennit and Irene Baldwin, m. October 22, 1772

BENTON.

Austen Benton, of Tolland, and Julia Ann Mathewson, of Coventry, m. September 22, 1830
Benjamin D. Benton, of Tolland, and Mary M. Mathewson, of Coventry, no date (probably 1831)
Chester Benton and Tirza P. Loomis, m. February 9, 1826

BESTER.

Daniel Bester and Dorcas Hibbard, both of Coventry,
m. August 1, 1782

BILL.

John Bill and Irene Swetland, m. July 18, 1754

BILLINGS.

Horatio Billings, of Somers, and Mary Ripley, of Coventry,
m. May 9, 1838

BINGHAM.

Horace P. Bingham and Emmeline Jones, of Coventry,
m. at Andover, March 10, 1824

BIRGE.

Alonzo W. Birge and Mrs. Eliza Ensworth, both of Andover,
m. December 20, 1846

BISSELL.

Solomon H. Bissell and Wealthy Learnerd, of Coventry,
m. September 16, 1824

BLACKMAN.

Beniamon Blackman, Jr., and Eunice Sawyer, of Windham,
m. February 12, 1756
Aaron Blackman and Mary Upham, m. September 21, 1775
David Blackman and Mary House, both of Coventry,
m. May 18, 1775
David Blackman and Anna Ensworth, both of Coventry,
m. June 28, 1787
Joel Blackman, of Florence, Ohio, and Wealthy Tilden, of Coventry, m. September 12, 1830

BLISH.

Aristarchus Blish and Sophia Chamberlin, m. January, 1824

BOLS or BOWLES.

William Bols and Carolina Sawyer, both of Coventry,
m. May 24, 1775

BOOTH.

Rev. Chauncy Booth, of Coventry, and Miss Laura Farnam, of Salisbury, m. November 16, 1815

BOYNTON.

Joshua Boynton and Rachael Carpenter, m. November 9, 1749
John Boynton and Tabithy Daues, m. November 6, 1740
Oliver Boynton, of Coventry, and Mary Brown,
m. August 6, 1770
John W. Boynton and Eunice Stanley, m. May 2, 1832
George Boynton and Cynthia Whittemore,
m. November 27, 1826

BRACE.

Mr. William Brace and Miss Elisabeth C. Chatfield, of Hartford, m. July 30, 1833

BRIANT.

Ebenezer Briant and Mehitable Dunham, m. July 29, 1736

BRIDGMAN.

Isaac Bridgman and Elisabeth Hatch, m. June 16, 1741

BRIGHAM.

Uriah Brigham and Anne Richardson, daughter of Amos Richardson, of Coventry, m. May 28, 1754
Thomas Brigham and Susannah Eells, m. February 5, 1769
Paul Brigham and Catharine Turner, m. July 1, 1741
Paul Brigham and Lydia Sawyer, both of Coventry,
 m. October 6, 1768
Don Carlos Brigham and Polly Greenleaf, m. June 7, 1789
Uriah Brigham and Emily Wright, m. April 26, 1825
Lewis Brigham and Louisa Tilden, m. February 19, 1833

BROWN.

Abraham Brown and Mary Dean, m. February 14, 1754
Abraham Brown, of Coventry, and Anna Church, of Mansfield,
 m. October 2, 1760
Joseph Brown, of Coventry, and the Widow Abigail Lamb,
 m. March 1, 1757
Moses Brown and Ruth Ingraham, m. December 25, 1751
Elijah Brown, of Coventry, and Lydia Gary, of Somers,
 m. February 12, 1755
Timothy Brown, of Coventry, and Esther Chapin, of Wilbraham, m. April 13, 1775
Elifilet Brown and Elisabeth Writer, m. June 13, 1745
John Brown and Ruth Fox, m. July 5, 1744
Jonathan Brown and Mary Sarels, m. April 30, 1740
Joshua Brown, Jr., and Prudence Welch, m. May 20, 1768
Col. Thomas Brown and Mary Lathrop, m. June 10, 1780
Rufus Brown and Triphene Fuller, m. May 4, 1824
Jonathan Clark Brown, of Coventry, and Sophia Bingham, of Ellington, m. October 8, 1807
Ebenezer Brown and Betsey Archer, m. May 26, 1835

BRUNSON

Mr. Watson W. Brunson and Miss Mary Ann Case, both of Coventry, m. at Andover, December 24, 1837

BUELL.

Elias Buell and Sarah Turner, m. August 6, 1758
Benjamin Buell and Elisabeth (Gone?) m. July 21, 1757
Lieut. Peter Buell and Martha Grant, m. January 7, 1728-9
Mr. Peter Buell and Hannah Wells, m. October 8, 1713
John Hubbell Buell, of Hebron, and Mary Olmstead Hollister, of Coventry, m. March 26, 1829
David M. Buell and Louisa Robertson, m. May 3, 1840

BURNAP.

John Burnap and Susannah, his wife, m. March 9, 1749
Abraham Burnap, Jr., and Irene Wright, m. November 8, 1753
Jeriah Burnap and Lois Lyman, m. October 4, 1781
Jeriah Burnap and Abigail Killeen, m. August 23, 1793
Daniel Burnap, Esq., and Mary Kingsbury, m. in Andover, May 28, 1823
Abner Burnap and Sarah Bingham, both of Andover, m. May 13, 1784

BURNS.

Thomas Burns and Eudotia Edwards were legally married; no date

CADY.

Cornelius Cady and Elisabeth Safford, m. June 25, 1759
Aaron Cady, Jr., and Ann Palmer, m. November 8, 1738
James Cady and Thomosine Simons, m. April 19, 1731
Jared Cady, of Ashford, and Mary Eells, of Coventry, m. September 12, 1832
Alpheus Cady, of Lebanon, and Emmeline Dickinson, of Norwich, m. November 2, 1828

CARPENTER.

James Carpenter and Irene Lad, m. April 5, 1763
Alvin Carpenter and Irene Carpenter, m. July 16, 1778
Elisha Carpenter and Deliverance Meraugh, m. April 14, 1748
Benjamin Carpenter, Jr., and Widow Catharine Brigham, m. October 18, 1750

MARRIAGES FROM TOWN RECORDS

Noah Carpenter (second time) to Widow Curtis,
m. September 1, 1744
Joseph Carpenter and Phebe Lad, m. August 4, 1757
Timothy Carpenter and Miriam Parker, m. February 8, 1759
Elijah Carpenter and Patience Bruster, m. October 31, 1764
Levi Carpenter and Elisabeth Parker, m. October 15, 1767
Eliphilet Carpenter and Elisabeth Andrus, m. November, 1727
Amos Carpenter and Deborah Long, daughter of Joseph Long,
m. October 23, 1718
Ebenezer Carpenter and Eunes Thompson, m. June 19, 1739
Benjamin Carpenter, Jr., and Rebeckah Smith,
m. April 12, 1727
Eliphalet Carpenter, Jr., and Esther Gurley, m. May 22, 1766
William Carpenter, of Coventry, and Rachael Badger,
m. February 19, 1767
Josiah Carpenter and Phebe Porter, m. December 20, 1770
Alvin Carpenter and Irena Carpenter, m. July 16, 1778
Charles Carpenter and Mary Chappel, both of Coventry,
m. October 11, 1790
Benjamin Carpenter and Martha Ranson (?)
m. October 13, 1822

CHAFFEE.

Elihu or Elisha Chaffee, of Ashford, and Emily Brunson, of Coventry, m. in Andover, January 30, 1836

CHAMBERLAIN.

James Chamberlain and Widow Abigail Palmer, daughter of Zachariah Boynton, m. January 27, 1757

CHAMPLIN.

Stephen Champlin, of Lebanon, and Mary Yound, of Coventry,
m. November 6, 1822
William M. Champlin, of Montville, and Emily Ripley, of Coventry, m. October 1, 1835

CHAPIN.

Asa Chapin, of Mansfield, and Louisa Burnap, of Coventry,
m. April 5, 1821
Asa Chapin, of Mansfield, and Esther Bishop, of Berlin,
m. in Andover, October 5, 1826

CHAPPEL.

Simeon Chappel, of Lebanon, and Abigail Sarl, of Coventry,
m. February 28, 1759

CHARTER.

Roswell Charter and Miss Olive Kimpton, m. March 27, 1843

CHATMAN.

Reuben A. Chatman and Caroline Loomis,
m. January 11, 1832

CHESBORO.

Martin Chesboro, of Vernon, and Lois Bissell, of Coventry,
m. August 28, 1821

CLARK.

David Clark and Christian Stedman, m. December 27, 1752
Seth Clark and Abigail Badger, m. February, 1736
Joseph Clark and Coziah Hearich, m. November 11, 1736
David Clark and Widow Sarah Badcock, m. March 6, 1736
Bahman Clark, of Elba, N. Y., and Mrs. Diadema Babcock, of Coventry, m. October 15, 1820
William Clark and Eunice Thomson, both of Hebron,
m. in Andover, August 24, 1823
Augustus Clark and Clarissa H. Hunt, m. February 26, 1827

COGESHALL or COGSHALL.

Joshua Cogeshall, Jr., and Lucy Dowe, m. April 21, 1748
Beniamon Cogshall and Serviah Thompson, daughter of John Thompson, m. December 25, 1751

COGSWELL.

Amos Cogswell and Rebecca Chamberlin,
m. December 19, 1777

COLE.

Calvin Cole, of Webster, Mass., and Melissa Slack, of Stonington, Ct., m. in Coventry, July 4, 1835

COLGROVE.

Benjamin Colgrove, of Bristol, and Amanda Smith, of Coventry,
m. June 27, 1831

COLMAN.

Timothy Colman, of Coventry, and Lora Hunt, of Stafford,
 m. February 5, 1839
Eleazer Colman and Mehitable Laus, (?)
 m. January 7, 1747-8
Gershom Colman and Mercy Alles, m. January 3, 1744-5
Ebenezer Colman and Sarah Brown, m. August 2, 1738
Samuel Colman, of Coventry, and Esther Bishop, of Norwich,
 m. October 30, 1765
Ephraim Colman and Widow Laviniah Curtis,
 m. October 25, 1764
Mr. Asa Colman and Miss Hannah Badcock,
 m. November 25, 1777
Ebenezer Colman and Phebe Carpenter, m. September 5, 1782
Solomon Colman and Nancy Manning, of Coventry,
 m. December 6, 1821

CONE.

Joseph E. Cone, of Manchester, and Mary M. Robertson, of
 Coventry, m. February 23, 1830

COOK.

Jesse Cook and Submit Root, m. April 7, 1743
Josiah Cook and Lucy Deman, (?) m. August 1, 1762
Moses Cook and Eunice Allin, m. January 17, 1760
Nathan Cook and Dorias Meacham, m. October 30, 1765
Shubael Cook and Catharine Edwards, m. February 2, 1758
Jesse Cook, Jr., and Presilla Talcott, m. March 31, 1785
Joseph Cook and Mehitable Badcock, m. November 30, 1785
Nathaniel N. Cook, of Bristol, and Lemira Hutchinson, of Coventry, m. in Andover, August 21, 1838
Sidney R. Cook and Pamelia R. Porter, of Manchester,
 m. November 16, 1829
Orin Cook, of Meriden, and Mary Hutchinson, of Andover,
 m. December 19, 1831

COWLS.

Timothy Cowls and Abigail Wordworth, m. May 25, 1775

CRANDALL.

Edward Crandall and Sarah Brown, m. September 22, 1784

CRANE.

John Crane and Abigail, m. October 29, 1712
John Crane and Prudence Belding, m. April 18, 1716
John Crane, of Columbia, and Maria Edgerton, of Coventry,
m. February 10, 1828

CROCKER.

John Crocker and Sarah Baldwin, m. May 30, 1751

CROSS.

Peter Cross and Mary Fuller, m. October 2, 1740

CROSSMAN.

Ebenezer Crossman and Mrs. Mercy Lyman, of Windham,
m. January 27, 1774
Ebenezer Crossman and Widow Mehitable Dow,
m. July 15, 1781

CUMMINGS.

John P. Cummings, of Mansfield, and Wealthy Dimmock, of Coventry, m. December 9, 1823

CURTIS.

Samuel Curtis, Jr., and Joanna Dimick, m. May 26, 1763
Henry Curtis and Elisabeth Root, m. November 6, 1751
Bildad Curtis, of Coventry, and Zeriah Bishop, of Norwich,
m. November 26, 1760
Henry Curtis and Silance Janes, m. January 3, 1727
Harry Curtis and Laura Wittemore, of Coventry,
m. January 27, 1825
Mr. James Curtis, Jr., of New York State, and Miss Prudence Mathewson, m. September 6, 1832

CUSHMAN.

Allerton Cushman, Jr., and Harmony Allen, m. June 2, 1761
Ephraim Cushman and Sarah Colman, m. December 20, 1764

CUTLER.

Spalding Cutler, of Mansfield, and Miss Fanny Albro, of Coventry, m. May 8, 1837

DAGGETT.
Isaiah Daggett and Esther English, m. December 9, 1784

DAMMAN.
Samuel Damman, Jr., and Thankful Root, m. March 31, 1730
John Daman and Elisabeth Grover, m. June 9, 1736

DANES or DEANS.
Solomon Deans and Ruth Neff, (?) m. April 20, 1756
Solomon Deans and the Widow Anne Brown,
m. December 3, 1770
Benajah Danes and Widow Brown, m. June 26, 1776

DANIELS.
Porter Daniels, of East Hartford, and Clariathy Carpenter, of Coventry, m. November 24, 1825

DAVENPORT.
Humphrey Davenport and Hannah Fitch, m. May 9, 1737
Bishop Davenport and Eliza Dimick, of Coventry,
m. August 11, 1825
Seymour Davenport and Fidelia Grover, m. May 27, 1832

DELANO.
Jonathan Delano and Susannah West, m. November 2, 1743

DEUTY or DUTY.
Matthew Deuty and Eunice Boynton, m. November 21, 1771
Nathan Deuty, of Vernon, and Phebe Mainard, of Tolland,
m. January 27, 1825

DEXTER.
Minerva Dexter, of Coventry, and Betsey Wheet, of Willington,
m. October 22, 1807
Nathan Dexter and Irena French, both of Coventry,
m. October 20, 1805

DICKINSON.
John Dickinson, of Middletown, and Mrs. Celia Galpin, of Berlin, m. in Andover, February 3, 1827

DIMOCK, DIMMICK or DIMICK.

Timothy Dimick and Desire Dimmick, m. March 11, 1749-50
Daniel Dimick and Anne Wright, m. November 16, 1786
Dr. Timothy Dimock and Miss Laura F. Booth,
m. May 8, 1839
Lewis A. Dimock and Celinda A. Gardner,
m. November 6, 1834

DORMAN.

Dudley Dorman and Eunice Hawkins, m. May 16, 1760
John Dorman and Elisabeth Grover, m. June 9, 1736
Amos Dorman and Keziah Brown, m. August 17, 1760
Joseph Dorman, of Coventry, and Lucy Aspenwall, of Lisbon,
m. June 19, 1800
Joseph Dorman and Hannah Dow, of Coventry,
m. March 10, 1825
William A. Dorman and Lucy F. Rose, m. May 19, 1836

DOW.

Daniel Dow and Mehitabel Palmer, both of Coventry,
m. March 11, 1773
Ephraim Dowe and Hepzibah Hawkins, m. August 15, 1752
Ephraim Dowe and Mary Ladd, m. August 24, 1775
Lemuel Dowe, of Coventry, and Anne Millinton, of Coventry,
m. April 27, 1758
Humphrey B. Dow and Tabitha Parker, m. October 8, 1767
Ulysses Dow and Anne Tilden, m. June 26, 1788
Lorenzo Dow and Peggy Holcomb, of Granville, Mass.,
m. September 3, 1804
Lorenzo Dow and Lucy Dolbeare, of Montville,
m. April 1, 1820
Joseph Newton Dow, of Mansfield, and Sally Trapp, of South
Coventry, m. in Andover, October 4, 1837
Eduard H. Dow and Henrietta C. Lyman,
m. November 25, 1840

DUMMER.

Peter Dummer, of East Hartford, and Sophia Evans, of Coventry, m. April 17, 1828

DUNHAM.

Austin Durham and Martha M. Root, m. May 26, 1830
Leonard G. Dunham and Lucy Baxter, of Mansfield,
m. March 27, 1839
Thomas Dunham, of Mansfield, and Eunice Morey, of Coventry, m. September 24, 1838

EDGERTON.

Hezekiah Edgerton 3d and Mary Colman, both of Coventry,
m. October 26, 1818
Gurdon Edgerton and Jennett Thompson,
m. December 6, 1841

EDWARDS.

Joshua Edwards and Dorkas Willow, m. December 16, 1758
Joseph Edwards and Anne Porter, m. August 23, 1759
William Edwards and Jane Harris, m. August 14, 1728
Adonijah Edwards and Mery Sarl, m. February 28, 1765
Joseph Edwards and Mary French, m. December 3, 1719

EELLS.

John Eells, Jr., and Lois Root, both of Coventry,
m. June 6, 1776
Capt. Chauncey Eells and Mary Janes, of Coventry,
m. June 28, 1824
Chauncey Eells, of New Fane, N. Y., and Dianthe Doan, of Coventry, m. May 12, 1830

FITCH.

Jeremiah Fitch, Jr., and Sybil Dimmick, m. September 8, 1776
Abner Fitch and Ruth Rose, m. February 17, 1736
Jeams Fitch and Febe Meraugh, m. October 6, 1738
Stephen Fitch and Ellener Strong, m. January 24, 1736-7
Jeremiah Fitch and Mercy Porter, m. January 6, 1729-30
Jeremiah Fitch and Widow Martha Giffords, m. June 4, 1744
Jeremiah Fitch 2d, of Coventry, and Abigail Whitmore, of Killingly, m. February 1, 1759
Elisha Fitch and Presilla Patten, m. May 27, 1736
Mr. Jephthah Fitch and Miss Ursula Root,
m. January 23, 1777
Chauncey Fitch and Mary, his wife, m. February 22, 1815

Apollos Fitch and Sybil Edgerton, both of Coventry,
m. August 30, 1801
Abiel G. Fitch and Asenath Andrews,   m. March 12, 1829
Newton Fitch and Jane C. Bidwell, of Coventry,
m. October 10, 1832
Mr. Alfred H. Fitch and Miss Martha Parker, both of Coventry,   m. April 27, 1842

FOSTER.

James P. Foster and Eunice Rose,   m. June 25, 1826

FOWLER.

Ichabod Fowler and Ruth Grover,   m. October 4, 1753
Daniel Fowler and Temperance Rogers,   m. June 18, 1752
Israel Fowler and Eunice Bissel,   m. September 16, 1755
Jonathan Fowler, Jr., and Abigail Bissell,
m. September 24, 1740
John Fowler and Widow Elisabeth Shaw,
m. November 16, 1753
Joseph Bissell Fowler, of Coventry, and Sarah Baldwin,
m. November 28, 1771
Harlow Fowler, of Bolton, and Susan Mathewson, of Coventry,
m. October 6, 1825

FREEMAN.

Henry L. Freeman and Sally M. Smith, m. September 11, 1831

FRENCH.

Ebenezer French and the Widow Rachael Boynton,
m. September 5, 1754
John French and Mehitable Root,   m. May 20, 1736
Mr. Aaron French and Miss Abigail Brown, m. May 18, 1775
Oliver French and Jane Doan, both of Coventry,
m. March 3, 1824

FRINK.

Mr. Luther Frink and Miss Mary Fitch, both of Coventry,
m. January 12, 1834

FRIZELLE.

Lorenzo Frizelle and Aura Ladd, of Coventry,
m. April 1, 1832

FULLER.

Josiah Fuller and Margaret Rose, m. March 22, 1753
Elijah Fuller and Mary Millinton, m. December 8, 1747
Shuball Fuller and Sarah Scott, m. June 24, 1726
Jonathan W. Fuller, of Mansfield, and Cynthia Austen, of Coventry, m. March 23, 1829
Goodwin Fuller and Harriet Robertson, m. March 2, 1831

FUNKER.

Elisha Funker and Mary Man, m. October 22, 1771

GAGER.

Simon Gager and Anne Porter, m. March 14, 1816
John W. Gager, of Tolland, and Susan Anna Brigham, of Coventry, m. December 29, 1831

GARDNER.

Simeon J. Gardner and Zilpha Lyman, m. August 11, 1820
Orrin W. Gardner, of Mansfield, and Clarissa L. Dunham, of Coventry, m. October 11, 1841

GEER.

Jedediah Geer and Sarah Dodge, m. February 20, 1755

GILBERT.

Thomas Gilbert and Rachael Gilbert, m. November 18, 1756
Nathaniel Gilbert, Jr., and Hannah Fowler, m. June 4, 1747
Samuel Gilbert, Jr., and Abigail, his wife, m. October 31, no date
Jasper Gilbert and Eliza H. Rose, m. April 21, 1825
Eduard Gilbert and Catharine F. Stebbins, m. April 11, 1831
George G. Gilbert and Augusta Russ, of Coventry, m. September 1, 1836

GILLIT.

Eleazer Gillit and Sarah Coos, m. November 3, 1751

GLEASON.

Mr. Charles Gleason and Miss Hannah Tucker, both of Pomfret, m. November 22, 1837

GODFREY.

Benjamin S. Godfrey, of Coventry, and Emily Thompson, of Columbia, m. February 22, 1827

GOODWIN.

Azel Goodwin and Clarissa Hunt, m. November 23, 1809

GRAVES.

Mr. Asa Graves and Miss Rhoda Carpenter,
m. October 10, 1824

GRAY.

Joseph Gray, of South Hadley, Mass., and Roxa Porter, of Coventry, Ct., m. October 16, 1827

GRIGGS.

Chauncey Griggs, of Tolland, and Harty Dimock, of Coventry, m. March 28, 1822

GRISWOLD.

Joseph Griswold and Margery Doggitt, m. March 28, 1753
Roger Griswold, of Simsbury, Hartford Co., and Eunice Wright, of Coventry, m. August 8, 1824

GROVER.

Matthew Grover, Sr., and Widow Sary Barnard, of Hartford,
m. November 26, 1735
John Grover and Elisabeth Miller, m. April 27, 1732
John Grover and Sarah Chapin (2d wife), m. January 18, 1738-9
Benjamin Grover and Mary Shailler, m. June 6, 1728
Ephraim Grover and Tabothy Manley, m. January 8, 1773
John Grover, Jr., of Coventry, and Abigail Flint,
m. August 25, 1762
Simon Grover and Phebe Grover, his wife, m. June 13, 1754
Matthew Grover and Lydya, m. August 19, 1725
Ebenezer Grover and Zuriah Larabe, m. January 25, 1742-3
Leonard Grover and Sarah Acley, m. November 29, 1738
Matthew Grover and Lydia Colman, both of Coventry,
m. July 1, 1767
Edmund Grover and Elisabeth Thomas, m. December 2, 1741

MARRIAGES FROM TOWN RECORDS

Isiah Grover, of Coventry, and Elisabeth Grover, of East Windsor, m. June 21, 1776
Benjamin Grover and Theodora House, m. May 6, 1783
Hembery Grover and Abigail Simon, m. January 14, 1768
Joseph Grover and Sarah Thompson, m. February 23, 1792
Ashbel Grover and Cynthia Morgan, of Coventry, m. October 31, 1825
Joseph N. Grover and Nancy H. Adams, both of Coventry, m. in Andover, December 29, 1826

GURLEY.

George Gurley, of Richland, N. Y., and Sophie Dimick, of Coventry, m. November 1, 1841

HALE.

Deacon Richard Hale and the Widow Abigail Adams, of Canterbury, m. June 13, 1769
Richard Hale and Elisabeth Strong, m. May 27, 1746
John Hale and Sarah Adams, both of Coventry, m. December 19, 1771
Lieut. Joseph Hale, of Coventry, and Miss Rebeccah Harris, of New London, m. October 21, 1778
Billy Hale, of Coventry, and Hannah Barker, of Norwich, m. January 19, 1785
Richard Hale, Jr., and Mary Wright, both of Coventry, m. March 16, 1786
David Hale, of Coventry, and Laura Hale, of Canterbury, m. at Canterbury, January 18, 1815

HALEY.

Charles L. Haley, of Groton, and Hannah Avery, of Coventry, m. January 9, 1822

HALL.

Adrastus Hall, of Coventry, and Lucretia Walton, of Willimantic, m. February 25, 1836
Libni Hall, of Long Meadow, Mass., and Eliza Brown, of Coventry, m. October 13, 1831
Marvin Hall, of Manchester, and Betsey Kimpton, of Norwich, m. September 16, 1838

HAMLIN.

Timothy Hamlin and Lucinda Brown, m. February 9, 1800

HAMMOND.

Elijah Hammond and Mary Kingsbury, m. October 12, 1732
Zephaniah Hammon and Mary Badcock, m. March 13, 1766
Nathaniel Hammond, of Bolton, and Lucy Hatch, of Coventry,
            m. January 1, 1822
Manton H. Hammon, of Vernon, and Mary E. Loomis, of Coventry,   m. November 10, 1831

HANOVER.

George Hanover and Malissa Goff,   m. November, 1825

HARRIS.

Isaac Harris and Priscilla Dunham,   m. September 20, 1795

HATCH.

Jesse W. Hatch and Caroline R. Eells, m. September 24, 1833

HAWKINS or HOLCKINS, same name.

Joseph Hawkins and Sarah Suthworth,   m. March 8, 1752
Ozias Hawkins and Anne Rose, both of Coventry,
            m. May 5, 1756
James Hawkins, Jr., and Phebe Dimmick, m. May 12, 1757
John Holckins and Naomy Shipman his wife, m. May 18, 1740
George Hockins, Jr., and Hepzibah Janes, m. March 11, 1729
James Hockins and Sarah his wife,   m. July 6, 1728
Joseph Hawkins and Zerviah Howard,   m. August 7, 1777

HEARICK.

Ezekiel Hearick and Mary,   m. December 10, 1724
Daniel Hearick and Lediah Rust,   m. February 18, 1734-5
Daniel Hearick and Elisabeth Rust,   m. May 20, 1731

HEATH.

Ebenezer Heath and Lidya Ultey,   m. September 18, 1728

HENDEE.

Jonathan Hendee and Martha Millinton,
m. February 12, 1740

HEWITT.

Daniel G. Hewitt, of Worthington, Mass., and Ursula R. Fitch, of Coventry, m. April 13, 1841

HIBBARD.

Selah Hibbard and Esther Loomis, m. December 29, 1791
Selah Hibbard, Jr., and Roxana Sweetland, both of Coventry,
m. October 9, 1816
Selah Hibbard and Lydia Jones, m. January 3, 1827

HINKLEY.

Barnabas Hinkley, of Rochester, N. Y., and Olive Ripley, of Coventry, m. November 19, 1835

HOLBROOK.

Mr. Luther Holbrook, of Vernon, Ct., and Miss Mary Ann Mitchel, of Cazenovia, N. Y., m. in Willimantic, August 12, 1838

HOLLISTER.

Samuel Hollister and Sally M. Loomis,
m. at Andover, November 18, 1824
Whiting H. Hollister, of Hartford, and Sarah Ann Buell, of Andover, m. November 11, 1829

HOLMAN.

Justin Holman, of Tolland, and Maria Tilden, of North Coventry, m. in Tolland, March 26, 1834

HOLMES.

Prince Holmes and Patty Jackson, both of Lebanon,
m. July 8, 1820

HOSMER.

James D. Hosmer, of Windham, and Dolly L. Kingsbury, of Coventry, m. January 19, 1826

HOUSE.

Samuel House, Jr., and Hannah Perry,
m. December 28, 1769
Joel M. House, of Coventry, and Celia Sheffield, of Glastenbury,
m. August 21, 1836

HOWARD.

Doctor Nathan Howard and Joanna Hale, m. January 22, 1784
John Howard and Lucy Ripley, both of Coventry,
m. April 19, 1809
Mr. William Howard and Miss Julia Porter,
m. November 17, 1822

HUBBARD.

Jonathan Hubbard and Caroline Root, m. October 18, 1824

HUNT.

William Hunt and Mary Crosby, m. August 1, 1762
Gad Hunt and Elisabeth Woodward, m. August 16, 1769
Eliphaz Hunt and Hannah Stiles, both of Coventry,
m. May 21, 1761
Gad Hunt, Jr., and Molly Bissell, m. March 30, 1802
Elijah Hunt and Mehitable Dexter, m. April 29, 1804
Eliphaz Hunt, Jr., of Coventry, and Anna Phelps, of Hebron,
m. April 5, 1804
Dr. Eleazer Hunt and Sibyl Pomeroy, both of Coventry,
m. September 19, 1809
Eleazer Hunt and Mariana Loomis, m. January 25, 1838

HUNTINGTON.

Joseph Huntington, Jr., and Mirza Dow, both of Coventry,
m. November 19, 1788
Septimus G. Huntington, of Coventry, and Mary Tyler Morse, of Sutton, Mass., m. February, 1810
Charles Huntington, of Windham, and Nancy B. Strong, of Coventry, m. November 30, 1829
Capt. Edward G. Huntington, and Miss Eliza Clark,
m. January 25, 1831

HUTCHINSON.

Ephraim Hutchinson and Elizabeth Jones,
　　　　　　　　　　　　　　m. December 24, 1778
Willard Hutchinson and Sophia Kingsbury, m. June 16, 1811
Jonathan Hutchinson, of Mansfield, and Rachael Williams, of
　　Coventry,　　　　　　　　　m. June 16, 1822

HYDE.

Lyman Hyde and Polly B. Hunt,　　　m. April 18, 1831

IRISH.

Joseph Irish, of Hebron, and Julia Richardson, of Providence,
　　R. I.,　　　　　　m. in Andover, March 16, 1826

JAMES.

Freeman James and Emily Stebbins,　　m. April 26, 1826

JANES.

Elisha Janes, Jr., and Elisabeth Davenport, m. April 28, 1763
Elisha Janes, Jr., and Desire Thompson, both of Coventry,
　　　　　　　　　　　　　　m. November 9, 1766
Elias Janes and Susannah Robertson, both of Coventry,
　　　　　　　　　　　　　　m. February 13, 1775
Samuel Janes and Rebeckah House,　m. December 4, 1791
Oliver Janes and Judith Rollo, both of Coventry,
　　　　　　　　　　　　　　m. February 22, 1775
Elijah Janes and Anne Hawkins,　　m. January 15, 1765
Elisha Janes and Widow Mary Dimick,　m. April 23, 1740
Seth Janes and Sarah Larabe,　　m. January 2, 1739-40
Benjamin Janes, of Coventry, and Irene Sawyer, of Windham,
　　　　　　　　　　　　　　m. May 6, 1773
Solomon Janes and Susanna Trapp,　　m. July 20, 1793
Sterling Janes and Huldah Loomis,　　m. January 25, 1826
Chauncey Janes and Laura Sweetland, of Coventry,
　　　　　　　　　　　　　　m. August 26, 1828
Sterling Janes and Idosia Lyman,　　m. September 29, 1830

JEWETT.

Ichabod Jewett and Mary Carpenter,　　m. April 4, 1761
Elam Jewett and Eunice Richardson,　　m. May 19, 1768

JONES.

Benajah Jones and Widow Brown,	m. June 26, 1776
Benjamin Jones, Jr., and Mehitable Terrill,	m. May 6, 1756
Ebenezer Jones and Abigail Long,	m. May 5, 1743
Ebenezer Jones and Zeriah Loomes,	m. December 4, 1745
Jonathan Jones and Abijah Strong,	m. March 12, 1747
Noah Jones and Dina Hichcock,	m. May 9, 1745
Adonijah Jones and Sarah Lyman,	m. March 15, 1770
Ebenezer Jones and Abigail Long,	m. March 5, 1743
Ebenezer Jones and Zuriah Loomis,	m. December 4, 1745
Azael Jones, Jr., and Eunice Hendee,	m. December 27, 1770

Eliakim Jones and Rebecca Webster, of Hebron,
m. November 11, 1784
Benjamin Jones, Jr., and Lydia Murdock, both of Coventry,
m. November 3, 1784
Noah Jones, Jr., of Coventry, and Dolla Hiltham, of Preson,
m. May 26, 1785
Amasa Jones and Lavinia Lyman, m. January 16, 1828
Justin Jones, of Coventry, and Eliza D. Woodward, of Columbia, m. September 11, 1831
George Jones, of Glastonbury, and Elvira Jane Goss, of Coventry, m. November 6, 1831
Harrance I. Jones, of Andover, and Huldah B. Ticknor, of Columbia, m. December 17, 1826

JUDD.

Thomas Judd, of Coventry, and Widow Mary Kaughley, of Hebron, m. August 5, 1773
Solomon Judd and Anna Carpenter, m. November 27, 1792

KEACH.

Asa Keach and Betsey Cogswell,	m. October 9, 1808
Jason Keach and Revilo Long,	m. April 1, 1834

KEENY.

George Keeny and Lydia Robertson,	m. November 4, 1791
Isaac Keeny, Jr., and Eudotia White,	m. November 30, 1820

KELLOGG.

Allyn Kellogg, of Vernon, and Eliza White, of Coventry,
> m. January 8, 1822

KIDDER.

Ephraim Kidder and Freedom Barnard,
> m. December 26, 1738-9

KING.

Jonathan King and Martha Wooduard, m. February 16, 1743

KINGSBURY.

Absolom Kingsbury and Rebeckah Rust,
> m. February 19, 1752

Jabez Kingsbury and Mary Phelps,   m. September 13, 1749
Elemuel Kingsbury and Elisabeth Loomis,   m. May 9, 1749
Thomas Kingsbury and Anne,   m. July 30, 1749 (?)
Nathaniel Kingsbury and Asenath Daggett, both of Coventry,
> m. March 5, 1778

Samuel Kingsbury and Olive Scribner,   m. January 6, 1771
Eleazer Kingsbury and Freelove Rust,   m. July 20, 1742
Ebenezer Kingsbury and Priscilla Kingsbury,
> m. November 28, 1743

Joseph Kingsbury, Jr., and Ruth Benton,   m. April 10, 1784
Joseph Kingsbury and Lois Porter,   m. February 21, 1780
Jabez Kingsbury and Freelove Kingsbury,
> m. December 10, 1789

Jabez Kingsbury and Fanny Davenport, both of Coventry,
> m. February 15, 1815

Harvey Kingsbury and Polly Wright,   m. April 7, 1824
Alvan Kingsbury and Emmeline Kingsbury,
> m. September 18, 1824

Rev. Nathaniel Kingsbury, of Mount Vernon, N. H., and Miss Eunice Dow, of Coventry,   m. February 9, 1825
Col. John Kingsbury, of Tolland, and Mary Brigham, of Coventry,   m. September 1, 1825
Charles Kingsbury and Pamela Porter, m. November 26, 1829

KIMPTON.

Martin Kimpton and Olive Hoxie,
m. in Smithfield, R. I., March 9, 1822

KNAP.

Richard Knap and Phebe Wentworth, m. (no date)

KNIGHT.

Alpheas Knight, of Willington, and Polly Cogswell, of Coventry, m. August 12, 1835

LAD or LADD.

Nathaniel Lad, Jr., and Elisabeth Rust, m. November 16, 1738
Ashbel Ladd, of Coventry, and Irena Babcock, of Mansfield,
m. April 4, 1782
Philipe N. Ladd and Betsey Davenport, m. October 15, 1795

LADD.

John Ladd and Prudence Sheperd, both of Coventry,
m. July 26, 1763
Dr. Henry Ladd and Abiel Richardson, m. June 26, 1766
Timothy Ladd and Rachael Spensor, m. May 7, 1761
Samuel Ladd and Anna Wooduard, m. October 18, 1750
Moses Ladd and Keziah Killeen, m. January 26, 1769
Samuel Ladd, Jr., and Elisabeth Redington,
m. March 18, 1775
Timothy Ladd and Ester Parker, m. June 17, 1734
Oliver Ladd, of Coventry, and Mary Badcock, of Mansfield,
m. December 19, 1782
Henry Ladd and Abigail Lilly, m. September 8, 1740
Nathaniel Ladd, Jr., and Rachael Tilden, m. March 11, 1773

LAMB.

Beniamon Lamb and Abigail Sims, m. December 18, 1754
Ebenezer Lamb and Abigail Larrabe, m. December 18, 1751

LAMPHEAR.

Isaac Lamphear and Mary Edwards, m. November 18, 1754

Isaac Lamphear, of Coventry, and Sarah Hamilton, of Lime,
m. April 19, 1762
Isaac Eduards Lamphear and Lois Johnes,
m. November 12, 1778

LARRABEE.

Enoch Larrabee, of Coventry, and Mary Gera, of Summers,
m. October 19, 1756
Richard Larrabee, of Coventry, and Mary Webster, of Lebanon,   m. February 20, 1767

LATHROP.

Francis Lathrop and Clarissa Janes, of Coventry,
m. November 7, 1825
Joel Lathrop and Anna M. Parrish, of Coventry,
m. February 17, 1829

LEE.

Jedediah Lee and Lucy Lorge, (?)   m. September 16, 1722
David Lee and Elisabeth,   m. May 27, 1719
Charles Lee, of Vernon, and Mary French, of Coventry,
m. March 16, 1837
Orin Lee and Eliza Boynton,   m. January 2, 1828

LILLY or LILLIE.

Samuel Lilly and Abigail Lad,   m. May 4, 1741
Samuel Lilly, Jr., and Elisabeth Terry,   m. January 18, 1776
Marcus Lillie and Eunice Porter,   m. May 24, 1836

LOCKWOOD.

Rev. Mr. Samuel Lockwood and Mrs. Anne May,
m. April 24, 1749

LONDON.

John London, of N. Hartford, and Phebe Mathewson, of Coventry,   m. at Bolton, September 20, 1838

LONG.

Samuel Long and Martha Bristor (daughter of Peter Bristor),
m. April 11, 1755
Joseph Long, Jr., and Sarah,   m. May 17, 1716
Jonathan Long and Azubah Cooly,   m. April 25, 1745

Silas Long and Lidia Euets, (?) m. September 28, 1726
Silas Long, Esq., and Mehitable May, m. October 12, 1758
Volney M. Long and Emily Brewster, m. October 19, 1833

LOOMIS.

Nathaniel Loomis and Sarah Riley, m. November 11, 1742
Zachariah Loomis and Huldah Jones, m. March 25, 1751
Dan Loomis and Sarah Field, m. November 22, 1774
Daniel Loomis, Jr., and Polly Hibbard, m. February 7, 1788
Israel Loomis and Sarah Addams, m. May 21, 1778
Ebenezer Loomis and Eunice Brown, m. December 27, 1786
Levi Loomis and Violette Metcalf, m. September 28, 1794
Eleazer Loomis and Lucretia Porter, both of Coventry,
  m. June 8, 1803
Mr. Silas Loomis and Miss Esther Case, of North Coventry,
  m. March 14, 1821
Amasa Loomis, Jr., and Amris Case, m. September 21, 1824
Eleazer Loomis 2d and Olive Palmer, both of Coventry,
  m. February 19, 1816
Francis Loomis and Fanny M. Rose, m. September 24, 1834
George Loomis and Mary A. Sweetland,
  m. December 29, 1835
Zenus Loomis, Jr., and Nisa Lillie, m. October 15, 1828
Chauncey Loomis, of Tolland, and Prudence Cook, of Andover, m. October 1, 1828
Orrin P. Loomis and Emily Wright, m. March 26, 1831
John A. Loomis and Mary Parker, m. April 13, 1840

LORD.

Solomon Lord and Meriam Colman, m. April, 1766

LOVETT.

Richmond C. Lovett, of Tolland, and Eliza R. Brigham, of
 Coventry, m. December 9, 1834

LUCAS.

George Lucas, of Hartford, and Susan Chatfield, of Coventry,
  m. November 19, 1840
Charles H. Lucas and Mary I. Chatfield, m. April 4, 1841

LYMAN or LIMAN.

Jacob Lyman, Jr., of Coventry, and Mary Woodward,
 m. December 19, 1771
Samuel Liman and Martha Long, m. November 7, 1745
Abiathar Lyman and Joanna Loomis, m. December 25, 1782
Ozias Lyman and Ruth Brown, m. November 24, 1774
Silas Lyman and Lydia Hutchinson, m. August 25, 1790
Mr. Flavel Lyman and Miss Harriet Cogswell,
 m. June 28, 1832
Harvey Lyman and Ann Trapp, both of Coventry,
 m. October 16, 1835

LYON.

Dr. Lockwood Lyon, of Wolcott, and Deborah Colman,
 m. January 28, 1828

MALBONE.

Godfrey Malbone and Dorcas Edwards, both of Coventry,
 m. October 15, 1789

MANLEY.

George Manly and Elisabeth Turner, m. November 8, 1733
Lazarus Manly and Hannah Clark, m. October 3, 1740
Joseph Manley and Deborah Green, m. November, 1786
Darius Manley, of Troy, Pa., and Susan Loomis, of Coventry,
 m. September 15, 1829

MANN.

Austen Mann and Cornelia E. Porter, m. October 3, 1840

MANNING.

Calvin Manning and Lydia Robertson, m. September 22, 1774
Mr. Royal Manning and Miss Sally Rose, of Coventry,
 m. March 21, 1821

MARSH.

Mathias Marsh and Prisilla Bridgham, m. January 2, 1725-6

MASON.

Abner Mason and Kilia Brigham, m. October 8, 1833

MATHEWSON.

Mr. Barnard Mathewson, of Coventry, and Miss Mary C. Norris, of Providence, R. I., m. in Mansfield, June 18, 1832
Edward Mathewson and Wealthy Topliff, m. May 17, 1826

MAXWELL.
Chester Maxwell and Lora Loomis, m. November 7, 1833

MEAD.
John Mead and Elisabeth Manley, both of Coventry,
m. October 3, 1765

MENS.
Simon Mens, of New York, and Mary F. Lyman, of Coventry,
m. June 18, 1838

METCALF.
Nathaniel P. Metcalf and Eliza Sprague,
m. November 23, 1825

MILLER.
Rev. Alpha Miller and Hannah Hunt, m. September 28, 1824

MORE.
Samuel More and Roxana Edwards, m. January 8, 1827

MORGAN.
James Sanford Morgan and Mary Bailey,
m. December 25, 1839

MURDOCK.
Jonathan Murdock and Hannah Wallbridge,
m. March 20, 1777

NEELY.
Barnard M. Neely, of Windham, and Susan Davis, of Coventry, m. September 13, 1821

NEWCOMB.
Albert Newcomb, of Tolland, and Eunice S. Brigham, of Coventry, m. April 10, 1837
Lucius Newcomb, of Columbia, and Mary Mead, of Coventry,
m. April 19, 1826

NICHOLS.
John W. Nichols, of New Albany, Pa., and Julia Ann Brunson, of Andover, m. January 28, 1838

NOBLE.
Leonard Noble, of Westfield, Mass., and Anna W. Loomis, of Coventry, m. November 28, 1835

NORTHROP.

Mr. Nelson W. Northrop, of Vernon, and Miss Lorenna Fitch,
of Tolland, m. November 17, 1836
Mr. Lewis K. Northrop, of Vernon, and Miss Freelove Usher,
of Coventry, m. May 26, 1841

NORTON.

John P. Norton and Harriet Hosmer, both of Coventry,
m. July 14, 1825

PAGE.

Thomas Page and Azubah Strong, m. February 13, 1750-51
Phineas Page, Jr., and Serviah Lamb, m. May 21, 1777
Elias Page and Ester Kingsbury, m. March 2, 1786
Gad Page and Abigail Loomis, both of Coventry,
m. November 27, 1788

PALMER.

Gershom Palmer, Jr., of Coventry, and Lucy Feald, of Mansfield, m. May 8, 1760
Aaron Palmer and Mary Chapin, m. January 10, 1748
John Palmer and Abigail Boynton, m. September 7, 1748
Elias Palmer and Elisabeth Stow, both of Coventry,
m. January 10, 1768
Gershom Palmer and Mehitable Badger,
m. February 2, 1737-8 (?)
George Palmer and Hannah Marsh, m. April 13, 1742
Nathan Palmer and Grace Palmer, his wife,
m. November 6, 1745
Benjamin Palmer and Ruth Bidwell, m. November 14, 1726

PARKER.

Nathan Parker and Deliverance Badcock,
m. October 26, 1780
Samuell Parker 2d and Sarah Badcock, m. March 1, 1753
Samuel Parker and Experience, m. March 24, 1726
James Parker and Elisabeth Skinner, m. November 30, 1732
Phinias Parker and Martha Meraugh, m. September 14, 1741
James Parker and Tabytha Strong, m. February 13, 1728-9

Harry Parker and Anna Peck, both of Coventry,
m. October 18, 1815
Sherman J. Parker and Fanny P. Dow,　m. August 23, 1832

PAYN or PAYNE.

John Payn and Jemima Hutherson,　m. May 7, 1747
Stephen Payn, of Coventry, and Rebeckah Bushnell, daughter of Nathan Bushnell, of Lebanon,　m. September 23, 1756
Stephen Payne and Harriet L. Coan, both of Coventry,
m. November 29, 1838

PAYSON.

Samuel Payson and Clarissa Weeks,　m. November 13, 1831
Hiram Payson and Philena Fuller,　m. August 8, 1832

PECK.

John Peck and Phebe Avery,　m. November 10, 1827
Ebenezer Peck and Phebe Kingsbury,　m. June 10, 1838

PERKINS.

Ebenezer Perkins and Ruth Fuller, daughter of Josiah Fuller, of Coventry,　m. September 17, 1776
Nathaniel P. Perkins, of Mansfield, and Lucia Boynton, of Coventry,　m. September 25, 1822
Timothy D. Perkins and Lucy P. Fitch, both of Coventry,
m. in Andover, March 28, 1835
Allen M. Perkins and Julia A. Robertson, of Coventry,
m. September 11, 1836
Mr. William A. Perkins, of Hebron, and Miss Eliza Boynton, of Coventry,　m. May 20, 1838

PERRY.

Daniel Perry and Mirza Barnabee,
m. in Coventry, February 2, 1823

PHELPS.

Beniamon Phelps and Widow Christian Yongs,
m. October 31, 1753
Benjamin Phelps and Joanna Colman,　m. March 27, 1740

PHILLIPS.

Gideon Phillips, of Ellington, and Amy Mitchel, of Smithfield, R. I., m. May 29, 1820

PINGREY.

Sylvanus Pingrey and Mary Sawyer, m. December 30, 1762

POMROY.

Eleazer Pomroy and Sybil Kingsbury, m. December 17, 1772
Eleazer Pomroy and Priscilla Kingsbury, m. November 24, 1786
Daniel Pomroy, Jr., of Coventry, and Eunice Grant, of Tolland, Ct., m. April 14, 1772
Eleazer Pomeroy, Jr., and Ruth Hunt, both of Coventry, m. September 24, 1800
Eleazer Pomroy, Jr., and Elizabeth M. Jones, m. December 5, 1837

POOL.

Elijah Pool, of Coventry, and Mary Dodge, of Glastenbury, m. April 3, 1804

PORTER.

Noah Porter 2d and Submit Cook, m. November 29, 1764
Jonathan Porter, Jr., and Lois Richardson, daughter of Amos Richardson, of Coventry, m. November 15, 1759
Jonathan Porter, Jr., of Coventry, and Widow Lydia Abel, of Lebanon, m. November 8, 1769
William Porter and Esther Carpenter, daughter of Benjamin Carpenter, m. February 26, 1756
Noah Porter and Irena Thompson, daughter of Andrew Dodge, of Windham, m. May 28, 1758
Daniel Porter, Jr., and Esther King, m. December 5, 1739
Jobe Porter and Sybil Hoskings, m. December 5, 1739
Thomas Porter and Rebeckah Turner, m. January 20, 1737
Samuel Porter and Sarah Skinner, m. June 15, 1735
Jonathan Porter and Sarah Lad, m. June 20, 1734
Isaiah Porter, of Coventry, and Jedida Chubbusch, of Ellington, m. January 10, 1787

Erastus Porter and Hannah Denton, m. April 13, 1786
Noah Porter and Polly Loomis, m. December 31, 1793
Noah Porter and Faith Loomis, m. March 8, 1808
Ebenezer Porter and Eunice B. Kingsbury, both of Coventry,
 m. November 24, 1802
Mr. Osman Porter and Miss Emily Flint,
 m. February 16, 1823
Francis Porter and Faith Marilla Porter, m. March 18, 1834
Mr. Wm. E. Porter, of Willimantic, and Miss Mary Blackman,
 of Andover, m. September 29, 1834
Thomas Porter, of Coventry, and Zilpah Lyman, daughter of
 Daniel Lyman, of Coventry, m. November, 1754

PRESTON.

Joseph Preston and Widow Abigail Badcock,
 m. February 14, 1754
John H. Preston, of Ashford, and Fanny Manning, of Coventry, m. November 29, 1832

PRICE.

Rufus Price and Marthew Grant, m. September 17, 1750
John H. Price, of Providence, R. I., and Clarissa Davenport,
 of Coventry, m. October 14, 1827

PRIOR.

Prosper Prior and Calista Loomis,
 m. December 3 (probably 1834)

REED.

Josiah Reed and Silviah Hearrich, of Coventry,
 m. November 29, 1754

RICHARDS.

Michael Richards and Sarah Andrews, m. July 3, 1804

RIDER.

Thomas Rider, of Wellington, and Cephronia Dunham, of
 Coventry, m. May 4, 1830

RIPLEY.

Elijah Ripley and Alice Adams, m. February 8, 1773

Jeremiah Ripley and Mary Gove, both of Coventry,
m. July 19, 1780
Chauncey Ripley and Lucretia E. Fitch,   m. July 4, 1832

RITCHARDSON or RICHARDSON.

Amos Ritchardson, Jr., and Ruth Stiles,   m. June 5, 1751
Nathan Richardson and Phebe Crocker,
m. November 18, 1748
Lemuel Richardson and Anne Rust,   m. August 30, 1747
Justus Richardson and Submit Throop, both of Coventry,
m. November 16, 1769
Hezekiah Richardson and Olive Thompson, both of Coventry,
m. January 27, 1774
Lemuel Richardson, Jr., of Coventry, and Rachael Lathrop, of Tolland,   m. June 2, 1774
Bila Richardson and Triphena Swetland,   m. March 18, 1782
Stephen Richardson and Mabel Marsh, m. February 22, 1763

ROBERTSON.

John Robertson 3d and Eunice Phelps,   m. February 2, 1764
Samuel Robertson and Martha Badcock,   m. March 20, 1746
Samuel Robertson and Mary Hindsdel, both of Coventry,
m. 20th day (no month) 1749
Samuel Robertson and Anne Curtis,   m. September 6, 1759
Samuel Robertson, of Coventry, and Anne Waters, of Colchester,   m. June 18, 1772
Daniel Robertson, Jr., and Triphena Janes,
m. February 18, 1773
Guy C. Robertson, of Bolton, and Julia Ann Lewis, of Coventry,   m. April 15, 1832
Capt. David Robertson, of Coventry, and Almira Starkweather, of Mansfield,   m. September 16, 1827
Joseph Robertson and Sybil Archer,   m. February 28, 1841
Horace Robertson and Laura Woodworth, of Coventry,
m. September 12, 1841

ROBERTSON or ROBERSON.

Samuel Robertson, of Coventry, and Anna Waters, of Colchester,   m. June 18, 1772

Daniel Roberson, Jr., and Hannah Hindsdel,
m. December 24, 1747
Daniel Robertson, of Coventry, and Susannah Robertson, of Newbury, m. November 21, 1755
Daniell Robeson and Lydia, m. June 24, 1719
Ephraim Roberson and Esther Rose, m. January 5, 1743-4

ROCKWELL.

Dr. William Rockwell, of Hartford, and Mrs. Maria F. Chapin, of Coventry, m. June 25, 1835

ROOT.

Joseph Root and Silance Curtis, m. December 20, 1753
Asal Root and Mehitable Warner, m. April 18, 1750
Ephraim Root and Elisabeth Carpenter, m. May 31, 1750
Eliakim Root and Mercy, m. December 15, 1724
Thomas Root and Elisabeth, m. November 18, 1719
Ebenezer Root and Sarah, m. May 19, 1718
Thomas Root, Jr., and Elisabeth Field, m. September 24, 1761
Samuel Root and Mercy Parker, m. March 12, 1728-9
Eliakim Root and Jemima Eells, m. August 5, 1731
Jonathan Root and Zirviah Fowler, m. May 27, 1779
Jonathan Root and Azubah Brown, m. May 1, 1766
Ebenezer Root, Jr., and Phebe Halkins, m. May 20, 1753
Medad Root and Rhoda Curtis, m. November 17, 1763
John Root and Deborah Hawkins, m. May 15, 1760
Mr. Jesse Root, of Coventry, and Mary Banks, of Newark, N. J., m. May 18, 1758
Thomas Root, Jr., and Elisabeth Lee, m. November 18, 1719
Thomas Root, Jr. (second time), Widow Hannah Hinsdale,
m. April 9, 1730
Thomas Root, Jr., and Elisabeth Field, m. September 24, 1761
Nathaniel Root and Elisabeth Kingsbury,
m. December 11, 1777
Nathaniel Root and Candace Hammond, m. May 26, 1791
Ephraim Root and Phebe Colbourn, m. February 3, 1785
Ebenezer Grant Root and Susan Gardner,
m. September 15, 1840

ROSE.

Nathan Hale Rose and Eunice Talcott, m. September 16, 1801
Nathan Hale Rose and Lydia Perkins, of Lisbon,
m. March 27, 1806
Major Richard H. Rose and Mary A. Dimick,
m. October 28, 1839
Samuel Rose and Elisabeth Hale, both of Coventry,
m. December 30, 1773
Joseph Rose and Desire Dimmick, m. August 9, 1769
Josiah Rose and Eunice Meecham, m. May 9, 1739
Joseph Rose and Millie Sweetland, m. November 27, 1799
William Rose and Irene Loomis, m. June 29, 1797
L. Perkins Rose and Ann R. Manning, of Coventry,
m. September 30, 1835

ROSWELL.

Alfred Roswell, of Colchester, and Emily Whittemore, of Coventry, m. November 24, 1825

RUST.

Joseph Rust, of Coventry, and Tabithe Kingsbury, of Norwich,
m. September 1, 1763
Ameziah Rust and Mary Marsh, m. August 26, 1753
Nathaniel Rust and Widow Mary Rose, m. September 9, 1754
Mathias Rust and Susa Fitch, m. February 6, 1749-50
Samuel Rust and Sarah, m. May 17, 1716
Nathaniel Rust and Hannah Hatch, m. April 19, 1716
Samuel Rust and Sarah Hockins, m. July 2, 1722
Noah Rust and Keziah, m. November 2, 1727
Nathaniel Rust and Widow Mary Rose, m. September 9, 1754
Daniel Rust and Mary Parker, m. February 16, 1762
Simeon Rust and Sarah Long, m. October 22, 1741
Nathaniel Rust, Jr., and Hannah Hatch, m. April 19, 1716
Daniel Rust and Anna White, m. April 26, 1732
Daniell Rust and Widow Mary Mead, m. October 27, 1748
Noah Rust and Keziah Strong, m. November 2, 1727
Samuel Rust and Marcy Parker, m. March 12, 1728-9
Nathaniel Wilson Rust and Rachael Babcock,
m. April 22, 1779

SABINS.

John Sabins and Margaret Rust, m. February 13, 1742-3

SAGE.

George Sage, of Vernon, and Almira Ingraham, of Middletown, m. in Andover, October 13, 1823

SARLS and SEARLE.

Ebenezer Sarls and Truelove Brown, m. July 20, 1741
Elisha Searle and Azubah Gates, both of Coventry, m. July 12, 1768
Elisha Sarls and Mary Acley, m. June 5, 1740
John Sarle and Margaret Coock, m. August 13, 1741

SCHOLTS.

Henry Scholts, of Tolland, and Syrena Hoxie, of Coventry, m. April 16, 1829

SCOTT.

Peter Scott and Hannah Edwards, m. November 5, 1740

SCRIPTURE.

John Scripture and Abigail Utley, m. May 15, 1712
John Scripture (second time), and Widow Mary Slater, m. December 30, 1728
Simeon Scripture and Ann Slatter, m. September 19, 1738

SHAFFER.

Dan Shaffer and Sophronia Goff, m. January 31, 1827

SHAW.

Benjamin Shaw and Elisabeth Edwards, m. June 9, 1736

SHEPARD.

Noah Shepard and Abigail Glason, m. March 9, 1747
Jonathan Shepard, of Coventry, and Loue Palmer, m. December 23, 1736

SIMPSON.

George W. Simpson and Caroline A. Robertson, both of Coventry, m. June 16, 1833
George W. Simpson and Julia A. Robertson, both of Coventry, m. March 26, 1840

SISSON.

Benjamin Sisson and Mary B. Eldridge, of Hartford, m. October 16, 1836

SKINNER.

Daniel Skinner and Abigail Burnap, m. February 14, 1754
Noah Skinner and Patiance Dunham, m. December 18, 1737
Noah Skinner and Mary Scott, m. March 12, 1741
Truman Skinner, of Van Buren, N. Y., and Lydia M. Jones, of Andover, m. October 4, 1832
Eli Skinner and Sally Griggs, m. October 22, 1826

SMITH.

Benjamin Smith and Mary Roberson, m. May 15, 1738
Deacon Recompense Smith and Elisabeth Kenney, m. (no date)
James Smith, Jr., and Esther Talcott, m. March 24, 1825
Sidney Smith and Lucy C. Chapman, m. September 15, 1841

SPENCER.

John Spencer and Jerusha Pease, of Coventry, m. November 27, 1823
Henry L. Spencer, of East Haddam, and Olive Brown, of Coventry, m. November 1, 1841

SPICER.

Abel Spicer, of Preston, and Lucy Babcock, of Coventry, m. December 23, 1826

SPRAGUE.

Joseph Sprague and Hannah Swetland, m. November 27, 1755
Samuel Sprague of Coventry, and Widow Ruth Clark, of Lebanon, m. December 21, 1772
Bila Sprague and Esther Parker, m. May 7, 1806

Elias Sprague and Lucinda Whaley, m. May, 1825
Ralph Sprague and Evelina L. Brown, m. September 15, 1833

STANLEY.
John Stanley and Lucy Edwards, m. November 14, 1748
Moses Stanley and Eunice Strong, m. June 12, 1768
John Stanley, Jr., and Mary Fuller, m. October 15, 1772

STAR.
Thomas Star and Hannah Edwards, m. October 23, 1729

STARKWEATHER.
James Starkweather, of Mansfield, and Sally Morey, of Coventry, m. January 13, 1825

STEDMAN.
John Stedman and Mary Merrill, daughter of Peter Merrill, of Norwich, m. May 25, 1758
Alexander Stedman and Sarah Cushman,
m. November 10, 1768

STORRS.
Mr. Leander Storrs, of Mansfield, and Miss Abby Edgerton, of Coventry, m. November 20, 1838

STORY.
Orasmus Story and Eliza Lyman, m. November 16, 1826.

STOWELL.
Stephen S. Stowell, of Mansfield, and Cornelia W. Stebbens, of Coventry, m. April, 1841

STRONG.
Oziah Strong, of Coventry, and Susanna West, of Tolland,
m. August 9, 1757
Phineas Strong, Jr., and Tabithy Bruster, daughter of Peter Bruster, m. January 25, 1748-9
Asa Strong, of Coventry, and Sarah Moody, of Newbury,
m. June 9, 1763
Phineas Strong and Mary Parker, m. November 5, 1724
Joseph Strong, Jr., and Elisabeth, m. May 12, 1724

Joseph Strong, Esq., and Ruth, m. September 15, 1724
Noah Strong and Widow Lideah Pers, m. January 29, 1740-41
Enoch Strong and Sarah Maraugh, m. October 14, 1742
Aaron Strong and Rachael Strong, m. January 6, 1731-32
Moses Strong and Sarah Long, m. February 4, 1730-31
Benajah Strong and Sarah Colman, of Coventry,
 m. April 29, 1784
Rev. Mr. Nathan Strong and Hester Mecham,
 m. October 2, 1746
Beniah Strong and Lucy Bishop, m. March 9, 1769
Bohan S. Strong, of Southampton, Mass., and Diana Colman,
 of Coventry, m. February 12, 1827

SWEATLAND or SWETLAND.

Ebenezer Sweatland and Sarah Leach, m. August 14, 1749
Ebenezer Sweatland and Widow Abigail Bliss, of Hebron,
 m. March 31, 1766 (?)
Israel Swetland and Dorias Dewey, m. May 6, 1756
Levi Sweetland and Ruth Ritchardson, m. December 28, 1780
Ebenezer Leach Sweetland and Meriah Badcock,
 m. April 13, 1780
Levi Sweetland, Jr., and Electa Kingsbury, both of Coventry,
 m. March 8, 1810
Daniel Sweetland and Miss Roxa McKee,
 m. November 19, 1829

SWIFT.

Brewster T. Swift, of Mansfield, and Charlotte Maxwell, of
 Coventry, m. June 9, 1825
Albert E. Swift, of East Windsor, and Miss Saphina C. Marsh,
 of Coventry, m. January 5, 1838
Barzilla Swift, of Mansfield, and Martha Gardner, of Coventry,
 m. April 20, 1841

TALCOTT.

Joseph Talcott, Jr., and Rebeckah, m. September 11, 1777
Arad Talcott and Anna Tracy, m. October 15, 1806
Erastus Talcott and Aurelli Loomis, m. September 19, 1820
Joseph A. Talcott and Mary Loomis, m. July 1, 1832
George H. Talcott, of Huron, N. Y., and Lucretia Colman, of
 Coventry, m. October 5, 1835

TARBOX.

Bill Augustus Tarbox and Sophia Loomis,
                                    m. November 14, 1820
Harvey Tarbox, of Coventry, and Sarah S. Jones, of Hebron,
                                    m. September 14, 1834

TAYLOR.

Stephen Taylor and Deliverance Rust,   m. May 16, 1746
John Taylor and Elisabeth Rose,   m. March 24, 1784

TERRILL.

Thomas Terrill and Triphene Terrill,   m. August 19, 1756
Thomas Terrill and Alathea Crocker,   m. August 15, 1769

THAYER.

Ephraim Thayer, Jr., of Burillville, R. I., and Adah Mathewson, of Coventry,   m. September 15, 1825
Elisha Thayer, of Vernon, and Lucy Burdwin, of Coventry,
                                    m. March 1, 1821

THOMSON or THOMPSON.

Amos Thomson and Irane Dodge,   m. May 17, 1750
Nathan Thompson and Hannah Dodge,   m. March 29, 1745
Thomas Thompson and Lucy Killam,
             m. in Stonington, November 24, 1773
John Thompson and Martha Remington, both of Coventry,
                                    m. December 26, 1823

TIFFT.

Jesse Tifft, of Hartford, and Almira Robinson, of Coventry,
                                    m. January 1, 1837

TILDEN.

Joshua Tilden and Caroline Carpenter, both of Coventry,
                                    m. September 19, 1837

TINKER.

Hazard Tinker and Adah Bump, of Mansfield,
                                    m. January 7, 1827

TOPLIFF.

Chauncey Topliff, of Coventry, and Miss Chloe Butler, of Mansfield,   m. in Andover, August 12, 1838

TOWNSEND.

William D. Townsend and Fanny Y. Sprague, both of Andover,
m. October 28, 1829

TRACY.

Trumbull Tracy and Dorcas Hibbard,   m. December 9, 1834
George Tracy and Maria L. Cummings, of Coventry,
m. March 28, 1841

TRAPP.

Samuel Trapp, of Coventry, and Alice Metcalf, of Mansfield,
m. June 30, 1808

TROWBRIDGE.

Ira Trowbridge, of Mansfield, and Cynthia Crossman, of Coventry,   m. August 21, 1808

TRYON.

George Tryon, of Tolland, and Lucy Abbot, of Coventry,
m. September, 1826

TUCKER.

Norman Tucker, of Suffield, and Mary Lyman, of Coventry,
m. September 20, 1830
Edwin D. Tucker and Abby J. Eells, of Coventry,
m. August 22, 1836

TURNER.

Jethro Turner and Sarah Badcock,   m. February 28, 1743-4
John Turner and Mary Wright, m. (no date) but child born February 21, 1766.
Daniel Turner and Hannah Boynton, both of Coventry,
m. April 10, 1771
Joseph Turner 2d and Elizabeth Bridgman,
m. November 7, 1762
Hab'k Turner, Jr., and Lydia Rose,   m. February 28, 1765
Amos Turner and Hannah Dorman, both of Coventry,
m. March 19, 1789
Stephen Turner, of Mansfield, and Naomi Palmer, of Coventry,
m. March 5, 1807
Orrin Turner and Lydia Woodward,   m. January 4, 1833
Isaac Turner and Lydia E. Arnold,   m. May 8, 1836

UPTON.

Turner F. Upton and Sophronia Bugbee, of Willimantic,
m. February 11, 1840

VIBBERT.

Mervin Vibbert, of East Hartford, and Mary Ann Ensworth, of Andover, m. January 8, 1842

VINTON.

Joel Vinton, of Willington, and Laura A. Loomis, of Coventry,
m. in Willington, March 14, 1831

VORRA.

Martin Vorra, of Germany, and Abigail Rust, of Coventry,
m. October 7, 1783

WADSWORTH.

Samuell Wadsworth and Mary Granger,
m. February 7, 1732-3

Samuel A. Wadsworth, of Hampton, and Jane E. L. Ormsby, of Coventry, m. June 22, 1837

WALDO.

Doctor John Waldo and Lucy Lyman, m. August 19, 1773
Lemuel Waldo and Sarah Marshall, m. January 3, 1827

WALKER.

Samuel Walker, of Willington, and Lucina Sweetland, of Coventry, m. November 19, 1823

WALLBRIDGE.

Samuel Wallbridge, of Coventry, and Sarah Page,
m. October 14, 1767

Lemuel Wallbridge, of Coventry, and Elisabeth Williams, of Preston, m. March 23, 1786

Henry Walbridge and Sarah Fowler, m. December 1, 1773 or 5

WATERMAN.

Benjamin Waterman and Harriet Porter, m. January 27, 1829

WATERS.

Jacob Waters and Mary Edwards, m. November 23, 1749

WEST.

Col. Samuel West, of Columbia, and Lucy Manning, of Coventry, m. April 26, 1832

WESTON.

George C. Weston and Alba Augusta Slack, of Coventry,
m. August 20, 1834

WHEELER.

Amasa Wheeler, of East Haddam, and Roxelana Hammond, of N. Coventry, m. September 21, 1830

WHELDIN.

Jonathan Wheldin and Anna Lyman, both of Coventry,
m. October 5, 1786

WHITE.

Samuel White and Widow Rachael Tilden, of Coventry,
m. March 14, 1756
Abner White and Jerusha Thompson, m. January 28, 1766
Montgomery White and Sally Coleman, m. May 13, 1812
Stanley White, of Andover, and Ann R. Rose, of Coventry,
m. November 30, 1841
George H. White, of Hebron, and Lucia Parker, of Coventry,
m. October 28, 1840
Nathaniel White and Maranda Ticknor, of Columbia,
m. November 8, 1826

WHITING.

Chester Whiting, of Ashford, Windham Co., Ct., and Levey Brown, of Columbia, m. January 6, 1833
Elijah Whiting, of Tolland, and Louisa Mathewson, of Coventry, m. at Bolton, May 24, 1838

WHITMAN.

James W. Whitman and Lucinda P. Stone,
m. December 25, 1836
Patrick F. Whitman, of Griswold, and Nancy Ladd, of Coventry, m. June 22, 1826

WILLIAMS.

Rufus Williams, of Columbia, Toll Co., Ct., and Harriet Allen, of Windham, m. (no date) 1833 (probably)

WILLSON or WILSON.

Francis Willson and Abigail Fellows, of Tolland,
m. February 10, 1757
Jacob Willson and Hannah Dimock, m. December 12, 1771
William Willson and Sarah Rust, m. July 26, 1749
Samuel Wilson, of Coventry, and Almira Dow, of Columbia,
m. October 12, 1830
Royal B. Wilson, of Vernon, and Maria L. O'Brien, of Middletown, m. November 4, 1838
Nelson Wilson, of Ashford, and Emily Topliff, of Coventry,
m. April 1, 1838
Joseph Wilson and Hannah H. Hunt, both of Coventry,
m. May 18, 1829
Samuel Wilson, of Coventry, and Almira Dow, of Columbia,
m. October 12, 1830

WINCHESTER.

Loring Winchester, of S. Mansfield, and Amelia Bidwell,
m. August 30, 1838
Daniel Winchester and Ruth Palmer, m. November 28, 1751

WINTWORTH.

Ebenezer Wintworth, Jr., and Sarah French, both of Coventry,
m. November 11, 1762

WOOD.

Roben Wood, negro slave of Peter Buell, and Judah Pallon, Indian servant to N. Buell, m. January 20, 1729-30

WOODRUFF.

Rev. Ephraim Woodruff and Sarah Aldin, m. October 7, 1801

WOODWARD.

Aaron Woodward, of Coventry, and Ellener Benton, of Tolland,
m. October 25, 1758
Nathaniel Woodward, Jr., and Surviah Ensworth,
m. May 31, 1781
Daniel Woodward and Lydia Edgerton, m. January 6, 1820

WOODWORTH.

Spencer Woodworth and Amanda Clark, both of Coventry,
　　　　　　　　　　　m. November 25, 1808
Simeon Woodworth, of Mansfield, and Lucy A. Dorman, of Coventry,　　　　m. December 11, 1833
William Woodworth and Mary Ann Knox,
　　　　　　　　　　　m. October 11, 1831
Harry Woodworth and Clarissa Bingham, of Columbia,
　　　　　　　　m. at Andover, September 28, 1826
Waterman C. Wordworth and Ann A. Parker,
　　　　　　　　　　　m. March 3, 1840
Jesse Wordworth and Almira Whittemore, m. March 15, 1840

WOOLCOTT.

Josiah Woolcott and Widow Lucy French,　m. April 23, 1740

WRIGHT.

Roswell Wright and Mary Jeffray,　　　m. June 9, 1785
Roswell Wright and Abigail Benton,　　m. June 1, 1789
Elijah Wright and Jane Richardson,　m. November 1, 1781
John Wright and Eunice Loomis, both of Coventry,
　　　　　　　　　m. at Andover, October 16, 1806
John Wright and Charlotte Mathewson, both of N. Coventry,
　　　　　　　　　　　m. June 7, 1831

YEOMANS.

William Yeomans and Betsey McLean, of Columbia,
　　　　　　　　　　　m. November 25, 1825
Sanford Yeomans, of Columbia, and Marinda Parker, of Coventry,　　　m. at Andover, Ct., March 26, 1836

YOUNG.

Eliphilet Young, of Windham, Ct., and Ruth F. Hammond, of North Kingston, R. I.　　　m. January 25, 1830

Copy of Deaths taken from Town Records, in Coventry, Conn., from 1711 to 1840.

ABBEY.

Abigail, daughter of Eliphilet and Lydia Abbey,
d. March 11, 1819
Edmund, son of Eliphilet and Lydia Abbey, d. March 1, 1820
Albert, son of Eliphilet and Lydia Abbey, d. June 9, 1830
Infant child, d. October 25, 1832
Infant child, d. October 28, 1835
George W. Abbey, d. April 20, 1832

ALLIN.

Samuel Allin, d. October 14, 1718
George Allin, d. May 31, 1756, in his 67th year

ANTISEL.

Sarah, daughter of Simon and Martha Antisel,
d. February 11, 1770

ARNOLD.

Robert, son of John and Elisabeth Arnold,
d. April 3, 1760, in his 8th year
Elisabeth, wife of John Arnold,
d. January 28, 1761, in her 40th year

BADCOCK.

Mary, wife of James Badcock,
d. April 1, 1735, in her 58th year
Martha, wife of John Badcock, d. May 18, 1728
John Badcock, Sr., d. August 17, 1731
Benjamin Badcock, d. February 28, 1751, in his 54th year
Abigail, daughter of Ebenezer and Mehitable Badcock,
d. May 27, 1735
Ebenezer, son of Ebenezer and Mehitable Badcock,
d. February 24, 1740-1
Daniel, son of Ebenezer and Mehitable Badcock,
d. August 23, 1750

Ebenezer Badcock, d. October 16, 1773, in his 75th year
Joseph, son of Ebenezer and Hannah Badcock,
　　　　　　　　　　d. May 11, 1759, in his 2d year
Jonathan Badcock, d. January 5, 1731-2, 80 years and 5 days
Sergeant Daniell Badcock, d. February 10, 1734, in his 45th year
Hannah, wife of John Badcock, d. March 10, 1779
Mary Badcock, daughter of Sergeant Daniell Badcock,
　　　　　　　　　　d. February 23, 1736
Jerusha, daughter of Daniell and Sarah Badcock,
　　　　　　　　　　d. April 2, 1722
Joshua, son of Daniell and Sarah Badcock, d. January 8, 1724-5
Robert, son of Jonathan and Mary Badcock, d. May 11, 1728
Lucy, wife of Robert Badcock, d. May 31, 1725
Simeon Badcock, d. November 30, 1751, in his 40th year

BADGER.

Ariel, son of Moses and Jerusha Badger,
　　　　　　　　　　d. May 3, 1778, in his 2d year
Mr. Enoch Badger (the elder),
　　　　　　　　　　d. September 4, 1793, in his 80th year
Mehitable Badger, wife of Abner Badger,
　　　　　　　　　　d. January 7, 1779, in her 31st year
Nathaniel Badger, son of Enoch and Mary Badger,
　　　　　　　　　　d. February 7, 1752
John Badger, d. July 28, 1762, in his 67th year
Mary, wife of Nathaniel Badger,
　　　　　　　　　　d. August 29, 1763, in her 87th year

BALDWIN.

Elamuell, son of Theophilus and Sarah Baldwin,
　　　　　　　　　　d. April 10, 1751
Theophilus Baldwin, d. January 3, 1750, in his 26th year

BARKER.

Rhoda, daughter of Oliver and Mary Barker,
　　　　　　　　　　d. January 24, 1764

BARNARD.

Esther, daughter of Benony and Freedom Barnard,
　　　　　　　　　　d. December 6, 1736

Abigail, daughter of Benony and Freedom Barnard,
                                d. December 8, 1736
Joseph Barnard,   d. November 14, 1752, in his 33d year
Benony Barnard,   d. September 6, 1750, in his 67th year

BENTLEY.

John, son of William and Phebe Bentley,   d. January 13, 1777

BISSELL or BISSEL.

Zariah, daughter of Capt. John and Sarah Bissel,
                                  d. March 6, 1739-40
Joseph, son of John and Sarah Bissell,   d. November 8, 1727
Sarah, wife of Captain John Bissell,   d. August 25, 1751

BLACKMAN.

Mary, wife of David Blackman,   d. August 23, 1784

BOOTH.

Elisabeth, daughter of Rev. Chauncey and Laura Farnam
    Booth,   d. January 4, 1821
Caleb, son of Rev. Chauncy and Laura F. Booth,
                                  d. October 30, 1840

BOYNTON.

Sarah, daughter of Zachariah and Sarah Boynton,
                                  d. October 6, 1723
Sarah, daughter of Zachariah and Sarah Boynton,
                                  d. October 6, 1724
Ace, son of John and Tabethy Boynton,
                         d. January 5, 1742, aged 14 days
Zachariah Boynton,   d. December 30, 1750, about 65 years old
Joshua Boynton,   d. October 16, 1752, in his 30th year

BRIDGMAN.

Dorothy, wife of Isaac Bridgman,   d. November 26, 1753
Isaac Bridgman,   d. June 22, 1756
John, son of Isaac and Dorothy Bridgman, d. February 20, 1717
Olive, daughter of Isaac and Elisabeth Bridgman,
                                    d. July 12, 1753

BRIGHAM.

Salinda, daughter of Thomas and Susannah Brigham,
    d. December 29, 1775, in her 4th year
Thomas, son of Thomas and Susannah Brigham,
    d. November 27, 1775
Paul Brigham,   d. May 3, 1746, in his 28th year
Mary, daughter of Paul and Lydia Brigham,
    d. March, 1773, in her 3d year
Anna, wife of Asa Brigham,   d. July 15, 1767, in her 21st year
Rogger, son of Uriah and Anne Brigham,
    d. November, 1760, in his 6th year
Uriah Brigham,   d. January 25, 1777, in his 55th year

BROWN.

Ephraim Brown,   d. November 16, 1750, in his 78th year
Ruth, daughter of John and Ruth Brown, d. November 15, 1749
Eunice, daughter of Jonathan and Mary Brown,
    d. in Summers, April 12, 1751, in her 16th year
Judah, daughter of Ephraim and Sarah Brown,
    d. February 6, 1741-2, in her 36th year
Abraham Brown,   d. June 28, 1769, in his 37th year
Hulda, daughter of Abraham and Anna Brown,
    d. January 11, 1770, in her 2d year
Mary, wife of Abraham Brown,
    d. April 25, 1760, in her 25th year
Abraham, son of Elijah and Lydia Brown, d. March 24, 1758
Bethiah, son of Elijah and Lydia Brown, d. January 30, 1760
Abraham Brown,   d. July 29, 1749
Tabitha, daughter of Ebenezer and Lucy Brown,
    d. December 22, 1751
Ebenezer, son of Timothy and Ester Brown, d. March 15, 1776
Oliver, son of Josiah and Mary Brown,   d. January 10, 1795
Mary, daughter of Josiah and Mary Brown, d. January 22, 1795
Abigail, daughter of Josiah and Mary Brown,
    d. December 25, 1782

BUELL.

Peter, son of Peter and Hannah Buell,   d. November 5, 1716
Hannah, wife of Peter Buell,   d. February 20, 1718-19

Ruth, daughter of Peter, Esq., and Martha Buell,
        d. December 30, 1736
Peter, son of Capt. Peter and Martha Buell,
        d. June 2, 1752, in his 23d year
Jesse Buell,   d. October 6, 1839

CARPENTER.

Benjamin Carpenter, Sr., d. April 18, 1738, in his 74th year
Hannah Carpenter, relict to Benjamin Carpenter, deceased,
        d. March 20, 1762, in her 92d year
Hannah, daughter of Eliphilet and Elisabeth Carpenter,
        d. October 8, 1742
Lois, daughter of Eliphilet and Elisabeth Carpenter,
        d. January 4, 1740
Hannah, daughter of Eliphilet and Elisabeth Carpenter,
        d. June 5, 1740
Anne, daughter of Eliphilet and Elisabeth Carpenter,
        d. June 7, 1740
Abigail, daughter of Eliphilet and Elisabeth Carpenter,
        d. June 8, 1740
Asahel, son of Eliphilet and Elisabeth Carpenter,
        d. June 9, 1740
Eunice, wife of Ebenezer Carpenter, d. January 21, 1777
Benjamin, son of Elijah and Patience Carpenter,
        d. January 29, 1770
Patience, wife of Elijah Carpenter, d. September 8, 1786
Joseph, Jr., son of Joseph and Phebe Carpenter,
        d. February 10, 1772, in his 6th year
Haretiah, daughter of Joseph and Phebe Carpenter,
        d. October 3, 1775, in her 6th year
Hannah, daughter of Joseph and Phebe Carpenter,
        d. October 8, 1775, in her 8th year
Joseph Carpenter, d. January 28, 1776, in his 41st year
Elisabeth, daughter of Joseph and Phebe Carpenter,
        d. September 18, 1776, in her 18th year
Phebe, relict of Joseph Carpenter,
        d. February 13, 1779, in her 39th year
Benjamin Carpenter, Jr.,
        drowned February 27, 1750, in his 29th year

Ebenezer Carpenter, d. January 30, 1777
Mabel C., daughter of Benjamin and Rebeckah Carpenter,
d. August 18, 1742

CASE.

Major Tabal Case, d. January 7, 1822

CLARK.

Thomas Clark, d. May 12, 1739, in his 94th year
Widow Ann Clark, d. December 14, 1750
David Clark, d. May 3, 1751
Sarah Clark, wife of David Clark, d. January 15, 1751
Abigail, wife of Seth Clark, d. September 2, 1740
Leakins, son of Joseph and Coziah Clark, d. April 19, 1740
Joseph Clark, d. January 15, 1738-9
Jacob, reputed son of Joseph Clark by Martha Millinton,
d. April 28, 1740

COLMAN.

Judah Colman, d. December 22, 1759, in his 72d year
Hannah, daughter of Ephraim, d. April 9, 1725
Ephraim, son of Ebenezer and Sarah, d. October, 1740
Gershom Colman, d. August 12, 1771, in his 55th year
Joseph, son of Ephraim and Lavinia Colman,
d. September 6, 1775, in his 5th year
Jesse, son of Ephraim and Lavinia Colman,
d. September 1, 1775, in his 3d year
John, son of Ephraim and Lavinia Colman,
d. September 13, 1775, in his 7th year

COOLEY.

Noah, son of Jonathan and Azubah Cooley,
d. September 13, 1760, in his 5th year

COWLS.

Samuel, son of Samuel and Abigail Cowls, d. July 23, 1741
Ruth, daughter of Samuel and Abigail Cowls,
d. August 9, 1741
Lydia, daughter of Samuel and Abigail Cowls,
d. August 10, 1741
Eunice, daughter of Samuel and Abigail Cowls,
d. September 10, 1741

CRANE.

John Crane's child, d. September 20, 1713
Daniell Crane, son of John and Abigail Crane,
           d. January 4, 1718-19.

CROCKER.

Mr. Andrew Crocker, d. July 4, 1778
Lois, wife of Mr. Andrew Crocker, d. September 22, 1775
Martha, daughter of Andrew Crocker, d. December 29, 1775
Roswell, son of Andrew Crocker, d. November 5, 1776
Samuel, son of Andrew Crocker, d. November 10, 1786
Simion, son of Andrew Crocker, d. February 24, 1777

CURTIS.

Sabrina, daughter of Samuel and Joanna Curtis,
           d. October 3, 1775
Joanna, daughter of Samuel and Joanna Curtis,
           d. October 29, 1775
Nathaniel Curtis, son of Henry and Silence Curtis,
           d. June 29, 1741
Rhoda, daughter of Henry and Silence Curtis, d. April 12, 1743
Silence, wife of Henry Curtis, d. November 2, 1745
Samuel Curtis, d. May 27, 1764, in his 84th year
Samuel, Jr., son of Samuel and Joanna Curtis,
           d. February 11, 1776
Anna, daughter of Henry, Jr., and Elisabeth, d. August 14, 1771
Henry Curtis, d. January 8, 1772
Bildad Curtis, d. November 2, 1762, in his 30th year
Nathaniel, son of Henry, Jr., and Elisabeth Curtis,
           d. July 21, 1760, in his 8th year
Hannah, daughter of Henry, Jr., and Elisabeth,
           d. November 27, 1762

CUSHMAN.

Stephen, son of Ephraim and Sarah Cushman,
           d. September 8, 1775
Hannah, daughter of Ephraim and Sarah Cushman,
           d. October 2, 1775, in her 9th year
Asa, son of Ephraim and Sarah Cushman,
           d. September 19, 1775, in his 7th year

Ephraim, Jr., son of Ephraim and Sarah Cushman,
      d. October 5, 1775, in his 5th year
Timothy, son of Allerton, Jr., and Harmony Cushman,
      d. May 8, 1766

CUTLER.

Sarah, daughter of Daniel Cutler,   d. January 19, 1758
Nathaniel, son of Daniel and Mary Cutler, d. July 9, 1758
Mary, wife of Daniel Cutler,   d. June 14, 1759
Eleazer, son of Daniel and Mary Cutler, d. August 1, 1759
Sarah, daughter of Daniel and Mary Cutler, d. August 22, 1759

DAGGETT.

Anna, daughter of Isaiah and Esther Daggett,
      d. February 12, 1795
Chester, son of Isaiah and Esther Daggett, d. February 21, 1795
Samuel Daggett,   d. August 24, 1798
Isiah Daggett,   d. August 24, 1835

DAMON.

Ebenezer, son of Lemuel, Jr., and Thankful Damon,
      d. February 17, 1733-4

DAVIS.

Benjamin, son of Thomas and Hannah Davis, d. April 19, 1728
Thomas, son of Thomas and Hannah Davis, d. May 24, 1725
Ebenezer, son of Thomas and Hannah Davis, d. July 16, 1726
Thomas Davis,   d. October 1, 1739, in his 63d year

DEANS.

Sarah, daughter of Beniah and Mary Deans,
      d. January 18, 1761, in her 22d year
Meriam, daughter of Benajah and Mary Deans,
      d. May 8, 1761, in her 19th year
Asa, son of Benaiah and Mary Deans,
      d. January 3, 1763, in his 17th year
Olive, daughter of Solomon and Ruth Deans,
      d. July 4, 1770, in her 2d year
Mary, wife of Benajah Deans,   d. April 5, 1776
Martha, daughter of Solomon and Anna Deans,
      d. December, 1774, in her 8th year

DIMICK or DIMOCK or DIMMICK.

Clara Maria, daughter of Capt. Daniel and Anna Dimmick,
　　　　　　　　　　　　　　　　d. August 21, 1849

DORMAN.

Mary, wife of Amos Dorman,　　　　d. April 16, 1749 (?)

DOW or DOWE.

Tabitha, wife of Humphrey Dow,
　　　　　d. in Coventry, December 11, 1803
Humphrey B. Dow,
　　　d. in Hebron, September 6, 1822, buried in Coventry
Anna, wife of Ulysses Dow,　　　　d. April 17, 1790
Lucy, daughter of Solomon and Tirzah Dow,
　　　　　　　　d. August 11, 1809, aged 17 months
Emily, daughter of Solomon and Tirzah Dow,
　　　　　　　　　d. June 3, 1811, aged 5 years
Solomon Dow,　　　　　　　　d. January 6, 1823
Peggy, wife of Lorenzo Dow,　d. in Hebron, January 6, 1820
Hepzibah, wife of Ephraim Dowe,
　　　　　　　　d. April 16, 1775, in her 44th year
Jesse, son of Ephraim and Hepzibah Dowe,　　d. May 3, 1755

DUTY or DEUTY.

Samuel, son of Matthew and Eunice Deuty,　d. June 27, 1772

EDWARDS.

Mary, daughter of Thomas and Mary C. Edwards,
　　　　　　　　　　　　　　　　d. March 15, 1748
Ephraim Edwards,　　d. September 25, 1761, in his 21st year
Oliver, son of Thomas and Mary Edwards,
　　　　　　　　　　d. October 13, 1761, in his 17th year
William, son of William and Jane Edwards,　d. October, 1732
Jerusha, daughter of William and Jane Edwards,
　　　　　　　　　　d. June 24, 1752, in her 25th year
William Edwards,　　　　　　　　d. July 7, 1752
Jane, daughter of William and Jane Edwards,
　　　　　　　　　　d. October 12, 1752, in her 19th year
William, son of Joshua and Dorcas Edwards,
　　　　　　　　　　　　　　　　d. November 20, 1759

Gideon, son of Joshua and Dorcas Edwards,
d. October 14, 1775
Joseph Edwards, d. December 16, 1750, in his 53d year
Ebenezer Edwards, d. September 11, 1754, in his 70th year
Mary, relict of Ebenezer Edwards,
d. March 2, 1769, in her 81st year
Thomas, son of Daniel and Hannah Edwards,
d. April 29, 1751
Daniel Edwards, d. December 30, 1756, in his 83d year
Thomas Edwards, d. September 25, 1761

ELLIS.

Naomy Ellis, who lived with Eliakim Root, who was said Root's wife's sister, d. January 26, 1739-40

EUERDON.

Walter Euerdon, d. July 11, 1740

EWISS or EUISS.

John Ewiss, d. October 1, 1719

FITCH.

Capt. Jeremiah Fitch, d. May 22, 1736
Febe, daughter of James and Febe Fitch, d. January 11, 1738-9
Deborah Fitch, d. August, 1742
John, son of Jeremiah and Marcy Fitch, d. May 25, 1743
Marcy, wife of Jeremiah Fitch,
d. January 27, 1743-4, in her 36th year
Deborah, daughter of Elisha and Presillah Fitch,
d. October 15, 1741
Mary, daughter of Jeremiah and Marcy Fitch,
d. May 7, 1749, aged 16 years and 3 months
Jeremiah Fitch, d. January 8, 1779
Ruth, daughter of Abner and Ruth Fitch, d. December 3, 1744
Jephthah, son of Apollos and Sybil Fitch, d. September 3, 1818

FLINT.

Prudence Flint,
d. October 18, 1834, aged 70 years, 1 month, 4 days
Abby Cardile, daughter of Ralph and Esther Flint,
d. December 12, 1834, aged 27 years, 6 months, 28 days

FOWLER.

Gurdon, son of Jonathan and Hannah Fowler,
d. May 24, 1737
Hannah, wife of Jonathan Fowler, d. October 8, 1756
Jonathan Fowler, d. October 22, 1756, in his 61st year
Dorothy, wife of John Fowler, d. March 10, 1751

FREEMAN.

Jonathan, son of Otis and Ruth Freeman, d. February 18, 1775

FRENCH.

Ezekiel, son of Joseph and Lucy French, d. August 10, 1740
Trifeny, daughter of Joseph and Lucy French,
d. August 2, 1740
Sarah, daughter of John and Mehitable French, d. May 24, 1737
Joseph French, d. August 11, 1740, 30 years old
Daniel, son of Joseph and Lucy French, d. August 7, 1740
Lucy, daughter of Joseph and Lucy French, d. August 12, 1740
Oliver, son of Aaron and Abigail French, d. March 7, 1791
Aaron French, Sr., d. June 8, 1807

FULLER.

David Fuller, d. April 12, 1750, in his 87th year
Constance Fuller, relict of David Fuller, late of Coventry, deceased, d. January 18, 1759
Mehitable, daughter of Elijah and Mary Fuller, d. July 5, 1768
Elizabeth, wife of Jeremiah Fuller, d. April 25, 1792

GRISWOLD.

Eunice, daughter of Joseph and Margery Griswold,
d. October 7, 1762, in her 9th year
Frederick, son of Joseph and Margery Griswold,
d. July 30, 1764, in his 2d year

GROVER.

Lidea, daughter of Matthew, Jr., and Lidea Grover,
d. October, 1740, in her 10th year

DEATHS FROM TOWN RECORDS

Daniel, son of Matthew, Jr., and Lidea Grover,
                                        d. November, 1740
Matthew, son of Matthew, Jr., and Lidea Grover,
                            d. August, 1748, in his 20th year
Abigail, daughter of Matthew and Lidea Grover,
                            d. May 12, 1761, in her 22d year
Lidea, wife of Matthew Grover,
                            d. January 30, 1767, in her 70th year
Mary, daughter of Benjamin and Mary Grover,
                            d. December 20, 1739
Sarah, daughter of Benjamin and Mary Grover,
                            d. December 28, 1739
Elisabeth, daughter of Benjamin and Mary Grover,
                            d. December 31, 1739
Mary, daughter of Benjamin and Mary Grover,
                            d. February, 1743
Sibel, daughter of Benjamin and Mary Grover,
                            d. December 5, 1761, in her 21st year
Mary, wife of Benjamin Grover,
                            d. November 17, 1764, in her 60th year
Mary, daughter of Matthew and Naomy Grover,
                            d. October 26, 1727
Leonard, son of Leonard and Sarah Grover,
                     d. at Havannah, August 26, 1762, in his 18th year
Micah, son of Leonard and Sarah Grover,
      d. returning from Havannah, Nov. 8, 1762, in his 21st year
Matthew Grover,   d. May 5, 1765, in his 89th year
Eunice, daughter of Leonard and Sarah Grover,
                            d. February 15, 1768, in her 17th year
Elisabeth, wife of John Grover,   d. August 14, 1737
Naomy, wife of Matthew Grover, Sr.,   d. October 12, 1732
Leonard Grover,   d. December, 1765
Jerusha, daughter of Ebenezer and Zeriah Grover,   d. 1750
Ebenezer, son of John, Jr., and Abigail Grover, d. July 17, 1776
Simon Grover,   d. at Fort Edward, October, 1757
Anne, daughter of Ebenezer and Zeruiah Grover,
                            d. October 7, 1753
Abigail, wife of Hembery Grover,   d. February 1, 1786
Benjamin Grover,   d. August 3, 1800, in his 52d year

Amasa, son of Joseph and Sarah Thompson Grover,
                                        d. October 26, 1802
Chauncey, son of Joseph and Sarah Grover,
                                        d. September 3, 1812

HALE.

John Hale, Esq.,   d. December 18, 1802, in his 55th year
Sarah, relict of John Hale, Esq.,
    d. at Hartford, November 6, 1803; buried in Coventry Nov. 8
Susannah, daughter of Richard and Elisabeth Hale,
                                        d. March, 1766
Elisabeth Hale, wife of Richard Hale,
                            d. April 21, 1767, in her 40th year
Capt. Nathan Hale, son of Deacon Richard Hale, was taken in
    the city of New York by the Britons and executed as a spy
    some time in the month of September, 1776.
Deacon Richard Hale,   d. January 1, 1802, in his 86th year
Lieut. Joseph Hale,   d. April 30, 1784, in his 35th year
Sarah, daughter of Lieut. Joseph and Rebeccah Hale,
                            d. June 27, 1784, aged 7 months
Billy Hale,   d. September 7, 1785, in his 27th year
Mary, daughter of Richard, Jr., and Mary Hale,
                                        d. December 10, 1791
Richard Hale, Jr.,
    d. at Island of Eustalia, February 12, 1793, in his 36th year
Polly, daughter of Richard, Jr., and Mary Hale,
                                        d. October 2, 1793

HATCH.

Sophia, wife of Ephraim Hatch,   d. April 13, 1818

HAWKINS or HOLCKINS.

James Hockins,   d. January, 1776, in his 7—th year
Sarah, relict of James Hockins,
                    d. September 3, 1777, in her 6—th year
James Hawkins, Jr.,   d. September 3, 1773, in his 40th year
Deborah Holckins, daughter of George and Hepzibah Hol-
    ckins,   d. February 14, 1747-8
George, son of George, Jr., and Hepzibah Holckins,
                                        d. February 14, 1747-8

Sarah, wife of Joseph Hawkins,
> d. January 25, 1775, in her 43d year

Joseph, Jr., son of Joseph and Sarah Hawkins,
> d. September 5, 1777, in his 15th year

HENDEE or HENDE.

Joshua, son of Joshua and wife, Hende,   d. August 30, 1740
Ruth, daughter of Joshua and wife, Hende, d. August 29, 1740
Jabez, son of Joshua and wife, Hende,   d. August 27, 1740
Ebenezer, son of Joshua and wife, Hende,   d. August 31, 1740
Rachael, daughter of Jonathan and Rachael Hende,
> d. December 31, 1739

HERRICK.

Ledia, wife of Joseph Herrick, d. March, 1764, in her 49th year
Ledia, daughter of Joseph and Ledia Herrick,
> d. September 28, 1739

Mehitable, daughter of Joseph and Ledia Herrick,
> d. November 5, 1738

Elisabeth, wife of Daniel Herrick,   d. December 15, 1741

HIBBARD.

David Hibbard,   d. in Coventry, August 13, 1800
Dorcas, relict of David Hibbard,
> d. July 31, 1801, in her 77th year

Clarissa, daughter of Selah and Ester Hibbard,
> d. November 22, 1796

Chauncey, son of Selah and Ester Hibbard, d. October 8, 1804

HOUSE.

Rebeckah, daughter of Jonathan and Ruth House,
> d. April 8, 1760, in her 4th year

James, son of Samuel, Jr., and Hannah House,
> d. March 19, 1775, in his 2d year

HOWARD.

Joanna, daughter of Dr. Nathan and Joanna Howard,
> d. May 4, 1788

Chauncey, son of Dr. Nathan and Joanna Howard,
> d. August 7, 1793

Anna, daughter of Dr. Nathan and Joanna Howard,
                              d. August 14, 1793
Richard Hale, son of Dr. Nathan and Joanna Howard,
                              d. October 3, 1803
Rufus, son of Dr. Nathan and Joanna Howard,
                              d. October 5, 1803
Dr. Nathan Howard,   d. April 21, 1838
Joanna, widow of Dr. Nathan Howard,   d. April 22, 1838
John Howard,   '   d. March 30, 1813, in his 29th year
John, son of John and Lucy Howard,   d. March 16, 1863
Chauncey, son of John and Lucy Howard, d. August 12, 1891

HUNT.

Ruth, wife of William Hunt,   d. January 18, 1761

HUTCHINSON.

Joseph Willard, son of Willard and Sophia Hutchinson,
                              d. December 17, 1814

ISHAM.

James Edgar, son of Oliver, Jr., and Minerva Isham,
                              d. October 22, 1823

JANES.

Abigail, wife of Samuel Janes,   d. October 18, 1791
Oliver Janes, of Coventry,
    d. at East Chester, in army, October 7, 1776, in his 23d year
Elisabeth, wife of Elisha Janes, Jr.,
                 d. November 16, 1765, in her 23d year
Elias, son of Elias and Susannah Janes, d. February 18, 1776
Daniel, son of Elisha Janes,
                 d. December 4, 1770, in his 21st year
Iraney Janes, daughter of Seth and Sarah Janes,
                 d. March 12, 1741, 5 weeks old

JONES

Asal, son of Benjamin and Patiance Jones, d. August 7, 1740
Sibel, daughter of Benjamin and Patiance Jones,
                              d. August 29, 1740
Dina, daughter of Benjamin and Patiance Jones,
                              d. September 8, 1740

Abigail, wife of Ebenezer Jones, d. December 16, 1743
Abigail, daughter of Ebenezer and Zuriah Jones,
  d. September 18, 1750
Sarah, wife of Adonijah Jones, d. May 1, 1771
Patiance, wife of Benjamin Jones,
  d. April 24, 1770, in her 75th year
Remembrance, son of Noah and Dina Jones,
  d. at Roxbury, December 15, 1775
Marting, son of Asael and Eunice Jones,
  d. October 14, 1775, in his 2d year
Millender, daughter of Asael and Eunice Jones,
  d. October 19, 1775
Joseph, son of Samuel Jones,
  d. February 25, 1801, in his 17th year

JUDD.

Thomas Judd, d. March 3, 1809

KEACH.

Benjamin Franklin, son of Asa and Betsey Keach,
  killed in Bolton by bursting of a cannon, September 23, 1828
Horatio Nelson, son of Asa and Betsey Keach, d. June 13, 1812

KINDRICK.

Thomas, son of Nathaniel and Judah Kindrick,
  drowned December 17, 1764, in his 16th year

KINGSBURY.

Jeremiah, son of Nathaniel Kingsbury, d. March, 1727
Ebenezer, son of Ebenezer and Priscilla Kingsbury,
  d. September 4, 1744
Hannah, daughter of Thomas and Anne Kingsbury,
  d. September 15, 1748
Priscilla, daughter of Ebenezer and Priscilla Kingsbury,
  d. January 5, 1751-2
Ruth, daughter of Nathaniel Kingsbury and wife,
  d. May 24, 1752, in her 15th year
Sarah, daughter of Thomas and Anne Kingsbury,
  d. May 9, 1753
Thomas Kingsbury, d. July 15, 1754

Widow Anne Kingsbury, relict of Thomas Kingsbury,
                                              d. May 10, 1755
Merah, daughter of Ebenezer and Priscilla Kingsbury,
                                          d. November 26, 1764
Jeremiah, son of Jabez and Mary Kingsbury,
                                 d. December 10, 1761, in his 5th year
Samuel Newel Kingsbury,   d. November 30, 1817

LAD or LADD.

Nathaniel Lad, Jr.,   d. December 19, 1744
Nathaniel Lad,   d. January 11, 1757, in his 73d year
Abigail, relict of Nathaniel Lad,
                                   d. August 7, 1778, in her 92d year
Abigail, daughter of Henry and Abigail Lad,
                                 d. March 22, 1768, in her 16th year
Henry Ladd,   d. April 6, 1768, in his 52d year
Jerusha, daughter of Henry and Abigail Ladd,
                                       d. October 8, 1741
Dr. Henry Ladd, l. August 9 (no date given), in his 33d year
Jerusha, daughter of Henry, Jr., and Abial Ladd,
                                       d. August 11, 1767
Jerusha, daughter of Henry and Abial Ladd,
                                       d. February 21, 1776
Lorin, son of Henry and Abial Ladd,
                                 d. December 10, 1777, in his 2d year

LAMB.

Ebenezer Lamb,   d. January 28, 1755
Abigail, wife of Benjamin Lamb,
                                   d. April 16, 1759, in her 25th year

LAMPHEAR.

Mary, wife of Isaac Lamphear,   d. July 31, 1761

LARABE or LARRABE.

Sarah Larabe,   d. June 15, 1738, about 75 years
Jabez, son of Joseph and Judah Larrabe,   d. July 3, 1750
Judith, wife of Joseph Larrabe,
                                 d. November 30, 1763, in her 69th year
Ruth, wife of Joseph Larrabe,
                                 d. January 30, 1765, in her 56th year

LATHROP.

Albert Lathrop, d. January 5, 1808
Mary Lathrop, d. August 9, 1814

LEA.

Lydia, wife of David Lea, d. July 16, 1718

LEACH.

Samuell, son of Ebenezer and Sarah Leach, d. June 30, 1742

LONG.

Jerusha Long, d. January 11, 1722-3
Silas, son of Silas and Lidea Long, d. October 4, 1757
Lydia, wife of Silas Long, d. November 5, 1757, in her 59th year
William Long, d. July, 1740, in his 72d year
Widow Mary Long, d. February, 1759, in her 87th year
Joseph, Jr., son of Samuel and Martha Long,
    drowned in Mistic River, July 8, 1775, in his 21st year
Stephen, son of Joseph, Jr., and Sarah Long,
    d. May 29, 1740, in his 8th year
Simeon, son of Joseph and Sarah Long, d. August 6, 1729
Rufus, son of Samuel and Martha Long,
    d. in Cambridge, September 8, 1775, in his 19th year

LOOMIS.

Polly, daughter of Daniel, Jr., and Polly Loomis,
    d. March 7, 1795
Nathaniel Loomis, d. February 10, 1758, in his 46th year
Zachariah Loomis, d. December 23, 1797
Huldah, wife of Zachariah Loomis, d. October 28, 1798
Mariah, daughter of Ebenezer and Eunice Loomis,
    d. December 12, 1800
Emily, daughter of Eleazer and Lucretia Loomis,
    d. March 27, 1815
Roxalana, daughter of Buel and Roxalana Loomis,
    d. October 14, 1816

LYMAN.

Hannah, daughter of Jacob and Mehitable Lyman,
    d. July, 1774, in her 15th year
Joseph, son of Jacob and Mehitable Lyman,
    d. at Camp Fort Burdett, September 5, 1776, in his 21st year

Jacob Lyman, d. January 15, 1802
Mehitable Lyman, d. May 10, 1814

MALBONE.

Sally, daughter of Godfrey and Dorcas Malbone,
d. March 28, 1802

MEACHAM.

Joseph, son of Rev. J. and Esther Meacham, d. August 31, 1720
John, son of Rev. J. and Esther Meacham, d. August 9, 1725
Joseph, son of Rev. and Esther Meacham,
d. February 15, 1729-30
Sybil, daughter of Rev. Joseph and Esther Meacham,
d. February, 1730-31
Esther, wife of Rev. Joseph Meacham, d. March 12, 1751
Rev. Joseph Meacham, d. September 15, 1752, in his 67th year

MEAD.

Anne, daughter of John and Elisabeth Mead,
d. September 25, 1775, in her 5th year
Hannah, daughter of John and Elisabeth Mead,
d. October 2, 1775, in her 8th year
John, son of John and Elisabeth Mead,
d. October 5, in his 2d year

MERAUGH.

Denis Meraugh, d. December 1, 1767, in his 79th year

MILLINTON.

Solomon, son of John and Martha Millinton, d. May 3, 1718

MURCH.

James Murch, d. June 3, 1726

MURDOCK.

Sarah, wife of Jonathan Murdock, d. April 7, 1776

NORTH.

Widow Sarah North, d. December, 1727

PAGE.

Mary, wife of Thomas Page, d. June 20, 1750

Elias, son of Thomas and Azubah Page,
 d. January 31, 1751-2, 1 month old
Azubah, daughter of Thomas and Azubah Page,
 d. October 19, 1760

PALLMER or PALMER.

Rebeckah, wife of Sergeant Benjamin Pallmer,
 d. March 22, 1726
Anne, daughter of Stephen and Elisabeth Palmer,
 d. January 20, 1737-8
Nathan, son of Stephen and Elisabeth Palmer,
 d. August 29, 1741
Elias, Jr., son of Elias and Elisabeth Palmer,
 d. November 9, 1779
Mehitable, wife of Gershom Palmer, d. September 22, 1760
John Palmer, d. January 26, 1785

PARKER.

Tabytha, wife of James Parker, d. November 20, 1730
James, son of James Parker, d. March 29, 1740
Tabethy, daughter of James and Elizabeth Parker,
 d. November 28, 1743
Deacon Samuel Parker, d. October 30, 1775, in his 94th year
Solomon Parker, d. August 3, 1799, in his 44th year

PHELPS.

Joanna, wife of Beniamon Phelps, d. July 7, 1752
Lidea, daughter of Beniamon and Joanna Phelps,
 d. January 23, 1753

PINGEY.

Abijah, wife of Moses Pingey, d. July 5, 1748

POMROY.

Sibyl, wife of Eleazer Pomroy, d. May 11, 1786
Esther, daughter of Daniel, Jr., and Eunice Pomroy,
 d. December 5, 1775
Daniel Pomroy, d. January 19, 1777
Daniel Starling, son of Daniel, Jr., and Eunice Pomroy,
 d. October 5, 1778
Daniel Pomroy, of Coventry, d. January 23, 1785

PORTER.

Thankful, wife of Thomas Porter, d. June 7, 1736
Daniell, son of Daniell and Hester Porter, d. January 31, 1742
Capt. Thomas Porter, d. August 7, 1752, in his 69th year
Irene, daughter of Jonathan and Sarah Porter,
      d. October 31, 1746, in her 8th year
Jonathan Porter, d. March 24, 1796, in his 77th year
Mr. Noah Porter, d. August 30, 1790, in his 75th year
Lois, wife of Jonathan Porter, Jr.,
      d. April 14, 1766, in her 25th year
Eunice, daughter of Thomas and Zilpah Porter,
      d. February 2, 1785, in her 18th year
Zilpah, wife of Thomas Porter, d. November 12, 1787, aged 54
Lemuel Porter,
    d. at Lake George, September, 1755, in his 31st year
Elisabeth, wife of Thomas Porter,
      d. October 28, 1755, in her 60th year
Thomas Porter, d. February, 1759, in his 63d year
Widow Abigail Porter, d. March 16, 1761, in her 87th year
Submit, daughter of Noah 2d and Submit Porter,
      d. February 14, 1768
Noah Porter, d. July 10, 1794
Joseph, son of Noah and Submit Porter, d. May 18, 1806
Erastus Porter, d. July 21, 1793, in his 30th year
Eunice, daughter of Erastus and Hannah Porter,
      d. November 3, 1794
Polly, wife of Capt. Noah Porter, d. October 25, 1806
Noah Loomis, son of Noah and Faith Porter, d. March 29, 1837
Henry Cheney, son of William and Sarah Porter,
      d. September 9, 1826
Charles Winslow, son of William and Sarah Porter,
      d. December 4, 1833

POTWINE.

Mary, wife of John Potwine, d. March 31, 1766, in her 68th year

PRICE.

Abigail, daughter of Rufus and Martha Price,
      d. March 29, 1755

RENALLS.

Samuel Renalls, drowned May 18, 1720

RICHARDSON.

———, son of Lemuel and Anna Richardson, d. February 22, 1757
Stephen, son of Lemuel and Anna Richardson,
d. November 4, 1765
Lemuel Richardson, d. April 22, 1777, in his 51st year
Phillip, son of Stephen and Mabel Richardson,
drowned May 13, 1793
Jennet Jewett, daughter of Stephen Richardson,
d. September 28, 1793
Mabel, wife of Stephen Richardson, d. August 4, 1798

RIPLEY.

Elijah Ripley, d. December 26, 1774
Elijah, son of Elijah, deceased, and Widow Alice Ripley,
d. October, 1775, in his 2d year
Jeremiah Ripley, Esq., d. February 11, 1812

ROBERTSON.

Anne, wife of Samuel Robertson, d. October, 1765
Anne, wife of Samuel Robertson, d. January 25, 1773
Lidea, daughter of Ephraim and Ester Robertson,
d. August 9, 1749
Ephraim Robertson, d. July 29, 1752, in his 31st year
Hannah, wife of Daniel Robertson, d. January 20, 1755
Daniel, Jr., son of Daniel and Susannah Robertson,
d. December 9, 1775, in his 14th year
Betty, daughter of Daniel and Susannah Robertson,
d. December 9, 1775, in her 7th year
(Mistake in records)
Daniel Robertson, d. February 6, 1793

ROBESON or ROBENSON.

Martha, wife of Samuel Robeson, d. April 29, 1749

ROCKWELL.

Daniel, son of Amariah and Martha Rockwell, d. May 2, 1777

ROOT.

Ephraim Root, d. September 25, 1713
Hannah, daughter of Ebenezer and Sarah Root,
            d. March 29, 1721
Mercy, wife of Eliakim Root, d. March 27, 1728
Elisabeth, wife of Thomas Root, d. November 30, 1726
Lowes, daughter of Thomas Root, Jr., d. January 1, 1741
Jonathan, son of Eliakim and Jemima Root,
            d. February 3, 1739-40
Thomas Root, d. November 13, 1756
Eliakim Root, d. January 19, 1759, in his 64th year
Rufus, son of Samuel and Mary Root,
            d. at Lake George, December 5, 1756
Hon. Jesse Root, d. March 29, 1822, aged 85
Thomas 3d, son of Thomas, Jr., and Elisabeth Root,
            d. December 20, 1775, in his 10th year
Azubah, wife of Jonathan Root, d. January 5, 1779
Lydia, daughter of Jonathan and Azubah Root,
            d. December 29, 1780
John, son of John and Deborah Root,
            d. January 14, 1775, in his 9th year
John, son of John and Deborah Root, d. September, 1776
Hannah, wife of Thomas Root, d. September 21, 1776
Thomas Root, d. December 2, 1782, in his 91st year
Nathaniel Root, d. September 21, 1840
Asal, son of Ephraim and Elisabeth Root, d. March 30, 1751
Elizabeth, wife of Nathaniel Root,
            d. August 3, 1790, in her 32d year
Lemuel and Martin, children of Nathaniel and Candace Root,
            died in infancy
Candace, wife of Nathaniel Root, d. June 1, 1835, in her 71st year
Nathaniel Root, d. September 21, 1840, in his 84th year

ROSE.

Dr. Samuel Rose, d. November 4, 1780
Eunice, wife of Nathan Hale Rose, d. February 10, 1805
Lydia, wife of Nathan Hale Rose, d. July 7, 1832
Josiah, son of Dr. Josiah and Eunice Rose,
            d. September 10, 1740

John, son of Dr. Josiah and Eunice Rose,
d. September 18, 1749-50
Eunice, wife of Dr. Josiah Rose, d. May 4, 1780
Dr. John, son of Dr. Josiah and Eunice Rose,
d. October 30, 1783, in his 28th year

RUSSELL.

John Russell, d. September 19, 1822, aged 64

RUST.

Mary, relict to Daniel Rust, deceased, d. September 23, 1775
Mercy or Mary, daughter of Daniel and Anna Rust,
d. August 15, 1739, in her 8th year
Anna, daughter of Daniel and Anna Rust,
d. August 23, 1739, in her 3d year
Anna, wife of Daniel Rust, d. July 23 (year illegible)
Mary, relict of Daniel Rust, d. September 23, 1775
Zebulon, son of Samuel and Sarah Hockins Rust,
d. September 23, 1740, aged 3 years, 2 months, and 13 days
Samuel, son of Samuel and Sarah H. Rust,
d. September 26, 1740, aged 12 years, 7 months
Nathaniel, son of Samuel and Sarah H. Rust,
d. September 30, 1740, aged 5 years, 4 months, 15 days
Mary, daughter of Amaziah and Mary Rust, d. April 1, 1758
Chauncey, son of Amaziah and Mary Rust,
d. November 5, 1776, in his 4th year
Margaret Rust, d. September 18, 1712
Mercy, wife of Nathaniel Rust,
d. January 21, 1754, in her 81st year
Cloah, daughter of Noah and Keziah Rust,
d. September 4, 1739
Noah Rust, Sr., d. December 11, 1746
Cloah, daughter of Noah and Keziah Rust, d. July 28, 1747
Elijah, son of Noah Rust, d. November 19, 1763, in his 24th year
Rebeckah, daughter of Mathias and Susa Rust,
d. February 6, 1752
Lore Rust, daughter of Nathaniel, Jr., and Rachael Rust,
d. October 15, 1803
Capt. Samuell Rust, d. September 6, 1773, in his 72d year

SABINS.

John Sabins, d. November 6, 1749, in his 27th year

SARGENT.

Widow Mary, relict to John Sargent, late of Mansfield,
d. December 18, 1773, in her 64th year

SCOTT.

Sarah Scott, who lived with Daniel Badcock, and afterwards with David Clark, d. August, 1747

SCRIPTURE.

Mary, daughter of John and Abigail Scripture, d. July 30, 1728
Daniel, son of John and Mary Scripture, d. March 14, 1736
Mr. John Scripture, d. July 24, 1779, in his 91st year
Mrs. Mary, relict of John Scripture,
d. July 20, 1780, in her 87th year

SEARL or SARL.

Martha, wife of Ebenezer Searl, d. November 7, 1756
Elisha, son of Elisha and Mary Searl,
d. September 26, 1749, in his 3d year
Mary, widow of Elisha Searl,
d. December 18, 1767, in her 50th year

SHEPARD.

Margaret, wife of Noah Shepard, d. March 1, 1746

SIMONS.

Elijah, son of Joshua and Anne Simons,
d. December, 1759, in his 3d year
Anne, daughter of Joshua and Anne Simons,
d. 1759, in her 5th year

SKINNER.

Patiance, wife of Noah Skinner, d. May 16, 1740
Patiance, daughter of Noah and Patiance Skinner,
d. May 7, 1740

SMITH.

Joanna, wife of Recompense Smith,
d. December 16, 1785, in her 72d year

SPRAGUE.

Eliakim, son of Samuel and Jerusha, d. June 28, 1762

STANLEY.

Caleb, son of Caleb, Jr., and Martha Stanley, d. March 15, 1776

STRONG.

Tabitha, wife of Preserved Strong,
              d. June 23, 1750, in her 73d year
Preserved Strong, d. September 26, 1765, in his 86th year
Joseph Strong, Esq., d. December 23, 1763, aged 91
Beulah, daughter of Phineas Strong and Mary,
              d. August 22, 1750
Mary, wife of Phineas Strong, d. April 13, 1757
Hannah, daughter of Phineas and Mary Strong,
              d. April 24, 1757
Jedediah Strong, d. May 22, 1733, in his 96th year
Beulah, daughter of Phineas and Mary Strong,
              d. August 22, 1750, in her 5th year
Mary, wife of Phineas Strong, d. April 13, 1757
Hannah, daughter of Phineas and Mary Strong,
              d. April 24, 1757
Billy, son of Benajah and Lucy Strong, d. July 23, 1782
Lucy, wife of Benajah Strong,
              d. November 27, 1783, in her 36th year
Deborah, wife of Noah Strong, d. November 30, 1739
Rev. Nathan Strong, d. November 7, 1795, in his 74th year
Irene, daughter of Phineas and Mary Strong,
              d. March 11, 1773, in her 32d year
Jemima Strong, d. February 3, 1760
Joseph Strong, Esq.,
              d. in Coventry, April 9, 1773, in his 72d year
Martha, daughter of Joseph, Esq., and Elisabeth Strong,
              d. October 4, 1775, in her 52d year
Elisabeth, late consort of Joseph Strong, Esq., d. May 1, 1792
Joseph, son of Joseph, Jr., and Elisabeth Strong,
              d. September 16, 1727
Cloe, daughter of Aaron and Rachael Strong,
              d. November 7, 1744

Rachael, daughter of Aaron and Rachael Strong,
    d. December 10, 1747, in her 14th year
Cloe, daughter of Aaron and Rachael Strong,
    d. November, 1745, in her 4th year
Sarah, wife of Asa Strong, d. August 4, 1770, in her 34th year

SWEATLAND.

Anna, daughter of Ebenezer and Sarah Sweatland,
    d. August 27, 1752
Sarah, wife of Ebenezer Sweatland,
    d. August 14, 1762, in her 34th year

TALCOTT.

Esther, daughter of Joseph and Eunice Talcott,
    d. February 17, 1765, in her 4th year
Capt. Joseph Talcott,   drowned June 10, 1789

TAYLOR.

Elisha, son of Stephen and Deliverance Taylor,
    d. August 1, 1747
John Taylor,   d. March (no date)
Elisabeth Taylor,   d. October 31, 1813

TERRILL.

Alathea, wife of Thomas Terrill,
    d. February 20, 1773, in her 25th year

THOMSON or THOMPSON.

Amos Thompson,   d. November 28, 1752
Amos, Jr., son of Amos and Irene Thompson,
    d. December, 1752, in his 2d year

TILDEN.

John, Jr., son of John and Bersheba Tilden, d. August 15, 1790

TOWNSEND.

Irene, wife of David Townsend,   d. January 16, 1761

TRAPP.

Aurelia, daughter of Samuel and Alice Trapp, d. April 30, 1836

TURNER.

Hannah, wife of Amos Turner,	d. November 19, 1797
Robert Turner,	d. August 4, 1797
Silance Turner,	d. August 14, 1798

VORRA.

Martin Vorra, d. May 2, 1792

WARD.

Oliver Ward, d. February 27, 1743-4, in his 56th year
Tabothy Ward, who lived with Recompense Smith,
d. December 2, 1775, in her 13th year

WEBSTER.

Eunice, wife of Benajah Webster, d. November 27, 1750

WENTWORTH.

Gad, son of Ebenezer, Jr., and Sarah Wentworth,
d. March 7, 1776

WILSON.

Dorothy, daughter of John and wife, d. June 2, 1739-40
Francis Willson, d. January 15, 1767, in his 55th year
John, son of John and wife, d. September 10, 1740

WOODWARD.

Nathaniel Woodward, d. April 15, 1792, in his 76th year
Henry Woodward,
killed by Indians, June 26, 1756, in his 36th year

WRIGHT.

Mary, wife of Roswell Wright, d. June 24, 1787
Roswell Wright, d. February 13, 1845
James, son of Elijah and Jane Wright, d. July 7, 1789

Records of 1st Church, Coventry, Conn., 1st page.

Children.	Baptisms.	Parents.
	1776.	
Oct. William,		Hab'k Turner, Jr.
Nov. Hannah,		Jonathan Root
Achsy,		Asa Manley
Dec. Daniel and Anne,		Daniel Rust
David,		Humphrey Dow
	1777.	
Apr. ———		Oliver Boynton
John,		——— Shepherd
Mary and William,		Deacon Porter
Martha,		Amos Dorman
Lucinda,		John Robinson
June Nathan Hale,		Dr. L. Rose
Stephen,		Zebulon Badcock
Elizabeth,		Daniel Rust
Sept. Three names illegible.		
Oct. Mary Bishop,		Allerton Cushman
Lydia,		Jonathan Root
Vina,		Humphrey Taylor
Nov. Jesse,		Ephraim Colman
Dec. Lorenzo,		Humphrey Dow
	1778.	
Jan. Stephen,		John Root
Feb. Nathan,		John Deuty
Apr. Septimus George, my son, born 15th, 5 o'clock in the morning,		Rev. Huntington
June Lucy,		Benajah Strong
July Henry, Herman, Peregrine, and Hiram Benoni,		Dr. Ladd
Marcia and Lucia,		Widow Brigham
Mary,		Jeremiah Fitch
Illegible,		Joseph Hawkins

Children.	Baptisms.	Parents.
	1778.	
July Illegible,		Medad Root
Dec. William,		David Greenleaf
	1779.	
Mar. Azubah,		Jonathan Root
Apr. Solomon,		Ephraim Dow
Esther,		Henry Shepard
May Fanny,		Dr. L. Rose
Elizabeth,		Zep'h Hammond
July Mary,		Oliver Boynton
Joseph,		Widow Boynton
Aug. Betty,		Deacon Porter
Oct. Barbary,		Timothy Rose
Nov. Clarissa,		Gershom Colman
Elias,		Elias Palmer
Dec. John,		Elias Palmer
Hannah, my daughter, born 22d inst., 6 o'clock, A. M.,		Rev. Huntington
	1780.	
Apr. John,		Ephraim Coleman
Joseph,		Alvin Carpenter
Eunice,		Medad Root
Martha and Mary,		Benajah Strong
May Lois,		John Robinson
Mary, Martha, Elisabeth, and Eunice,		Elias Palmer
June Elisabeth,		Joseph Hale
Stephen,		Amos Dorman
Lucy,		Joseph Hawkins
David,		Humphrey Taylor
Josiah,		Timothy Rose
July Asenath, Amasa, and Tirzah,		Widow Mehitable Dow
Oliver,		Gershom Colman
Aug. Luther,		Ephraim Cushman
Walter,		Jehiel Rose
Mary,		Jabez Ripley
Oct. Cynthia, Lois, and Moses,		John Eells, Jr.
Samuel,		Samuel Badcock
Abigail and Thomas,		Thomas Root
Fanny,		Alvin Carpenter

Children.	Baptisms.	Parents.
	1780.	
Oct. Jerusha and Billy,		Billy Root
Dec. Phebe,		John Richardson
	1781.	
Feb. Philomela,		Widow Perkins
Apr. Amelia,		John Root
Rebecca,		Joseph Hale
Esther,		Samuel Colman
May Benjamin,		Oliver Boynton
June Daniel,		Asa Manley
July Martin, Luther, Mary, Bishop, Henry, Lavinia, Prosper, and Theodamia,		Henry Boothe
Caleb,		William Badcock
Elizabeth,		Timothy Carpenter
Salome, Peter, Mehitable, Samuel, Jesse, Daniel, Bille, and Nathan,		Samuel Rose
Betsey,		Abel Palmer
Aug. David,		Hezekiah Robertson
Harry, my son, born the 20th, 2 A. M.,		Rev. Huntington
Sept. Zuriah,		Samuel Badcock
Marjaram and Clarinda,		Pelatiah Dow
	1782.	
Feb. Vine,		Abner Fitch
Mar. Bille,		Benajah Strong
Apr. Eliza and Bennet Field,		Thomas Root
June Joseph,		Ephraim Coleman
Joseph,		Joseph Hawkins
Stephen,		Ephraim Cushman
July Anne,		Amos Dorman
Nehemiah,		Billy Root
Aug. Anne, Polly, and Daniel,		Nathaniel Brown
Betsey, Royal and Calvin,		Calvin Manning
Nancy,		Nathan Cook
Sept. Tabitha,		Humphrey Dow
Oct. Orpah,		Ebenezer Crossman
	1783.	
Jan. Joshua Woodworth,		Adult
Sophie and Spencer,		Joshua Woodworth
Mar. Benajah,		Deacon Strong

RECORDS OF FIRST CHURCH 203

Children.	Baptisms.	Parents.
	1783.	

June Asa, — Abel Palmer
      Hannah, — Nathan Cook
      John, — Oliver Boynton
      Ada, — Joshua Edwards
      Mary, — Joseph Hale
July Elias, — Elias Palmer
      Joseph, — John Robinson
      Mary, — Calvin Manning
Aug. Cynthia. — Ebenezer Crossman
      Gurdon, — Bennet Field
      Chloe, — Asa Manley
      John, — Samuel Badcock
      Josiah, — Josiah Alcott
      Mary, — Ephraim Root, Jr.
Oct. Lucretia, my daughter, born September 29, 11 o'clock,
      Rev. Huntington
   Thomas, Elizabeth, Dianthe, and Cornelius, Abner Fitch

1784.

Jan. Enoch, — Elias Judd
Feb. Sarah, — Joseph Hale
June Eunice, — Capt. I. Ripley
Aug. Ephraim, — Ephraim Colman
      Solomon Lathrop, — Samuel Colman
Sept. Sarah and Elijah, — Hezekiah Robertson
   Diadamia, Ephraim, Apollos, and Phebe,
      Jephthah Fitch
      Amos, — Samuel Rose
      Jehiel and Daniel Pomeroy, — Timothy Rose
      Hannah, — George Hawkins
Dec. Joseph, — Benjamin Grover

1785.

Feb. Sarah, Gideon, and John, — Joshua Edwards
April John and Dean, — John Fisk
      Lydia and Lucy, — Calvin Manning
      Alpheus, — Billy Root
June Sylvester, — Sylvester Manley
July Wealthy, — Amos Palmer
      George, — Abel Palmer

Children.	Baptisms.	Parents.

1785.

July	John,	Dr. Howard
Aug.	Oliver and Enos,	Oliver Boynton
	Rebecca,	Ephraim Cushman
	Eben,	Ebenezer Crossman
	Fanny,	Asa Manley
Sept.	Betsey,	John Taylor
Nov.	Eunice,	Joshua Wordworth
Dec.	Alpheus,	Bennet Field

1786.

Feb.	Billy,	Billy Hale
April	Samuel,	William Trapp
May	Fanny, John Young, and Phoene,	Nathan Cook
July	Latham,	Abner Fitch
Sept.	Rufus and Gordon,	Joseph Hawkins
	Mary,	Dudley Dorman
Oct.	Benjamin,	John Robinson
	Darius,	Sylvester Manley
Nov.	Betsey,	Silene Burns

1787.

Feb.	David,	Nathan Cook
Mar.	Samuel,	Oliver Boynton
May	Benjamin,	Medad Root
June	Ira,	Ebenezer Crossman
	Hezekiah,	Calvin Manning
Aug.	Mason, Lucy, Mercy, and Dolly,	Stephen Turner
	Esther,	Capt. Howard
	Louisa,	Abel Palmer
Sept.	Elisabeth and Emminia,	C. Root, Esq.
	Sarah,	Elias Palmer
	Sarah,	Jabez Ripley
Oct.	Mary,	Richard Hale, Jr.
	Betsey,	William Trapp
	Billy,	Abner Fitch
Nov.	Epaphras,	Timothy Rose

1788.

Feb.	Mercy,	Widow Dorothy Turner
April	Mercy Penelope, my daughter, born the 25th inst., 9 A. M.,	Rev. Huntington

| Children. | Baptisms. | Parents. |

1788.

May Ruth, Jephthah Fitch
Joanna, Dr. Howard
Elizabeth, Bennet Field
July Sally, Deacon Strong
Aug. Nathan, Chester, Alpheus, and Polly, Josiah Fuller, Jr.
Sarah and Deborah, Nathan Colman
Sept. Cornelia, Widow Manley
Paul, William, Anson, and Harvey, Levi Dow
Oct. Asa, Joshua Wordworth
Horace, Jehiel Rose
Asynthe, John Robinson
Nov. Orinde, Philomela, Deborah, Lucy,
Phebe, and Isaac, Widow Elisabeth Robinson
Joseph, Stephen Turner
Dec. Darius, Sylvester Manley

1789.

May Mira, Ebenezer Crossman
Sept. David, Mr. Taylor
Lora, Richard Hale
Anne, Dr. Howard
Lucy, Capt. Ripley
Annie, Calvin Manning
Polly, Abner Fitch, Jr.
Oct. Hannah, Clarissa, Jesse, and Lavinia,
Grandchildren of Eliphilet Brown
Nov. David, Benjamin Grover

1790.

Jan. William and Nathaniel, Asahel House
Mar. Esther, Isaac Robertson
May Erastus, Jabez Ripley
Laura and Jesse, Samuel Rose
Benjamin and Salome, Benjamin Colman
June Clarissa, Josiah Fuller
July Orin and Alfred, Timothy Rose
Anne, Ulysses Dow
Lucy, Joshua Woodworth
Aug. Betsey, Lydia, Hannah, Patty, Elvira,
Asa, and Anna, Asa Colman

Children.	Baptisms.	Parents.

1790.

Aug. Don Alonzo and Zenas, — Isaac Robertson
    Sarah, Fanny and Mary, — Ebenezer Colman, Jr.
Sept. Royal, — Stephen Turner
Nov. Anna, — Barzaillac Ames
    My son James, born 9th inst., 2 o'clock, A. M.,
    — Rev. Huntington

1791.

Jan. Ruth Lyman, — Adult
Feb. Jephtah, Persis, William, Jesse, Edna, and Jemima,
    children of Mrs. Lyman
    Isabella, — William Root
    Ephraim Colburn, — C. Root, Esq.
    Seth Pierce, — Bennet Field
Mar. John, — Frederick Rose
    Solomon, — Isaac Robertson
July Lydia, — Asahel House
Aug. Warren, Polly, Lavinia, and Betsey, Elisha Hutchinson
Oct. Temperance, — William Robertson

1792.

Mar. Eleazer, Lavinia, Horace, Elisabeth, and Sally,
    — Solomon Parker
    John, Polly, and Jesse, — John Eells
    Anne, Nathan, Dyar, Fanny, Milton, and Electa,
    — Jedediah Geer
    John, William, and Isabella, — Joseph Manley
    Betsey, — Mrs. Hazleton
May Chauncey, — Dr. Howard
    Luther, — Ephraim Hutchinson
July Polly, — Nathan Colman
    Elias, — Joshua Woodworth
Aug. James, — Calvin Manning
    Elisabeth and Electa, — Timothy Rose
    Lucy, — Joseph Fuller
    Ursula, — Abner Fitch
Oct. Jeremiah, — Judge Ripley
    Lydia and Elisabeth, — John Root
Nov. Polly, — Richard Hale, Jr

RECORDS OF FIRST CHURCH

| Children. | Baptisms. | Parents. |

1793.

Jan. Flavius Josephus,   Joseph Huntington, Esq.
April Martha, Clarissa, Fanny, and Samuel,
        grandchildren of Jonathan House
May Elisabeth,   Jabez Ripley
    Anne, Lucia, and Sally,   Cephas Brigham
Sept. Roswell,   Stephen Turner
    Phebe,   Nathan Colman
    Dianthe,   Uriah Palmer
    Joanna,   Bildad Curtiss
Oct. Olive,   Asa Colman
    Chauncey,   Capt. Jeremiah Fitch
    Phebe,   Ebenezer Colman, Jr.
    Hannah,   Joseph Fuller
    Clarissa,   Shubael Cook
    Philena, Billy, and Nathan,   Widow Cook

1794.

    Chauncey,   John Eells
June Samuel, Marvin, and Augustus,   Bildad Curtiss
Sept. Timothy Cushman and Harmony Allen,
        Mr. Brockway, New York State
Oct. Jesse,   Joshua Woodworth

1795.

    Chauncey,   Judge Ripley
    Nathan,   Dr. Nathan Howard
    Jethro Turner,   aged 74 (private)
    William Buell,   son of Benjamin Sprague (Andover)

1796.

June 12 Anna Jones,   daughter of William Holt (Milton)
July 24 Joel,   son of Amasa Jones
    Harry and Harriet,   Joshua Woodworth
Aug. 21 Rebeckah,   —— Reynolds (Greenfield, N. H.)
Oct. 2 Josiah,   Josiah Fuller, Jr.
    Billy,   Nathan Coleman
    Sally,   Nathaniel Woodward (N. S.)
Nov. 13 Daniel Clark and Belsey,
        children of Ephraim Dow (deceased)

Children.	Baptisms.	Parents.

1797.

Mar. 21	Jeremiah Fitch, Jr.,	
July 22	Elisabeth,	Dr. Howard
Sept. 24	Joseph Huntington,	son of Amasa Jones
Dec. 3	James Buell,	grandson of Judge Root

1798.

Jan. 12	Eunice,	wife of S. Dewey
April 5	Neal, Sarah, and Anne,	Widow Mercy Robinson
June 24	Maria,	Nathan Coleman and wife
July 22	Guerdon,	
29	Elisabeth,	daughter of Rev. Abiel Abbot and wife Jane Richardson,
		daughter of William Lyman and wife
Nov. 12	Esther,	wife of Elijah Sweatland

1799.

Aug. 22	Tryphena,	Josiah Fuller
	Temperance,	Asa Coleman
	William and Rebeckah,	Asa Coleman
	Roderick and Lucy,	Lieut. Bildad Curtis
Sept. 15	Rufus,	Dr. Nathan Howard
	Fanny Huntington,	Amasa Jones
	Abigail,	Rev. Abiel Abbott
	Miranda,	William Lyman

1800.

	Wealthy,	Nathan Coleman

1801.

Feb. 13	Joseph Janes,	Adult
Aug. 30	William Augustus,	Capt. Curtis
Sept. 13	Margaret and Emmeline,	Amasa Jones
	Dorcas and Sarah,	Rev. Abiel Abbott
Nov. 13	Augustus,	Josiah Fuller
	Jesse, Leonard, Betsey, Harry, and Laura,	
	Sally,	Widow Hulda Curtis
		wife of Benjamin Coleman

1802.

Jan. 26	Walter,	Walter Rose
Mar. 21	Eunice,	Joseph Dow
July 25	George,	Benjamin Coleman
Sept. 5	Richard Hale,	Dr. Nathan Howard

Children.	Baptisms.	Parents
	1802.	
Oct. 3 Alicia,		William Lyman
Polly Deuty,		Adult
	1803.	
Jan. 16 Rebeckah,		Joseph Dow
Sept. 25 Maria,		Amasa Jones
Oct. 16 John,		Capt. Bildad Curtis
30 Nathan,		Nathan Coleman
	1804.	
May 22 Hannah,		Joseph Dow
June 1 Zilpah (negro)		
Aug. 5 Idocia,		William Lyman
19 Betsey, Stephen. and Cephonia,		Stephen Dunham
23 Eunice;		Joseph Dorman
Sept. 2 Laura,		Sinmuel Babcock, Jr.
Oct. 5 Eunice Talcott,		N. H. Rose
Elisabeth,		Betsey Manning
	1805	
May 5 Elisabeth,		Amasa Jones
July 28 William,		Samuel Babcock, Jr.
Oct. 6 John Dorman,		Francis Norton
Joseph,		Joseph Dorman
20 Maria,		Joseph Dow
Nov. 3 Mary,		William Lyman
	1806.	
Jan. 25 Anne Deuty,		Adult
Sept. 14 Caroline,		Stephen Dunham
	1807	
Mar. 3 Nabby Grover,		Adult
April 21 Samuel and Polydore,		Nathan H. Rose
July 12 Samuel,		Amasa Jones
Oct. 18 Lucy,		William Lyman
	1808.	
June 5 Harriot,		Nathan Colman
28 Lucy Aspinwall		Joseph Dorman
July 3 Emily and Caroline,		Capt. Bildad Curtis
Aug. 28 Lucia A. Ward,		Hezekiah Edgerton, Jr.
Oct. 9 Lydia, Dolly Levens, John, and Ezra,		
		John Kingsbury
Nov. 15 Olive Richardson,		James White

Children.	Baptisms.	Parents.
	1809.	
Mar. 12 Lucia and Anna Maria,		Hezekiah Edgerton, Jr.
Oct. 8 Joseph and Newton,		Joseph Dow
Mary and Joanna,		Amasa Jones
Levi Perkins,		Capt. N. H. Rose
	1810.	
Feb. 2 Elisabeth,		Rodney White
	1811.	
Mar. 15 Nathan Morrison and Chauncey,		William Lyman
Lucy Davenport,		Adult
Nov. 3 Abiel Abbott,		Amasa Jones
	1812.	
Mar. 22 Richard Hale,		N. H. Rose
George Edgerton, Lucy Eliza, Ursula Root, Ephraim Alson, Newton, and Lucretia,		Apollos Fitch
William Augustus,		Joseph Dorman
	1813.	
Charles Dow,		Adult
Martha Matilda,		grandchild of J. Root, Esq.
Jephtha,		Apollos Fitch
	1814.	
Sally Robert,		Adult
Eunice Balcomb,		Adult
Eunice, Maria, and Charles,		Marcus Balcomb
George, Lucius, Marcus, Austen, and Walter,		Thaddeus Boynton
	1815.	
Lucy,		Major Rose
Sept. 24 Pauline Colman,		adult, Levi Colman
Oct. 1 Anne,		Joseph Dorman
Phebe,		Apollos Fitch
Julia Ann,		William Lyman
Maxon, Ashbel George, Amasa, Eliza, and Henrietta,		Seth Roberts
Hezekiah, Lucia, and Augustus,		Capt. Joseph Dow

| Children. | Baptisms. | Parents. |

1816.

Jan. 11 Frederick, Josephus, George, Wyllys,
   Jasper Gilbert, Charles Dabney,   John Dresser
Mar. 1 Lucy Clark,   Adult
   Sally Root,   Spencer Woodworth
   30 Jefferson Carpenter,
April 28 Mary,   David Hale (Boston)
June 2 Lucia, Marcia, and Eliza,   Jesse Boynton
   23 Harriet Amanda, Lucy, and John Spencer,
          Spencer Woodworth
   Caroline and Mary,   George White
Aug. 18 Joseph, Amos, Polly, Frederick, Olive,
      Sally, and Erastus,   children of Elijah Ripley
   Hezekiah and Joseph Warren,   Amos Richardson
Aug. 28 John Olds, Roxana, and Emily,   Ruel Loomis
Sept. 1 Selah Brown,   Adult
   29 Selah Ashley, Eliza, and Mary, Lewis
      Dunham and Andrew Kingsbury,   Selah Brown
Oct. 6 Cynthia Goodwin.
   Belsey Sanford.
   Hannah Palmer.
   Eliza Needham.
   Daniel Brigham.
   Bishop Davenport.
   Rufus Davenport.
   Evelina Liba Brigham.
Oct. 25 Anne,   Calvin Manning
   William Armstrong.   Rev. Chauncey Booth
Dec. 8 Chauncey,   Rev. Chauncey Booth
   Celinda, Nancy, Angeline, and William Henry,
          William Armstrong
   Caroline, Laura, and Mary,   John Eells

1817.

Mar. 10 Harry Dow.
   Milton Clark.
   Anna T. Clark.
May 18 Elisha Morgan, Lydia Abbey, Solomon
      Goodrich, and Olive,   Solomon Gilbert

COVENTRY RECORDS

| Children. | Baptisms. | Parents. |

1817.

May 18 John Wilton, Daniel Dimmick, and
       Maria Ann,   Milton Clark
       Eliza,   Samuel Dow 2d
June 1 Edward,   Joseph Dow
       Solomon, George, Beverley, Abbot, and
           Ezra,   Solomon Dow
June 29 Rufus, William, Fanny, and Charles,   Harry Dow
Aug. 17 Marcina and Emma,   Reuel Loomis
       John Ripley and Chauncey,
                     grandchildren of Dr. Howard
       Sally and Frederick,   Montgomery White
    19 Mary Elisabeth, Louisa, and Henry S. G. Huntington
Sept. 7 Eunice Williams.
       Charles,   Amos Richardson
Dec. 9 Rufus,   Spencer Woodworth
Dec. 28 Salome Emerit, Ephraim Abbot, and
       Lucy Ann,   Ephraim Colman, Jr.
       William,   Seth Roberts

1818.

Feb. 1 Benjamin Armstrong.
May 10 Abby Jane,   John Eells
    24 Laura Farnam,   Rev. Chauncey Booth
       Sybil,   Apollos Fitch
June 21 Emily,   Joseph Dorman
       Nancy,   Samuel Dow 2d
July 26 Sylvester,   Selah Brown
Oct. 4 Maria,   Montgomery White
Nov. 1 John,   George R. White

1819.

Feb. 16 Chauncey,   Milton Clark
Mar. 1 Elisabeth,   Capt. Joseph Dow
May 23 Chauncey Booth,   Spencer Woodworth
June 6 Joseph,   Ephraim Colman, Jr.
       Robert,   Clark Robinson
    13 Julius,   Septimus G. Huntington
Aug. 29 Eunice,   Samuel Dow 2d

| Children. | Baptisms. | Parents. |

1820

Jan. 4	Emily and Norman,	Widow Elijah Ripley
May 7	Cynthia Lyman.	
July 2	Almira Cady,	Col. James White
Aug. 13	Elizabeth,	Rev. Chauncey Booth
Sept. 3	Elijah,	Widow Elizah Ripley
	Benjamin,	Benjamin Armstrong
Dec. 3	Sarah Ann,	Apollos Fitch

1821

Jan. 21	James Richardson,	Capt. Joseph Dow
June 10	Ephraim,	Samuel Dow 2d
July 1	Lucy Strong,	Amos Richardson
15	Laura,	Montgomery White
16	Salome, Norman, and Austin,	Thaddeus Boynton
Aug. 1	Daniel Watson,	Daniel Brigham
Sept. 9	Phebe Sprague.	
	William Edgar,	William Coleman

1822

June 16	Caleb,	Rev. Chauncey Booth
Sept. 1	Olive,	Selah Brown
Nov. 17	Julia,	Lanflear

1823

Mar. 7 William Lyman.
    9 Wealthy Dimmick.
      Charlotte Maxwell.
May 3 Oliver H. Isham.
    4 Wife of Azel Edgerton.
      Wife of Samuel Dow 2d
      Fanny Boynton.
      Jane Doan.
      Maria Dimmick.
      Delia Grover.
      Eliza Dimmick.
      Desire Dimmick.
      Harriet Hosmer.
      Mary Brigham.
      Lavina Moore.
      Augustus Clark.
      Eber Dunham.

COVENTRY RECORDS

Children.   Baptisms.   Parents.
1823.

June 15 Frederick Haughton,   Mrs. Solomon Dow
        Rufus,   Milton Clark
        Mary Ann,   Simeon J. Gardner
        Wealthy Topliff.
        Eliza Topliff.
        Wife of Stephen Dunham, Jr.
        Maria Topliff.
        Mrs. Avery.
        Wife of Joseph Doan.
        Wife of Solomon Bidwell.
        Mary Carpenter.
        John and Sally Brale, his wife.
        Edward,   Amos Richardson
        Henry,   Daniel Brigham
Aug. 24 Walter Adams,   Reuel Loomis
     31 Elisabeth White.
Sept. 7 Abner Mason
        Susan Daggett.
        Almira Whittemore.
Sept. 21 Helen, Sophia, Sidney, Lucian, William,
         and Charlotte,   Marvin Curtis
         Emily Brigham.
         Darius Randolph, Abel Sylvester, Charles
            Gilbert, Abby Ann, and Almira, Darius Manley

1824.

April 30 Maria;   Apollos Fitch
May 30 Elizabeth,   Col. James White
June 27 Frederick Gibson,   Darius Manley
July 11 Thomas Fitch,   Rev. Chauncey Fitch
        Henry Newton and Oramel,   Phineas Post
Sept. 5 Louisa, Penelope, and Samuel,
                                    Capt. Edward G. Huntington

1825.

Feb. 18 George,   Marvin Curtis
May 29 Louisa Maria,   John P. Cummings
June 12 Ruth,   Amos Richardson
Aug. 14 Charlotte,   Col. James White
     28 Mary Jane,   Oliver French

Children.	Baptisms.	Parents.
	1826.	

July 16 Harriet,   Marvin Curtis
Dec. 10 Henry Martyn,   Rev. C. Booth

1827.

July 1 Lucy Maria,   Joseph Dorman
Aug. 26 Maria Ann,   Ralzaman Belknap
         Olive White,   Amos Richardson

1828.

May 2 Roxana Emily,   Daniel Loomis
June 1 James,   Col. James White
July 1 Hannah, wife of Elias Janes.
        Sally, wife of Royal Manning.
        Eliza Clark.
        Maria Clark.
        Joseph Emerson and Edwin,   Rufus Dimmick
        Emily Wright,   Daniel Brigham
        Nancy and Solomon Lathrop,   Solomon Colman

1829.

Feb. 20 Sarah Adams and Joseph,   Sterling Janes
May 24 Kirtland Farnam,   Rev. Chauncey Booth
        Horace, Austin, Henry, Louisa, and
             William Everett,   Gardiner Lord
        Mary,   Capt. Joseph Dow
Aug. 28 Caroline,   Rufus Davenport

1830.

June 6 Eliphilet Ward and William Morgan,
                                                  Eliphilet Harris
     27 Sarah Howe,   Simeon Woodworth

1831.

July 3 Mary Ann Moody,   Dr. Dimock
     17 Martha Sergeant,   Austin Dunham
        James White,   Amos Richardson
Sept. 4 Dr. Timothy Dimock.
        William H. Godfrey.
        Fanny Manning
Sept. 28 Charlotte,   Col. James White
        Mary Elisabeth,   Rufus Dimmick
        Frederick Benton, George, and Edwin, twins,
                                                  Daniel Brigham

| Children. | Baptisms. | Parents. |

1831.

Sept.   Richard Augustus,   Joseph Dorman
   16 William Howard,   Rev. Chauncey Booth
   30 James Manning,   Solomon Colman
Nov.   6 Stedman W. Hanks.
       Mary Parrish.
       Martha Gardner.
       Eliza Davenport.
       Emmeline Davenport.
       Francis Lyman.
       William Lyman,   Sterling Janes

1832.

Sept.   2 James,   Capt. E. G. Huntington
       Amos,   Amos Richardson
   16 James Marvin,   Marvin Curtis

1833.

Jan. 18 Joel Lyman,   Sterling Janes
July   5 Mary,   Watson Boynton
Sept. 22 George Judson,   Washington Barrows
      Josiah Everitt,   Gardiner Lord

1834.

Feb. 28 Francis,   Rufus Dimmick
July   3 James Ormand and Francis Lewellyn,   James Dyke
Aug.   2 Lucinda,   John W. Murphy
      Wealthy and Henry Kirk and Nathan Colman,
                                              Montgomery White

1835.

      Daniel Wright,   Dr. Timothy Dimock
      Simeon Cornelius,   Daniel Loomis
Nov.   1 Dianna Strong.

1836.

Mar.   6 John Dresser and Abbey, his wife.
   27 Ebenezer Kellogg,   Samuel P. Rose
April 17 Mercy Almira and Francis Hermon,
                                            Bohan S. Strong
June 19 Cornelia,   Widow Eliza Murphy
      John,   John Winchester
      Addison,   Alvan Kingsbury
Sept.   2 James Dorman,   Simeon Woodworth
Nov.   4 John Everell and James Henry,   John W. Boynton
      Ellen Maria,   Rev. Chauncey Booth

| Children. | Baptisms. | Parents. |
|---|---|---|–

RECORDS OF FIRST CHURCH

1837.

Children		Parents
	Alford Bliven.	
	Melissa Bliven.	
	Lydia Joanna,	William Dorman
Aug. 24	Nathan and Walter,	Sterling Janes
Sept. 24	Clarissa Sabin,	James Dike

1838.

May	Cleanthe Kinne.	
June 3	Andrew Backus,	Alvan Kingsbury
July 1	Remick K. Arnold.	
	James S. Morgan.	
	Silas F. Clark.	
	Ethan Barrows.	
	Chloe Morgan.	
	Sarah E. Brace.	
	Lovinne Mason.	
Aug. 26	Edward Griffin,	Edward G. Huntington
Sept. 2	Cynthia Grover.	
	Julia Ann Dunham.	
	Sarah Manning.	
	Eliza Manning.	
	Charlotte Manning.	
	Mary Landfear,	William Babcock
	Mason Morgan.	

1839.

	Elisabeth Rose,	Samuel P. Rose
Jan.	Clement J. Godfrey.	
	E. Grant Root.	
	Mary Watrous.	
	Henrietta Lyman.	
July 7	Mrs. Julia Mason.	

1840.

Mar. 17	George W. Fitch.	
June 25	Mary Jane,	Sterling Janes
July 3	Edward Stanley and Eliza,	John W. Boynton
	Joseph Rose,	William Dorman
	Maria Elizabeth,	Dr. Timothy Dimock
	John Francis,	John P. Loomis

Children.	Baptisms.	Parents.
	1840.	
July 25 Charles Myron,		Charles P. Talcott
Clarissa Storrs,		Frederick Freeman
	1841.	
Roxana Bingham,		Ralzamon Belknap
	1842.	
Jan. Oliver Peckham.		
Mary, wife of John Albro.		
Daniel Albro,		John Albro
Nov. 5 Henry Farnam,		Dr. Timothy Dimock
Emma Matilda,		John O. Loomis
	1843.	
June 30 Edward Arthur,		Frederick Freeman
Mary Ellen,		James S. Morgan
Emily Elizabeth,		John Winchester
Richard Dimock,		Col. Richard H. Rose
	1844.	
June 12 Lucy Richardson,		Sterling Janes

"BILL OF MORTALITY."

1763.

July Wife of Denis Maraugh.
Oct. Child of Ebenezer Wentworth.
      Child of William Taylor.
Dec. Wife of Joseph Larrabee.
      Nathaniel Gove.
      Joseph Strong, Esq.

1764.

Mar. Wife of Joseph Harris.
May   Aged Mrs. Davenport.
      Child of Simeon Chapel.
      Aged Samuel Curtiss.
July John Rose.
Aug. Child of Levi Dow.
Nov. Wife of Benjamin Grover.
Dec. Thomas Kindrick.

1765.

Aged Widow Brigham.
Wife of Joseph Larabe.
May Child of Medad Root.
July James White.
Sept. Preserved Strong.
Oct. Wife of Captain Robertson.
Nov. Wife of Elisha Janes, Jr.
Child of Lot Dimmick.

1766.

Feb. Widow Basset.
Child of Peltiah Dow.
Mar. Joseph Turner.
Child of Deacon Hale.
May Child of William Taylor.
Joseph Turner, Jr.
Child of Allerton Cushman.
Rachael Crossman.
June Widow Judd.
Oct. Aged Mr. Pierce.
Dec. Widow Root.

1767.

Feb. Wife of Matthew Grover.
Mar. Child of Jonathan Root.
Widow Mary Edwards.
April Wife of Deacon Hale.
Child of James Hawkins, Jr.
Child of Jer. Ripley.
May Wife of Jer. Ripley.
Aug. Child of Dr. Ladd.
Oct. Wife of Denis Maraugh.
Nov. Child of Amos Dorman.
Dec. Denis Maraugh.
Samuel French.
Wife of Elisha Searle.

1768.

Jan. Wife of Lazarus Manley.
Child of Solomon Lord.

1768.

- Jan. Hudson Babcock.
- Feb. John Everton.
- July Child of Elijah Fuller.
  - Child of Josiah Fuller.
- Aug. Child of Josiah Fuller.
  - Child of Capt. Robertson.
- Sept. Child of Levi Dow.
  - Child of Widow Babcock.
  - Aged Mrs. Turner.
- Dec. Gideon Bridgman.
  - George Hawkins.

1769.

- Jan. Aged Mr. Pierce.
- Feb. Hannah Root.
- Mar. Child of Elijah Janes.
  - Widow Edwards.
  - Captain Buell.
- June Wife of John Robertson.
- July Benjamin Grover.

1770.

- Jan. Child of Gershom Colman.
- Feb. Child of Simon Antizzal.
- July Child of Thomas Judd.
- Aug. Wife of Asa Strong.
  - Wife of Caleb Stanley.
- Dec. Daniel Janes.

1771.

- April Jerusha Root.
- Aug. Wife of Daniel Lyman.
  - Gershom Colman.
  - Child of Henry Curtiss, Jr.
- Sept. 25 4.30. " My dear, dear Consort," &c., &c. (Huntington)

1772.

- Jan. Dr. Curtiss.
- Feb. Child of Joseph Carpenter.
  - Widow Cogshall.
  - Child of Isaac Root.
  - Wife of Richard Davenport.
- June Wife of Thomas Judd.

1772.

Oct. Widow Hawkins.
Nov. Joseph Rose.

1773.

Jan. Wife of Samuel Robertson, Jr.
     Wife of John Badcock.
Mar. Child of Nathaniel Rose.
     Child of Samuel Parker.
     Wife of Nathaniel Rose.
     Benjamin Janes.
April Joseph Strong, Esq.
     Jehiel Rose.
Sept. James Hawkins, Jr.
     Capt. Rust.
     Child of Isaac Root.
Oct. Widow Badcock.
     Aged Ebenezer Badcock.
Nov. Daughter of Asa Manley.
Dec. Widow Sergeant.

1774.

Jan. Sarah Scot.
Mar. Child of Joseph Root.
April Tabitha Janes.
Oct. Child of William Edwards.
Nov. Polly Robertson.
     Widow Turner.
Dec. Child of Capt. Robertson.
     Daniel and Betty Robertson.
     Elijah Ripley.

1775.

Jan. Peter Buell, Esq.
     Salome Robertson.
     Child of John Root.
     Wife of Matthew Grover.
     Wife of Joseph Hawkins.
Feb. Sarah Buell.
Mar. 3 Children of Enoch Larrabee.
April Wife of Eph. Dow.
     Lydia Turner.
     Widow Rust.

1775.

- May Wife of G. Palmer.
- Sept. Three children of Eph. Colman.
  - Four children of E. Cushman.
  - Child of Amos Ames.
  - Widow Rust.
  - Child of John Mead.
  - Child of Allerton Cushman.
  - Child of Amos Ames.
  - Gideon Edwards.
  - Child of John Mead.
  - Child of Joseph Carpenter.
  - Jedediah Turner.
  - Child of Henry Curtiss.
  - Child of Samuel Curtiss.
  - Patty Strong.
  - Child of John Mead.
  - Child of Joseph Carpenter.
  - Stephen Palmer.
  - Child of Samuel Colman.
  - Child of Mrs. Ripley.
  - Widow Palmer.
  - Child of Nathaniel Palmer.
  - Child of Isaac Root.
  - Child of Samuel Curtiss.
  - Child of Samuel Curtiss.
  - Aged Deacon Parker.
- Nov. Child of Thomas Brigham.
  - Child of Eliphilet Edwards.
  - Child of Samuel Colman.
- Dec. Child of Benjamin Grover.
  - Wife of Benjamin Grover.
- Dec. Child of Thomas Root.
  - Child of Thomas Brigham.

1776.

- Jan. Child of Abner White.
  - Child of Ebenezer Badcock, Jr.
  - James Hawkins.
- Feb. Child of Elias Janes.
  - Child of Otis Freeman.

1776.

Feb. Samuel Curtiss.
    Child of Dr. Ladd.
Mar. Child of Caleb Stanley.
    Child of Amos Ames.
    Son of Pelatiah Dow.
June Joseph Carpenter.
Aug. Aged Widow Rust.
Sept. Child of Samuel Colman.
    Child of Major Buell.
    Elisabeth Carpenter.
    Child of John Root.
Sept. 23 "Septimus, my son," &c.,   Huntington
    Wife of Thomas Root.
    Moses Eells.
    Child of Mr. Oaks.
    Child of Allerton Cushman.
Oct. Child of Medad Root.
    Child of Oliver Boynton.
    Aged Widow Colman.
    Oliver Janes.
    Eliezer Webster.
    Oliver Eells.
    Capt. Hale's death ascertained.
Nov. Child of Benajah Strong.
    James White.
    Child of Elisha Janes, Jr.
Dec. Son of Enoch Larabee.
    Child of Daniel Turner.
    Thankful, one of the town's poor.

1777.

Jan. Jesse Curtiss.
    Uriah Brigham.
    Allerton Cushman.
    Benjamin Root.
Mar. Peter Pelham.
April Moses Boynton.
May Daniel Dow.
June Abigail Eells.

1777.

Aug. 10, " At 8.40, my son, George Washington," &c.,
                                                    Huntington
  David Parker.
Sept. Child of Timothy Rose.
  Child of Dudley Dorman.
  Widow Hawkins.
  Joseph Hawkins, Jr.
  Child of Samuel Parker.
Dec. Child of Dr. Ladd.
Aug. Wife of Asa Manley.

1778.

Jan. Joseph Larabe.
Feb. Wife of Ephr. Cook.
Mar. Mark, negro.
April Child of Daniel Turner.
Aug. Dr. Ladd.
Sept. Child of Ebenezer Badcock.
Oct. Child of Ned (mulatto).
Nov. Child of John Robinson.
  Hannah Pelham.

1779.

Jan. Wife of Jonathan Root.
  Jeremiah Fitch.
Feb. Widow Carpenter.
Mar. Child of Elias Janes.
  Elisha Janes.
April Samuel Boynton.
May Wife of John Robertson.
July Lucy Dimmick.
Aug. Meriah Turner.
Sept. Child of Humphrey Taylor.
Oct. Child of Ben. Badcock.
Nov. Child of Elias Palmer.

1780.

May Wife of Dr. Rose.
Sept. Child of Patience (mulatto)
Nov. Wife of Hab'k Turner.
  Dr. Samuel Rose.
Dec. Child of Jonathan Root.

DEATH RECORDS OF FIRST CHURCH

1781.
Jan. Widow Gary.
Feb. John Ripley.
May James Parker.
June Child of Jonathan Root.
July Widow Maraugh.

1782.
Jan. Humphrey Taylor.
Mar. Widow Curtiss.
May Polly Root.
July Child of Deacon Strong.
Aug. Norman Brigham.
    Three children of Dan. Brown.
    Aged John Robertson.
Sept. Child of Richard Brown.
Nov. Wife of Capt. Fitch.
Dec. Deacon Thomas Root, 92 years.

1783.
Jan. Hannah Coleman.
    Child of E. Colman.
May Mrs. Boothe.
Aug. Child of Capt. Robertson.
Sept. Widow Gove.
Oct. Dr. John Rose.
Nov. Wife of Deacon Strong.

1784.
Feb. Rhoderia Skinner.
    Aged Mrs. Carpenter.
Mar. Wife of Capt. Robertson.
    Abigail Curtiss.
April Jenne (Indian).
    Child of Solomon Buell.
    Joseph Hale.
May Eunice Eells.
June Child of Widow Hale.
Aug. Child of Gideon Badcock.
    Hannah Robertson.
    Wife of Samuel Badcock.
Nov. Eliezer Colman.
Dec. Hectar (mulatto).

1785.

Jan. Child of Jedediah Geer.
Feb. Eunice Porter.
     Wife of Joshua Edwards.
Mar. Mulatto woman.
April Child of Deacon Strong.
May Child of Gideon Badcock.
     Child of Gideon Badcock.
     Child of Jehiel Rose.
June Wife of Solomon Robinson.
     Anne Burns.
July Phœbe Robertson.
Sept. Billy Hale.
     Samuel Boynton.
Oct. Mary Turner.
Nov. Ebenezer Wintworth.

1786.

Jan. Wife of Hembry Grover.
Feb. Sally Hawkins.
Mar. Wife of Medad Root.
July Child of Henry Curtiss.
Oct. Dr. Rose.
     Widow Edwards.
     Silence Burns.
Dec. Joseph Turner.

1787.

Jan. Bildad Colman.
Feb. Child of George Manly.
     Child of Nathan Cook.
     Child of Solomon Buell.
     Child of Samuel Rose.
Mar. Child of Major Buell.
April Child of Stephen Turner.
May Child of Billy Root.
Sept. Polly Turner.
Nov. Wife of Thomas Porter.

1788.

- Jan. Child of Richard Davenport, Jr.
- Feb. Child of Keyes (negro).
  Esther Dow.
- Mar. Wife of Ebenezer Colman.
  Asa Manley.
- April Child of Widow Manley.
- May Child of Jephthah Fitch.
  Jeremiah Dow.
- Nov. Widow Rose.
  Widow Parker.
- Dec. Aged Widow White.

1789.

- Feb. Wife of Elihu Babcock.
- April Child of Abner White.
- May Two Infants of Ebenezer Colman.
- June Caleb Stanley.
  John White.

1790.

- Mar. Solomon Robertson.
  Mrs. Rindge.
  Child of Abner White.
  Aged Widow Dow.
  Aged Mrs. Meacham.
- April Hembery Grover.
  Wife of Ulysses Dow.
- May Child of Samuel Rose.
- June Aged Mrs. Dean.
  Wife of Benjamin Colman.
- July Child of Daniel Turner.
- Aug. John Tilden.
  Seth Janes.
  Noah Porter.
- Dec. Child of Timothy Dimock, Jr.

1791.

- Mar. Aged Mr. Preston.
- May Wife of Thomas Judd.
- June Eunice Janes.

1791.

- July — Aged Mrs. Huett.
- Oct. — Child of Samuel Janes.
  - Wife of Samuel Janes.
- Dec. — Jonathan Gurley.
  - Child of Richard Hale.
  - Aged Widow Edwards.

1792.

- Jan. — Ambry (negro).
  - Aged Hab'k Turner.
- Mar. — Widow Colman.
- April — Timothy Cushman.
- May — Aged Widow Strong.
  - Martin Worry.
- July — Child Pelatiah Dow.
  - Aged Amos Carpenter.
  - John Root.
  - Child of Joshua Woodworth.
- Aug. — Child of Joseph Grover.
- Oct. — Horatio Carpenter.

1793.

- Feb. — Daniel Robertson.
  - Nathan Cook.
- Feb. — Richard Hale, in the Island of Eustatius, his death ascertained in March.
- Mar. — Sally Greenleaf.
- May — Gershom Palmer.
- July — Erastus Porter.
- Aug. — Two children of Dr. Howard.
  - Child of Timothy Rose.
  - Child of Timothy Rose.
  - Child of Widow Gurley.
- Sept. — John Robertson.
  - 9, My youngest son, James (Huntington).
  - Jonathan House.
  - Child of Benjamin Davenport.
  - Timothy Carpenter.
  - Child of Bildad Curtiss.
  - Wife of Ebenezer Colman, Jr.
  - Child of Daniel Robertson.

1793.

- Sept. Gurdon Field.
- Child of Benjamin Colman.
- Oct. Child of Widow Cook.
- Child of Widow Hale.
- Child of Uriah Palmer.
- Lois Eells.
- Wife of George Manley.
- Aged Widow Badcock.
- Son of Ephraim Colman.
- Nov. Samuel Janes.
- John Mead.
- Child of Mr. Field.

1794.

- Jan. Capt. Robertson, Sr.
- Mar. Child of Oliver Cook.
- April Henry Curtiss.
- Aug. Child of Ebenezer Crossman.
- Triphene Janes.
- Child of Elisha Fitch.
- Sept. 17 Joseph Huntington, in Charleston, S. C.
- Oct. Child of Henry Fitch.
- Nov. Child of Widow Porter.
- Wife of Ebenezer Crossman.
- Dec. 12 "Deceased, at half after 10 o'clock, P. M., my dear daughter Penelope, in her 7th year."
- 15 Monday, 9 o'clock, Hannah, about 15 years, both children of Rev. W. Huntington.
- 25 Dr. Joseph Huntington.

1795.

- Jan. Eunice Dorman.
- Feb. Capt. Dimick.
- Child of Jesse Boynton.
- Child of Betty House.
- Abner White.
- Polly Root.
- Ephraim Hutchinson.
- May Child of Elisabeth Dow.
- June Mrs. Gurley.
- Mrs. Stanley.

1795.

July Child of Mr. Sanford.
　　 Child of Richard Davenport, Jr.
Aug. Shubael Cook.
　　 Child of John Eells, Jr.
Sept. Child of Ephraim Badcock.
　　 Child of —— Janes.
Nov. Child of Timothy Gurley.
　　 Aged George Manley.

1796.

Jan. 23	Jethro Turner,	74 years
Feb. 9	Child of J. J. Kingsbury,	3 months
May 21	Ephraim Dow,	63 years
Aug.	Frederic Palmer,	24 years
Sept.	Child of Samuel Babcock,	1 year 6 months
	Child of Levi Colman,	Stillborn
Nov. 26	Nathaniel Wright,	85 years 9 months
	—— Herrick,	85 years

1797.

Jan. 3	Widow Turner,	71 years
4	Polly Ripley,	19 years
15	Phineas Parker,	77 years 9 months
17	Female child of Timothy Dimmick,	1 month
20	Female child of S. Greenleaf,	3 months
Feb. 14	Wife of Mr. Jones,	38 years
Mar. 23	Abner Fitch, Jr.,	47 years
25	Jeremiah Fitch, Jr.,	18 years
June 17	Male infant of G. Badcock,	1 day
23	Capt. Abner Fitch,	94 years 11 months
July 20	Capt. Samuel Robertson,	50 years
22	Elisabeth, child of Dr. Howard,	1 day
Aug. 27	Josiah Fuller,	69 years
Sept. 4	Male child of L. Colman,	Stillborn
5	Wife of E. Dewey,	63 years
29	Son of Joseph Fitch,	8 years 9 months
Oct. 21	Female infant of J. Kingsbury,	3 days

1798.

Aug. 23	Widow A. Fitch,	82 years
Sept.	Cæsar Peters (negro),	18 years
Nov. 19	Mary Rose,	79 years
29	Wife of E. Sweetland (Andover),	21 years

DEATH RECORDS OF FIRST CHURCH

1799

Mar. 26	Widow Janes,	76 years
July 23	Son of Daniel Robertson,	10 months
Aug. 2	Solomon Parker,	43 years
July	Child of J. Topliff,	Stillborn
Oct. 30	Widow Mary Coleman,	77 years
Nov. 26	Robert White,	25 years

1800.

April 6	Ambrose Deuty,	22 years
May 10	Capt. Thomas Brigham,	58 years
June 5	John Palmer,	25 years
Aug. 3	Benjamin Grover,	51 years
29	Harriet, daughter of J. Woodworth,	4 years
Aug. 2	Nathan Davenport,	19 years
Sept. 15	Female child of M. Dimock,	0
Oct. 24	Widow Susan Robertson,	68 years
Nov. 11	Abijah Curtis,	33 years
Dec. 7	Eunice Badcock,	27 years
13	David Greenleaf,	63 years

1801.

Feb. 20	Jabez Ripley,	46 years
25	Joseph Janes,	17 years
Mar. 6	Benajah Edwards,	70 years
April 1	Male child Mr. Sanford,	3 months
10	Libbeous Boynton,	30 years
19	Son of Samuel Babcock,	3 days
May 5	Augustus, son of Capt. Curtis,	7 years 6 months
June 29	James Buell,	12 years
Sept. 16	Wife of Asa Manley,	32 years
Oct. 4	Rufus, son of E. Judd,	9 months
	James, son of Jesse Boynton,	2 years
6	Ebenezer Coleman,	90 years
Nov. 1	Olive, daughter of S. Dunham,	8 years
9	Louis, son of S. Dunham,	3 years

1802.

Jan. 17	Female infant of William Dowe,	6 hours
Feb. 4	Joseph Turner,	84 years
3	Mary Boynton (E. Hartford),	30 years
Mar. 20	Lucinda Parker,	18 years

1802.

May	10	Widow Desire Dimmick,	70 years
June	1	Deacon Richard Hale,	85 years 3 months
	5	Polly Deuty,	22 years
	16	Walter Rose,	24 years
Aug.	1	Male infant of N. H. Rose,	Stillborn
		Zebulon Babcock,	88 years 9 months 22 days
	10	Walter, son of Wal. Rose,	9 months
Sept.	21	Female infant of J. Dresser,	1 hour
Oct.	10	Son of Levi C. Colman,	7 months
		Amasa, son of Joseph Grover,	9 years
	28	Two daughters of Joseph Turner,	3 and 2 years
Nov.	3	Daughter of Joseph Turner,	1 year
	11	Son of J. Morey,	5 years
	28	Widow Dorothy Turner,	73 years
Dec.	18	John Hale, Esq.,	54 years
	23	Daughter of E. Bacon,	1 year 4 months

1803.

Jan.	26	Lydia Herrick,	57 years
April	26	Widow Fitch, born in Coventry,	90 years
June	20	John Rose,	31 years
July	3	Jared, son of Capt. Fitch,	4 years 3 months
	10	Daughter of Widow D. Rose,	2 or 3 hours
Aug.	7	Mrs. Brown,	77 years
	13	Mrs. Eells,	84 years
	22	Amos Brown,	72 years
Sept.	8	Oliver Boynton,	18 years
Oct.	3	Richard Hale Howard,	1 year 8 months
	5	Rufus Howard,	4— years
	11	Daughter of J. Mead,	1 day
	12	Ephraim Dow,	41 years
	15	Laura Rust,	13 years
	16	Richard Davenport,	87 years
	19	John Curtis,	1 year
Nov.	6	Widow Sarah Hale,	50 years
Dec.	1	Ezekiel Wentworth,	58 years
	15	Wife of Humphrey Dow,	56 years
	16	Widow Babcock,	78 years
	17	Widow Preston,	94 years

1804.

Jan	4 Daughter of Capt. Curtis,	10 days
	5 Son of Fred. Rose,	2 days
	18 Widow Follet,	82 years
	19 Daughter of Solomon Janes,	5 years
	20 Son of D. C. Brigham,	2 years
	27 Daughter of M. Dimock,	Stillborn
Feb.	6 Polly Robertson,	29 years
Mar.	7 Son of Dr. Howard,	30 minutes
April	24 Son of Samuel Babcock,	3 months
June	11 Gurdon, son of D. C. Brigham,	12 years
	22 John Christie,	59 years
July	25 Rebecca, daughter of Joseph Dow,	2 years
Aug.	28 Eunice, daughter of Joseph Dorman,	3 years
Sept.	4 Nathan Thompson,	78 years
Nov.	12 Meda Robertson,	47 years
Dec.	10 Son of Phineas Ladd,	1 year 6 months

1805.

Jan.	1 Laura, daughter of Widow Curtis,	4 years
Feb.	10 Wife of N. H. Rose,	21 years
Mar.	25 Son of Benjamin Davenport,	7 weeks
May	12 Daughter of S. Chappell,	10 years
Nov.	1 Eunice Brigham,	22 years 11 months
	2 Solomon Janes,	48 years 9 months
	21 Wife of John Carpenter,	75 years

1806.

Jan.	18 Male infant of P. Ladd,	2 days
Feb.	1 Emmeline, daughter of A. Jones,	4 years 6 months
	4 Harry Huntington,	24 years
	7 Widow Cook,	67 years
	17 Widow Elisabeth Huntington,	58 years
Mar.	13 Daughter of Benjamin Davenport,	6 weeks
	15 John Carpenter,	85 years
April	30 John Eells,	90 years
July	23 Wife of Guy Robertson,	26 years
Aug.	16 Widow Susan Grant,	84 years
Sept.	8 Ephraim Fitch,	27 years
Oct.	11 Daughter of M. Waldo,	17 years

1806.

Oct. 14	Son of M. Waldo,	4 years
	Widow Herrick,	75 years
Dec. 16	Male infant Silas Guild,	1 day

1807.

Feb	Female infant of J. Turner,	3 days
Mar. 6	Nabby Grover,	35 years
Oct. 3	Wife of E. Colman,	65 years
Nov. 10	Wife of Ph. Ladd,	29 years
2	Harvey Dow,	25 years
9	Wife of Joseph Herrick,	57 years

1808.

Mar.	Female child of J. Morey,	2 months
Nov. 14	Wife of James White,	26 years
Dec. 24	Ozias Lyman,	56 years

1809.

Feb. 9	Male infant of Capt. M. Dimock,	Stillborn
19	Zebulon Richardson,	52 years
Mar. 3	Thomas Judd,	88 years
14	Wife of Hezekiah Edgerton, Jr.,	39 years
June 10	Widow Boynton,	97 years
18	Anna Edwards,	79 years
19	Daughter of E. Bacon,	11 months
July 1	Widow Phebe Lincoln,	45 years
Aug. 11	Daughter of Solomon Dow,	1 year 6 months
Nov. 25	Benajah Strong, Esq.,	69 years
Dec. 25	Widow of J. Ripley,	95 years

1810.

Jan. 6	Emily, daughter of J. C. Manning,	3 years
Feb. 16	Widow Wright,	93 years
April 19	Female child of Thad's Byington,	1 year 1 month
24	Female child of William Thomson,	3 days
June 29	Eunice Talcott Rose, daughter of Capt. N. H. Rose,	6 years 10 months
22	Frederic White (at Orange, N. J.),	24 years
Sept. 26	Widow Christie,	66 years
Nov. 28	Infant child of Capt. Mason Dimick.	
Dec. 1	Female child of Guy Robertson,	12 days
	Child of J. Morey.	
	Child of S. Badcock.	

DEATH RECORDS OF FIRST CHURCH

1811.

Mar. 30	Chauncey, son of William Lyman,	—
April	William Morey,	85 years
June 2	Emily, daughter of Solomon Dow,	5 years
6	Wife of Hezekiah Richardson.	
Sept. 1	Peg, a negro, at Judge Root's.	
Nov. 16	Wife of Samuel Allen.	

1812.

Feb. 10	Medad Root,	76 years
11	Jeremiah Ripley,	70 years
24	Diarca Curtis.	
Jan. 7	Samuel Judd (Otsego, N. Y.),	21 years
April 15	Female infant of Calvin Manning, Jr.,	1 month
May 5	Wife of Asa Parker,	50 years
June 2	Wife of Duthan Kingsbury,	72 years
5	Anna Simons,	49 years
20	Infant of S. Colman, Jr.,	13 days
July 2	Electa, daughter of F. Stedman,	18 years
Aug. 13	Jacob Brown.	
Sept. 3	Child of Joseph Grover,	2 years
12	Child of Spencer Woodworth,	6 days
Oct. 3	Wife of Azel Edgerton,	44 years
Nov. 19	Lucinda Robinson.	
Dec. 10	Dudley Dorman,	78 years
16	Chauncey Badcock,	20 years
26	Daniel Dimick, son of Milton Clark,	1 year 2 months

1813.

Jan. 9	Elisabeth Murray,	64 years
23	David Loomis,	23 years
Mar. 30	John Howard,	28 years
	Wife of Nathan Parker.	
May 5	Widow Mary Dow,	70 years
8	Anna Grover,	24 years
June 7	Jehiel Rose,	65 years
27	Charles Dow,	22 years
Aug. 2	Hannah, daughter of J. Boynton,	17 years
12	Sally, daughter of H. Christy,	4 years
17	Male child of Joseph Turner,	3 days

COVENTRY RECORDS

1813.

Aug. 5	Wife of Hon. Jesse Root, Esq., Widow Brigham.	81 years

1814.

Jan. 7	Samuel Allen,	83 years
Feb. 27	Orra, son of Elijah Robertson,	6 years
April 8	Prudance Brown.	
10	Abraham Brown.	
11	Chloe Rust.	
19	Anna Robertson.	
	Anson Dow (at New London).	
May 10	James Edwards.	
June 26	Pierepont, son of Samuel Badcock,	14 years
23	Hezekiah Richardson,	60 years
Aug. 24	Mariah, daughter of Bela Boynton,	15 years
30	Austin, son of Thadeus Boynton,	3 years
Nov. 18	Lucy Fish,	26 years
29	Son of Amos Richardson,	16 months
Dec. 10	Female child of Caleb B. Slocum,	14 months
16	Wife of Jonathan Hutchinson.	

1815.

Mar. 11	Wife of Joseph Edgerton,	22 years
April 28	Widow Abigail Vorry,	57 years
May 9	Wife of Elijah Simons.	
July 24	Wife of Capt. Bildad Curtis,	48 years
Aug. 18	Wife of Capt. Gershom Brigham,	66 years
Dec. 3	Infant child of M. Chamberlain.	

1816.

Jan. 9	Infant child of Joseph Dow,	19 days
26	Infant child of Edward G. Huntington.	
Feb. 1	Sally Loomis,	30 years
6	Samuel Sprague,	57 years
7	Delight Dresser,	43 years
20	Daniel Robertson,	60 years
Mar. 9	Hezekiah Robertson,	73 years
10	Sally Root, daughter of Spencer Woodworth,	6 months
23	Elisabeth Albro,	63 years
30	Jefferson Carpenter,	14 years

DEATH RECORDS OF FIRST CHURCH

1816.

April	1 Joanna Curtis,	80 years
	4 Mary Sanford,	13 years
	28 Henry C. Card, at Mr. Woodworth's, from R. I.,	20 years
June	4 Capt. Hezekiah Edgerton,	73 years
Sept.	28 Mary, wife of Duthan Kingsbury,	58 years
Oct.	4 Roxana'Emily, daughter of Roderick Loomis,	2 years and 5 months

1817.

Mar.	3 Widow Irene Porter,	90 years
	11 Esther Williams,	88 years
Aug.	17 Daniel Brown,	18 years
Sept.	30 Samuel Turner.	
Oct.	20 Sarah Crandall,	75 years
Nov.	8 Elizabeth Palmer,	73 years
	25 Asa Lyman,	63 years

1818

Feb.	2 Esther Colman,	76 years
Mar.	28 Maria Ann, daughter of Milton Clark,	1 year 9 months
April	20 Esther Colman,	37 years
Sept.	5 Jephtha, son of Mrs. Fitch,	5 years
Oct.	13 Thomas Porter,	83 years
	22 Elizabeth Curtis,	89 years
	27 Widow Theodore Grover,	64 years
Dec.	16 Thomas Holbrook,	84 years

1819.

Feb.	28 Oliver, son of Capt. Daniel Robinson,	9 months
Mar.	1 Elizabeth, daughter of Capt. J. Dow,	2 months
	2 Ann Dorman,	76 years
May	24 Levi Dow,	84 years
Aug.	13 Thomas Dorman,	80 years
	19 Nancy Colman,	14 years
	31 Jonathan Herrick,	44 years
Sept.	8 Anne Rudd,	86 years
	Eunice Duty.	
Oct.	5 Phebe Dow,	78 years
Dec.	13 Maria, child of Samuel Colman, Jr.,	2 years
	19 Robert Babcock,	87 years
	28 Fanny, daughter of John Y. Cook,	5 years

1820.

Jan.	1 Elijah Ripley,	37 years
	8 Daniel Albro 3d,	3 years 6 months
Mar.	30 Sally, wife of Frederick Rose.	
May	6 Widow Lydia Austin,	83 years
Sept.	12 Joseph, son of Edward G. Huntington,	20 years
	24 Eunice, daughter of Mrs. Williams,	12 days
Dec.	6 Barnard Phillips,	70 years
	25 Wife of John Kingsbury,	54 years

1821.

Jan.	23 Deborah Wright,	82 years
Mar.	27 Joseph Grover,	49 years
April	3 Infant child of Simeon J. Gardner,	Stillborn
	5 Wife of Samuel Colman, Jr.	
June	4 Elisabeth Booth,	11 months
	27 Ann Robinson.	
Aug.	16 Susannah Grant,	70 years
	18 Infant of W. Clark,	9 days
	19 Wife of Jephtha Fitch,	66 years
Nov.	13 Daniel, son of Capt. Daniel Robertson,	2 years

1822.

Jan.	1 Silas King,	76 years
	13 Marcus Boynton,	14 years
	28 Infant son of Jesse Colman,	8 years
Feb.	10 David Hale, Esq.,	60 years
	Joshua Edwards.	
	17 Samuel Colman,	78 years
Mar.	14 Capt. Roger Strong,	48 years
	16 Julia Bracket (negro),	19 years
	24 Elias Palmer,	77 years
	29 Hon. Jesse Root,	85 years
April	1 Wife of Chauncey Fitch,	27 years
	16 Rufus Clark,	28 years
	20 —— Utley.	
	24 Wife of Moses Stanley,	79 years
	27 Wife of Dudley Dorman,	8— years
May	1 Moses Stanley,	8— years
	3 Joseph Dorman,	53 years
	26 Walter Loomis,	19 years

DEATH RECORDS OF FIRST CHURCH 239

1822.

June 18	Widow Mead,	old age
July 9	Duthan Kingsbury,	79 years
12	Widow of Medad Root,	67 years
13	Infant child of Capt. Daniel Robertson,	2 weeks
Oct. 12	Eunice Deuty,	31 years
24	Widow Margaret Fuller,	89 years
Nov. 9	Joseph Herrick,	84 years
27	Irene Wright,	70 years
Dec. 8	Joel Wright,	80 years

1823.

Jan. 6	Solomon Dow,	44 years
11	Widow Elizabeth Thomas,	82 years
24	Elihu Babcock,	8— years
Feb. 5	Widow Mary Rose,	73 years
28	Perus Sprague,	84 years
Mar. 25	Joshua Woodworth,	66 years
April 20	Rachael Davenport,	77 years
May	David Skinner,	7— years
July 18	Widow Martha Parker,	101 years
Oct. 16	John Albro,	67 years
22	Infant child of Dr. O. H. Isham,	7 weeks
Dec. 2	Calvin Manning,	77 years
11	Anne Sprague,	60 years

1824.

Jan. 20	Benjamin Davenport,	61 years
April 17	Samuel Hale,	77 years
18	Abigail Palmer,	82 years
Sept. 16	Widow Jerusha White,	79 years
30	Ephraim A. Fitch,	17 years
Nov. 20	Josiah Carpenter,	80 years
Dec. 21	Clarissa Babcock,	22 years

1825.

Feb. 18	George, son of Marvin Curtis,	11 days
Mar. 7	Wife of Capt. C. Eells,	34 years
26	Patty Lyman,	4— years
April 22	Widow Elisabeth Blackman,	6— years
June 9	Wife of Lester Colman,	27 years
July 1	Lester Colman,	34 years

1825.

July	12 Levi Colman,	62 years
	13 Mary Augusta, child of H. Edgerton, Jr.,	5 weeks
	23 Beulah, wife of Elias Judd,	66 years
	24 Betsey, widow of Hezekiah Edgerton,	80 years
Aug.	15 Mrs. Hariet Malone,	32 years
	16 Zenas Doan,	20 years
	21 Matthew Deuty,	80 years
	22 Mary Ann (S. J. Gardner),	2 years 8 months
	31 Eliphilet C. Hall,	15 years
Sept.	24 Albigense Philips,	2 years 6 months
Nov.	1 Widow Miriam Carpenter,	86 years
	20 Infant child of Harry Woodruff,	1 year

1826.

Feb.	2 John Ingraham, son of Abner Mason,	4 months
	5 Widow Hannah McDonell,	68 years
	17 Widow Abigail Burns,	98 years
Mar.	7 Widow Abigail Turner,	83 years
	26 Mrs. Emily Bingham,	30 years
	29 Benjamin Cogswell,	98 years
May	2 Diantha Topliff,	5— years
July	12 John Rose,	35 years
Sept.	10 Henry Francis Porter,	1 year 5 months
	Ira Spafford,	6 months
	14 William Grover,	21 years
Oct.	2 Elisha Mason Sanford,	
	Stephen Perkins,	27 years
	17 Ephraim Robinson,	80 years
Nov.	30 Wife of Joseph Robertson,	40 years

1827.

Jan.	3 Emily Eliza Robertson,	14 years
Mar.	7 Daughter of Stephen Morey,	2 years
April	8 Widow of Robert Babcock,	93 years
	13 Ebenezer Crossman,	85 years
	26 Ephraim Colman,	85 years
May	10 Wife of Capt. David Robinson,	39 years
	31 John Robertson,	87 years
June	15 Starkweather.	
July	11 Female child of Mr. Neff,	11 months

1827.

Aug.	23 Rufus Green,	35 years
	25 Infant child of Horace Lincoln,	4 hours
	31 Wife of Elias Sprague,	27 years
Sept.	22 Polly Christie,	50 years
Oct.	13 Wife of Ephraim Babcock,	60 years
	31 Wife of Captain E. G. Huntington,	33 years

1828.

Jan.	17 Timothy Cheney,	27 years
Feb.	26 Ephraim Babcock,	65 years
Mar.	14 Widow Sprague,	83 years
	21 Anne Dorman,	13 years
	26 Wilson Rust,	7— years
June	25 Eliza Tucker,	19 years
July	26 Widow Alsworth,	84 years
Sept.	20 Infant child of M. Sillamer.	
Oct.	5 Harry Burns, son of Capt. E. D. Robinson,	1 year 6 months
	7 Widow Esther Grant,	75 years
Nov.	23 Sarah, daughter of Asa Parker,	3 years
Dec.	12 Emily, daughter of Lucius Carpenter,	2 years
	13 Louisa, daughter of Capt. E. G. Huntington,	77 years
	16 Elisabeth, daughter of Daniel Albro,	1 year 6 months

1829.

Jan.	14 Mary Godfrey,	3 months
	26 William Selheimer,	15 weeks
	Infant son of Cyril Parker,	12 days
	Pelatiah Dow,	89 years
Feb.	20 Joseph Janes,	4 months
	28 Esther Woodworth,	73 years
Mar.	1 Widow Phebe Carpenter,	79 years
April	26 Nathan Colman,	73 years
May	5 Huldah Janes,	32 years
	6 Jephtha Fitch,	77 years
June	17 Jesse Gardner,	46 years
	24 Jeremiah Fitch,	81 years
Aug.	16 Lucius Cone,	1 year 6 months
	17 Wife of Frederick Rose,	56 years
	21 Jerome Topliff,	3 years
Sept.	4 Mason Dimmick Sanford,	1 year 6 months

1829.

Sept. 18	Harlan Herrick,	28 years
Nov. 8	Samuel Bacon,	58 years
13	Josiah Carpenter,	31 years

1830.

Mar. 8	John Eells,	85 years
	Widow Herrick,	73 years
April 25	Charlotte White,	5 years
28	James White,	2 years 6 months
May 3	Leonard Curtis,	4 months
June	Infant child of Elijah Babcock.	
23	George Dow,	26 years
July 2	Wife of Bela Boynton,	72 years
Aug. 14	Capt. David Babcock,	35 years
Oct. 3	Female child of Benjamin Dimmick,	2 years
25	Caroline Dunham,	25 years
Sept. 5	—— Vinton.	

1831.

Jan. 3	Isabella Y. Robertson,	18 years
Feb. 27	James Babcock,	45 years
April 4	Cynthia Morgan,	65 years
5	Caleb Austin,	70 years
6	Harry Curtis,	33 years
19	Mason Roberts,	26 years
19	David Smith,	70 years
20	Infant son of Leonard Jones,	5 months
21	Widow Mary Colman,	65 years
22	Sarah Loomis,	73 years
May 18	Widow Crossman.	
June 12	David Topliff,	7 years
July 29	Samuel Guild,	81 years
Aug. 10	Eliza Topliff,	25 years
Nov. 20	Widow Mary Russel,	63 years
25	William Lyman, son of S. Janes,	14 days 14 hours 24 minutes
Dec. 29	Frederick Rose,	74 years

1832.

Jan. 6	Widow Tryphena Robertson,	77 years
26	Anne Dimmick,	65 years
Feb. 23	Tabitha Edwards,	87 years

DEATH RECORDS OF FIRST CHURCH

1832.

Mar. 2	Oliver Dow,	10 years
July 7	Wife of Nathan H. Rose,	57 years
	Widow Nareysa Davenport,	60 years
Sept. 7	Wife of Wm. Willips (?).	
22	Juliet Root,	18 years
Oct. 16	Emma Phillips.	
	Female child of Harry Parker,	11 months
Nov. 17	Wife of Abner Mason,	38 years
Dec. 13	Male child of Goodwin Fuller,	9 months

1833.

Jan. 3	John Fuller,	4 years
Feb. 14	Phebe Dow,	3 years
Mar. 13	Martin Carpenter,	52 years
April 4	Widow Eunice Robertson,	89 years
21	Tryphena Brown,	35 years
May 28	Aaron Topliff,	11 years
July 3	Child of Cyril Parker (Julia),	6 months
29	Ezekiel French,	63 years
31	Sarah Ann Hall,	18 years
Aug. 1	Capt. Daniel Dimmick,	68 years
11	Elias Janes,	82 years
25	Child of Mr. Neff.	
Sept. 20	Nelson Grover,	25 years
Nov. 20	Wife of George Simpson,	22 years
Dec. 6	Male child of William Porter.	9 months
10	Louisa J. Mead.	
12	Elijah Tinker (?),	67 years
	Widow of Hezekiah Robertson,	92 years
20	Lucy Mead,	16 years

1834.

Jan. 6	Jesse Chappel,	51 years
22	Betsey House,	66 years
23	Elisha Sanford,	78 years
Feb. 3	Wife of Elias Janes,	71 years
22	Israel Loomis,	80 years
25	Calvin Dow,	87 years
26	Clarissa Dimmick,	15 years
April 19	Abraham Babcock,	64 years
May 1	Widow of Capt. J. Fitch,	77 years

1834

May 14	Susan F. Kingsbury,	2 years
June 7	Lucy Peck,	24 years
28	Harry Dow,	48 years
29	Capt. Daniel Robertson,	45 years
July 12	Shubael Whittemore,	63 years
Aug. 1	Evet Seward Boynton,	1 year 5 months
2	Charles Lyon,	1 year 1 month
7	Lucinda Murphy,	10 months
Aug. 10	Warren Holt,	6 years
15	Mary Louisa White,	5 weeks
21	M. Louisa Woodward,	4 years
23	Timothy Dwight Robinson,	4 years
Sept. 26	Lewis White,	6 years
Nov. 5	Stephen S. Bushnell,	39 years
10	Ephraim O. Robinson,	55 years
Dec. 18	Elizabeth Judd,	80 years

1835.

Jan. 4	Infant daughter of Guy Robinson,	2 days
	Wife of Lorenzo Frizelle,	26 years
Feb. 10	Sarah Ripley,	22 years
22	Mary Bidwell,	20 years
24	Widow Chappel,	94 years
26	Phineas Post,	57 years
Mar. 28	Tryphene Woodworth,	1 year 1 month
31	Damarius Freeman (colored)	13 years
May 1	Widow of John Eells,	88 years
June 26	Wife of Stephen Dunham,	7— years
Aug. 5	Sally White,	21 years
19	Child of Eunice Topliff,	2 years 8 months
22	Male child of Gurley Judd,	2 months
Dec. 28	Widow Shepard.	

1836.

Feb. 18	Sophronia Mead,	27 years
Mar. 14	Ruth Whitman,	54 years
19	Josiah Everett Lord,	3 years
Mar. 23	Ezekiel Grover,	62 years
26	Lois Judd,	69 years
April 7	Capt. Joseph Dorman,	30 years
22	George Tucker,	28 years

DEATH RECORDS OF FIRST CHURCH

1836.

April 30	Aurelia Trapp,	27 years
May 6	Wife of E. L. Sweetland,	76 years
24	Rachael, wife of Owen Jewell,	30 years
27	Ebenezer Loomis,	72 years
July 13	Salome Tickner,	23 years
28	Female child of Charles Palmer,	9 months
Aug. 14	Olive Kinne,	53 years
Sept. 20	James Kingsbury,	2 years
Nov. 28	Elijah Simonds,	76 years

1837.

Jan. 19	Henrietta Roberts,	24 years
Feb. 7	Male child of Philo Parker,	3 days
10	Alfred Bliven,	3 months 15 days
Mar. 6	John Henry Dow,	9 months
10	Female child of Benoni Austin 2d,	1 day
24	Wife of Benoni Austin 2d,	21 years
May 4	Rebecca Janes,	74 years
July 31	Newton Post,	19 years
Aug. 12	Widow Sarah Strong,	91 years
18	Mary Ann Baker,	3 years
Sept. 5	Mrs. Mudge (of Scotland),	74 years

1838.

Jan. 8	Widow Clarissa Post,	50 years
22	Timothy L. Janes,	73 years
Mar. 13	Lydia R. Manning,	4 years
21	J. W. Loomis,	2 years 7 months
29	Elizabeth White,	14 years
April 4	Ralph Sprague,	30 years
21	Nathan Howard,	77 years
22	Joanna Howard,	74 years
	Sheldon Whittemore,	25 years
28	Infant child of Justin Lathrop,	1 day
May 2	Wife of Justin Lathrop,	33 years
4	Nathan H. Rose,	61 years
28	Widow Elizabeth Sprague,	78 years
June 12	Hezekiah Robertson,	22 years
28	Wife of Timothy Coleman, Jr.,	36 years
July 2	Male child of Lucius Carpenter,	7 months

1838.

July	23	Elias Sprague,	44 years
	31	Female child of Dr. T. Dimock,	1 day
Aug.	11	Esther Roswell,	5 years
	16	Wife of Dr. T. Dimock,	28 years
Aug.	28	Wife of William Babcock,	25 years
	30	Female child of John Coggins,	2 days
Sept.	2	Gideon Badcock,	84 years
Oct.	4	Infant daughter of William Babcock,	5 weeks
	10	Son of E. G. Huntington,	1 year 1 month
Nov.	14	Joseph Doan,	67 years
Dec.	4	M. Emma Loomis,	21 years
	30	Daughter of Silas Brown,	2 years

1839.

Jan.	30	Sally Grover,	62 years
Feb.	7	Clarence Mason,	1 year 1 month
Mar.	16	Amasa Roberts,	30 years
Mar.	18	Infant child of Augustus Clark,	30 minutes
	20	Infant son of Augustus Clark,	36 hours
April	18	Leander W. Curtis,	4 years
	21	Silas Guild,	64 years
May	2	Elijah Warren,	21 years
June	29	Widow of Gideon Babcock,	75 years
Aug.	22	Sybil Fitch,	21 years
Sept.	26	Widow of Nathan Colman,	76 years
Nov.	29	Lucy Ann Robertson,	19 years
Dec.	8	Asher Morgan,	77 years.

1840.

Jan.	9	Harvey Shepard,	57 years
	29	Wife of Jesse Woodworth,	47 years
Feb.	16	Wife of Charles Carpenter,	69 years
Mar.	11	Female child of Rufus Brown,	1 year
April	26	John Snow,	33 years
May	18	William Cummings,	79 years
June	12	Widow Crossman,	82 years
Aug.	9	Levi Perkins Rose,	30 years
	17	Lucy Ann Colman,	24 years
	28	Ann Amelia Morey,	9 months
	31	Wife of Solomon Edwards,	45 years
Oct.	3	Wife of Elisha Morey,	44 years

1840

Oct.	20 George W. Fitch,	32 years
	30 Caleb Booth,	18 years
Nov.	26 Female child of Charles D. Dresser,	11 days

1841

Jan.	14 Sarah Babcock,	16 years
	15 Ebenezer Root,	58 years
Mar.	4 Male child of Ziba Warren, Jr.,	10 weeks
	25 Chauncey C. Austin,	1 year 3 months
	28 Asa Parker,	82 years
April	2 Female child of E. G. Huntington.	
May	17 Cepha Brigham,	75 years
	21 Elijah Dunham,	55 years
Aug.	12 John Kingsbury,	73 years
	16 Jonathan Warren,	25 years
	21 Andrew B. Kingsbury,	4 years
Sept.	24 Ebenezer L. Sweetland,	88 years
	26 Charles Spaulding,	11 months
Oct.	16 Matilda Phillips,	16 years
Nov.	24 Female child of Addison Dimock.	
Dec.	9 Infant son of Joseph Robinson,	10 days 5 hours

1842.

Jan.	25 Eliza Roberts,	35 years
Feb.	4 Wife of John Dow,	63 years
	7 Jerome Topliff,	75 years
	16 Almira Sprague,	22 years
Mar.	6 Moses Kilbourne,	65 years
	10 Sarah A. Janes,	15 years
	15 Widow Manning,	89 years
	29 Elizabeth Dimock,	2 years
April	18 Daniel Albro,	57 years
May	20 Wife of Timothy Colman,	76 years
	27 Harry Parker,	53 years
June	1 John H. Austen,	4 years
	12 Jeremiah Ripley,	51 years
	22 Ellen Louisa Dow,	3 years
	28 Mary L. Albro,	22 years
July	3 Newton Robertson,	32 years
Aug.	19 Apollos Fitch,	62 years

1842.

Aug. 28 Clarissa Palmer,	42 years
Sept. 6 Son of Loring Winchester,	2 months
G. E. Eaton,	38 years
Female child of Augustus Clark,	2 weeks
14 Wife of John Clark,	32 years
Nov. 1 Infant son of Elijah Badcock,	14 days 1 hour
Dec. 19 Harriet Woodworth,	10 years

1843.

Mar. 7 John Dresser,	71 years
15 Helen T. Curtis,	26 years
27 Don C. Brigham,	80 years
April 16 Elizabeth Porter,	20 years
May 26 Son of T. Coleman, Jr.,	10 months
28 Thomas F. Booth,	19 years
Aug. 15 William Roberts,	26 years
Sept. 22 Wife of Rev. M. Chapin,	24 years
Nov. 13 Jesse Colman,	66 years
18 Joseph Whitman,	59 years
Dec. 21 Hezekiah Edgerton,	74 years

1844.

Jan. 17 Daniel Brown,	74 years
Feb. 9 Capt. Caleb Matheson,	72 years
April 20 Maria Dow,	39 years
21 Thaddeus Boynton,	67 years
June 20 Asher Wright,	90 years
29 George Robertson,	18 years
July 29 George Dunham,	18 years
Dec. Mrs. Lyman,	24 years
Mrs. Grover.	

Marriages from Records of First Church, Coventry, Conn., from 1763 to 1843.

1763.
Nov. 14 Stephen Tuttle, of Sunderland, and Elizabeth Geer, of Coventry.
    17 Medad Root and Rhoda Curtiss, both of Coventry.
Dec. 29 Denis Maraugh and Mary Sprague, both of Coventry.

1764.
Jan.   Daniel Lyman and Rachael Southworth, of Coventry.
Feb. 2 John Robinson, of Windham, and Eunice Phelps, of Coventry.
Mar. 23 Joseph Larabee and Widow Bill, of Coventry.
May 23 Daniel Cutler, Norwich, and Betty Fitch, of Coventry.
July 11 Samuel Turner, Mansfield, and Mehitable Wentworth, of Coventry.
Oct. 25 Ephraim Colman and Zurviah Curtiss, of Coventry.
Dec. 2 Ephraim Cushman and Sarah Colman, of Coventry.

1765.
Jan. 10 Elijah Janes and Anne Hawkins, of Coventry.
Feb   Habakuk Turner, Jr., and Lydia Rose, of Coventry.
    28 Adonijah Edwards and Mary Searl, of Coventry.
Sept. 7 Samuel Rose and Rebecca Palmer, of Coventry.
Oct. 3 Dr. Josiah Rose and Abigail Rose, of Coventry.
       John Mead and Elizabeth Manley, of Coventry.
    24 Simeon Edwards, of Coventry, and Elizabeth Kinne, of Hartford.
Dec. 20 Eliphalet Edwards and Anna Porter, of Coventry.

1766.
Jan. 28 Abner White and Jerusha Thompson, of Coventry.
Feb. 16 John Badcock and Eunice Janes, of Coventry.
Mar. 27 Humphrey Taylor and Violet Hawkins, of Coventry.

1766.

April 2 Samuel French and Hannah White, of Coventry.
      3 Solomon Lord and Miriam Colman, of Coventry.
May 1 Jonathan Root and Azubuh Brown, of Coventry.
Sept. 4 Ebenezer Kindrick and Anne Davenport, of Coventry.
Oct. 13 Abraham Thurell, of Newbury, and Lydia Boynton, of Coventry.
Nov. 20 Elijah Lyman and Patty Chamberlain, of Coventry.

1767.

Hudson Babcock and Mercy Preston, of Coventry.
Ebenezer Bacon, of Dudley, and Phebe Parker, of Coventry.
July 2 Abraham Collins and Sarah Harris, of Coventry.
Matthew Grover and Lydia Colman, of Coventry.
Sept. 27 or 29 Simon Antizzal and Martha Fuller, of Coventry.
Oct. 8 Humphrey Dow and Tabitha Parker, of Coventry.

1768.

Jan. 10 Elias Palmer and Elizabeth Stow, of Coventry.
     18 Hembry Grover and Abigail Symonds, of Coventry.
Feb. 24 —— Fenton, of Willington, and Anne Carpenter, of Coventry.
April 28 John Arnold and Miriam Root, of Coventry.
May 5 Sylvanus Owen (Hebron) and Eunice Roberts, of Coventry.
July 12 Elisha Searle and Azubah Gates, of Coventry.
Oct. 6 Paul Brigham and Lydia Sawyer, of Coventry.

1769.

Feb. 5 Thomas Brigham and Susanna Eells, of Coventry.
Mar. 26 George Hawkins and Hannah Kingsley, of Coventry.
Aug. 9 Joseph Rose and Desire Dimmick, of Coventry.

1770.

Mar. 15 Adonijah Jones and Sarah Lyman, of Coventry.
June 28 Levi Lyon, of Woodstock, and Ruth Fitch, of Coventry.
Nov. 14 William Robertson and Lucy Edwards, of Coventry.

1771.

Feb. 14 Maltiah Bingham, of Windham, and Mercy Wright, of Coventry.

MARRIAGE RECORDS OF FIRST CHURCH 251

1771.

April 3 Benjamin Grover and Lois Curtiss, of Coventry.
      11 Daniel Turner and Hannah Boynton, of Coventry.
May 22 Ephraim Brown, of Springfield, and Apphia Boynton, of Coventry.
June 13 Jehiel Rose and Mary Ripley, of Coventry.
Nov. 17 Timothy Rose and Elizabeth Pomeroy, of Coventry.
      25 Matthew Deuty and Eunice Boynton, of Coventry.
Dec. 18 Israel Gurley, of Mansfield, and Eunice Dimmick, of Coventry.
      19 John Hale and Sarah Adams, of Coventry.

1772.

Mar. 19 Joseph Cook and Jerusha Turner, of Coventry.
June 18 Ezra Kingsley, of Windham, and Anne Kingsbury, of Coventry.
July 9 Caleb Stanley and Martha Robertson, of Coventry.
Oct. 26 Cæsar and Molly, negroes, of Lebanon.
      28 William Roberts, of Hartford, and Abigail Stanley, of Coventry.
Dec. 2 Elisha Fitch and Rahamah Allen, of Lebanon.

1773.

Feb. 8 Elijah Ripley and Alice Adams, of Coventry.
      18 Daniel Robertson and Triphene Janes, of Coventry.
June 16 —— Dewey (Springfield) and Elisabeth Turner, of Coventry.
July 28 Benjamin Badcock and Julia Judd, of Coventry.
Dec. 30 Dr. Samuel Rose and Elisabeth Hale, of Coventry.

1774.

Jan. 13 Gershom Brigham and Anne Parker, of Coventry.
      26 Joel Hannum (N. Hampton) and Esther Colman, of Coventry.
April 21 John Daggett, Jr. (Lebanon), and Sarah Hawkins 3d, of Coventry.
June 15 John Arnold, Jr., and Hannah Loomis, of Coventry.
Sept. 22 Calvin Manning and Lydia Robertson, of Coventry.
Dec. 6 Rev. Ebenezer Gurley (Gilford) and Mrs. Desire Rose, of Coventry.
      20 —— Clap (N. Hampton) and Mary Strong, of Coventry.

1775.

Jan. 12 —— Dimmick (Mansfield) and Alice Ripley, of Coventry.
Feb. 22 Oliver Janes and Judith Rollo, of Coventry.
May 5 William Boynton and —— Turner, of Coventry.
June 1 Moses Badger and Jerusha Janes, of Coventry.
Aug. 24 Ephraim Dow and Mary Ladd, of Coventry.
Oct. 26 Isaac Robinson and Joanna Colman, of Coventry.

1776.

Mar. 27 Gershom Colman and Abigail Eells, of Coventry.
April 9 Elisha Tracy (Kent) and Dinah Brigham, of Coventry.
June 4 John Eells and Lois Root, of Coventry.
    19 Jabez Ripley and Mary Hawkins, of Coventry.
Sept. 8 Jeremiah Fitch, Jr., and Sibel Dimmick, of Coventry.
Oct. 31 Frary (?) Hale (Glastonbury) and Eunice Atherton, of Coventry.

1777.

Jan. 23 Jephthah Fitch and Ursula Root, of Coventry.
May 29 Abraham Merryfield and Bethia Johnson, of Lebanon.
Sept. 24 Amos Badcock and Mary Williams, of Coventry.
Nov. 25 Asa Colman and Hannah Badcock, of Coventry.
Dec. 11 Nathaniel Root and Elis-Kingsbury, of Coventry.
    31 Jedediah Geer and Phebe Hawkins, of Coventry.

1778.

Jan. 8 William Root and Rebecca Hawkins, of Coventry.
April 29 Josiah Fuller and Triphene Colman, of Coventry.
May 27 Josiah Alcott (Hartford) and Mary Badcock, of Coventry.
Aug. 13 Nathaniel Robinson (Windham) and Phebe Colman, of Coventry.
    23 —— Woodworth (Lebanon) and —— Fuller, of Coventry.
Oct. 5 Adonijah Skinner (Hebron) and Judith Janes, of Coventry.
    22 Samuel Badcock and Hannah Dow, of Coventry.

MARRIAGE RECORDS OF FIRST CHURCH 253

1779.

Feb. 1 John Fitch and Anne Buell, of Coventry.
    25 Stephen Turner (Mansfield) and Lois Dimmick, of Coventry.
Sept. 9 Asa Perkins (Lebanon) and Olivet Manley, of Coventry.
    15 Azariah Skinner (Windsor) and Deborah Cushman, of Coventry.
Nov. 18 Simon Loomis and Patty Buckingham, of Lebanon.
Dec. 30 Samuel Perkins (Lebanon) and Mary Cook, of Coventry.

1780.

Dr. Amos Carpenter (Tydingham) and Hannah Hunt, of Coventry.
Feb. 21 Joseph Kingsbury and Lois Porter, of Coventry.
    27 Mr. Mayhew (Goshen) and Cynthia Reynolds, of Coventry.
Mar. 16 Asa Manley and Eunice Gurley, of Coventry.
April 13 Ebenezer Leach Sweatland and Meribah Badcock, of Coventry.
June 29 Samuel Robertson, Jr., and Mercy Porter, of Coventry.
Oct. 23 Moses Hannum and Jerusha Parker, of Belchertown.
Nov. 2 Lewis Tyrrel (Tolland) and Susanna Simonds, of Windham.
Dec. 20 William Johnson (Tolland) and Mary Rust, of Coventry.

1781.

Jan. 23 Solomon King (Becket) and Elis-Manley, of Coventry.
Feb. 15 Samuel Allin (Lebanon) and Hannah Fuller, of Coventry.
April 19 Davis Williams and Lois Eells, of Coventry.
May 17 Lemuel White and Nancy Brigham, of Coventry.
July 15 Ebenezer Crossman and Mehitable Dow, of Coventry.
Oct. 30 Daniel Murray (Granville) and Elizabeth Rose, of Coventry.

1782.

Jan. Zacheus Downer (Sharon) and Bethiah Brigham, of Coventry.

1782.
Feb. 16 Elisha Sanford and Mary Dorman, of Coventry.
July 18 Jonathan Gennings (Windham) and Mindwell Colman, of Coventry.
Sept. 5 Ebenezer Colman, Jr., and Phebe Carpenter, of Coventry.
Nov. 11 Son of Robert Badcock, to daughter of Elihu Babcock, of Coventry.
27 William Lawrence (Hartford) and Alice Ripley, of Coventry.
Dec. 5 Robert Badcock, Jr., and Hannah Arnold, of Coventry.
15 Elias Judd and Beulah Larrabe, of Coventry.
16 Perez Sprague and Azubah Carpenter, of Coventry.

1783.
Feb. 19 Samuel Rudd (Norwich) and Anne Brigham, of Coventry.
July 2 Asahel House and Sarah Wallbridge, of Coventry.
Oct. 23 —— Johnson (Mansfield) and Abial Harris, of Coventry.
Nov. 18 John Christie and Mabel Rose, of Coventry.

1784.
Jan. 22 Dr. Howard and Anne Hale, of Coventry.
Mar. 24 John Taylor and Elisabeth Rose, of Coventry.
April 22 William Trapp and Susanna Robertson, of Coventry.
28 Diarche Curtis and Hepzibah Fuller, of Coventry.
29 Deacon Strong and Miss Sarah Colman.
May 6 Benjamin Grover and Theodora House.
Oct. 14 John Brown and Elizabeth Dorman, of Coventry.
Nov. 10 Rev. Moses C. Welch and Chloe Evans, of Mansfield.
18 Solomon Robertson and Patty Hawkins, of Coventry.

1785.
Mar. 12 Talcott Camp and Anne Hale, of Glastonbury.
23 Isaac Robertson and Polly Dow, of Coventry.
April 3 Annie Doubleday (N. Lebanon) and Lois Tilden, of Coventry.
20 John Carpenter and Abijah Pingree.
May 10 Philip Turner (Mansfield) and Sibil Geer, of Coventry.

MARRIAGE RECORDS OF FIRST CHURCH 255

1785.

Nov. 17 Roger Fuller (Hebron) and Violet Taylor, of Coventry.
    24 James Welles (Windsor) and Molly Badcock, of Coventry.
    30 Joseph Cook and Mehitable Badcock, of Coventry.
Dec. 1 Nathan Colman and Deborah Turner, of Coventry.
      Ephraim Dow, Jr., and Alice Davenport, of Coventry.
    20 Timothy Colman and Eunice Fuller, of Coventry.

1786.

Jan. 5 Jubal Case and Esther Parker, of Coventry.
Mar. 16 Richard Hale and Polly Wright, of Coventry.
April 25 Elijah Turner (Mansfield) and Ruth Badcock, of Coventry.
May 14 Cephas Brigham and Amelia Robertson, of Coventry.
Sept. 7 Joshua Barrows (Mansfield) and Anne Turner, of Coventry.
Oct. 12 Bildad Curtiss and Hepzibah Dow, of Coventry.
Nov. 2 Joseph Manley and Deborah Green, of Coventry.

1787.

Jan. 18 Manson Dimmick and Anne Robertson, of Coventry.
    29 Samuel Turner and Abigail Rose, of Coventry.
Feb. 4 Abel Hinds, Esq. (N. Milford), and Abigail Rose, of Coventry.
Mar. 15 Benjamin Colman and Sally Dorman, of Coventry.
      Medad Root and Anne Gurley, of Coventry.
May 3 Thomas Abel (Franklin) and Rebecca Hale, of Coventry.
Aug. 20 Richard Davenport, Jr., and Catharine Fuller, of Coventry.
Nov. 8 Samuel Huntington (Tolland) and Sally Howard, of Coventry.
Dec. 10 Warham Edwards and Elizabeth Scripture, of Coventry.

1788.

Mar. 10 Josiah Caswell (Rutland) and Christiana Hawkins, of Coventry.
June 26 Ulysses Dow and Anna Tilden, of Coventry.
Aug. 26 Warren Mark (Pittsfield) and Polly Lord, of Coventry.

COVENTRY RECORDS

1789.

Mar. 15 Amos Turner and Hannah Dorman.
April 23 Luther Woodworth (Lebanon) and Harmony Badcock, of Coventry.
Oct. 15 Godfrey Malbone and Dorcas Edwards, of Coventry.
Nov. 8 John Anthony and Ruth Harris, of Coventry.
    12 Abijah Prince (Glastonbury) and Anne Harris, of Coventry.
Dec. 2 Nathaniel Andrus and Polly Ladd, of Coventry.

1790.

Feb. 8 Alpheus Chapman (Hartford) and Jerusha Carpenter, of Coventry.
Oct. 11 Charles Carpenter and Polly Chapel, of Coventry.
Nov. 18 Nathaniel Cushman (Stafford) and Hannah Parker, of Coventry.

1791.

Feb. 17 Jonathan Gurley (Mansfield) and Abigail Rose, of Coventry.
Mar. 17 Samuel Blackman (Pittsfield) and Jerusha Badcock, of Coventry.
July 7 Zephaniah English (Andover) and Mary Babcock, of Coventry.
Aug. 1 Samuel Badcock and Susanna Badcock, of Coventry.
Oct. 27 Elisha Root and Patty Palmer, of Coventry.
Nov. 17 Medad Root, Jr., and Olive Hawkins, of Coventry.
    24 George Keeny (Ellington) and Lydia Robertson, of Coventry.

1792.

Jan. 26 Job Sherman and Lucy Root, of Coventry.
Mar. 22 William Boynton and Ruth Perkins, of Coventry.
April 1 Benjamin Blackman and Pamela Murdock, of Coventry.
Aug. 12 Ebenezer Baron (N. Marlboro) and Betsey Turner, of Coventry.
Sept. 20 David Hilliard (Ashford) and Eunice Robinson, of Coventry.
Dec. 12 Joshua Edwards, Jr. (Coventry), and Wait Russel, of Springfield.

MARRIAGE RECORDS OF FIRST CHURCH 257

1793.

Jan. 24 Bemsley Edwards (Franconia) and Sally Cushman, of Coventry.
Feb. 11 —— Scovill (Skeensborough) and Anne Kingsbury, of Coventry.
    21 Shubael Whittemore and Eunice Turner, of Coventry.
April 2 James Adams (Tinmouth) and Mercy Turner, of Coventry.
Oct. 27 Abijah S. Curtiss and Huldah Fuller, of Coventry.
Nov. 4 Eleazer Grant, Esq. (N.| Lebanon), and Esther Rose, of Coventry.
    24 Josiah Talcott (Williston) and Abigail Gurley, of Coventry.
Dec. 5 Frederic Palmer and Abial Turner, of Coventry.
    11 —— Hammond (Tolland) and Polly Parker, of Coventry.
    19 William Baxter and Elisabeth Babcock, of Coventry.

1794.

Mar. 6 Timothy Gurley and Mary Mead, of Coventry.
May 8 John Fuller (Stafford) and Amelia Perkins, of Coventry.
July 25 Solomon Janes and Susanna Trapp, of Coventry.
Aug. 17 Charles McLean (Hartford) and Anne Babcock, of Coventry.
Oct. 2 James Thrall (Bolton) and Esther Robinson, of Coventry.
Nov. 27 Joseph Turner and Patty Robertson.
    9 Amasa Jones and Elisabeth Huntington, of Coventry.

1796.

Feb. 4 Timothy Gurley and Eunice Rose.
April 10 Daniel Robertson, Jr., and Amelia Janes.

1797.

Jan. 26 Ebenezer Root Fitch and Sally Dow.
    Jonathan Hutchinson (Hebron) and Temperance Colman, of Coventry.
Aug. 26 Elijah Porter and Jedidah Turner.
Sept. 14 Ebenezer Colman, Jr., and Margaret Fuller.

COVENTRY RECORDS

1797.
Sept. 19 William Lyman and Susan Richardson.
Dec. 7 Phineas Ladd and Anna Grover.

1798.
Jan. 14 Rev. Joseph Warren Crosman (Salisbury) and Lucy Strong.
Mar. 5 William Shaw (Canterbury) and Lydia Davidson (Mansfield).
April 18 Francis Norton (Hebron) and Tabetha Dorman.
    26 John Rose and Desire Gurley.
Nov. 26 Frederick Phelps (Hebron) and Mercy Robertson.
    29 Elijah Dewey and Anna Murdock (Windham).

1799.
Jan. 1 Dr. Samuel White (Andover) and Wealthy Pomroy (N. S.).
    28 Benjamin Lord (Rutland) and Fanny Buell (N. S.).
Mar. 28 Amasa Loomis and Pamela Loomis (N. S.).
April 9 Libbeus Boynton and Betsey Robertson.
Oct. 6 Lieut. Ezra Abbot (Wilton, N. H.) and Rebeckah Hale.
    19 Thomas Turner and Jemima Woodworth, both of Lebanon.
Nov. 27 Joseph Rose and Mille Sweatland, both of N. S.
Dec. 25 Sanford Hunt and Fanny Rose (N. S.).

1800.
Jan. 19 Jeremiah Brown (Long Meadow) and Abigail Deuty, of Coventry.
Feb. 19 Daniel White (Andover) and Eunice Stanley.
Mar. 8 Oliver Kingsley (Lebanon) and Mary Dorman.
    23 Josephus Fitch (Lebanon) Susannah Peters (negroes).
June 3 William Lamphear and Huldah Adams.
Aug. 28 James Thomson (Lebanon) and Hannah Dow, of Coventry.
    31 Dr. Rice (Glastonbury) and Lucia Brigham, of Coventry.
Nov. 27 Clarke Robertson and Vina Babcock.

1801.
Feb. 3 Martin Carpenter and Theodama Boothe.
May 28 James Phillips and Hitty Kidder.

MARRIAGE RECORDS OF FIRST CHURCH

1801.

July 9 Nathan Adams (Canterbury) and Mary Hale, of Coventry.
Aug. 27 William Dowe and Cynthia Eells.
    30 Apollos Fitch and Sybil Edgerton.
Sept. 16 Jeriel Root and Sally Coleman.

1802.

Nov. 7 Don F. Brigham and Lois Palmer.
    18 Gurdon G. Young (Windham) and Polly Robertson.
    25 Nathan Fuller and Hannah Fowler.
Dec. 28 Samuel Guild, Jr. (Lebanon), and Hannah Coleman.

1803.

April 3 Silas Perry (Hebron) and Sally Hamlin, of Coventry.
May 3 William Alworth (Hampton) and Mrs. Sarah Jewett, of Coventry.
June 16 John Mead and Betsey Dow, of Coventry.
Oct. 6 John N. Parker (Mansfield) and Harriot Sanford.
Dec. 4 Eleazer Baldwin (Mansfield) and Harriot Robertson, of Coventry.

1804.

Jan. 1 Leolay Rodgers (E. Hartford) and Rhoda Dimock, of Coventry.
Mar. 6 Asa Lyman, Jr., and Lydia Colman, of Coventry.
    24 Joseph Thomson (Mansfield) and Ruby Rust, of Coventry.
Sept. 18 Selah Brown and Betsey Dunham, of Coventry.
Oct. 17 Asa Colman, Jr., and Betsey Trapp, of Coventry.
Nov. 14 Elijah Ripley and Phebe Richardson, of Coventry.
Dec. 24 Nathaniel Stocking (Colchester) and Camilla Carpenter.

1805.

Jan. 10 David Robertson and Anna Burns, of Coventry.
Feb. 3 Samuel French (Hardwick, Vt.), and Tabitha Dow, of Coventry.
Mar. 28 Daniel Clarke Dow and Melinda Dimmick, of Coventry.
May 19 James Bailey (Glastonbury) and Sarah Puffer, of Coventry.

1806.

Jan. 19 James White and Olive Richardson, of Coventry.
Feb. 16 Elisha Adams (Canterbury) and Clarissa Cook, of Coventry.
April 2 Israel Loomis, Jr., and Lydia Sprague, of Coventry.
May 7 Bela Sprague and Esther Parker, of Coventry.
June 10 Joseph G. Norton and Lucretia Huntington, of Coventry.
    18 Joseph Robertson and Polly Fuller, of Coventry.
Aug. 31 Samuel Swetland and Milly Cook, of Coventry.
Oct. 9 Roderick Dimmick (Mansfield) and Anne Brigham.
Dec. 17 Ephraim Colman, Jr., and Salome Colman, of Coventry.
    18 Elijah Robertson (Coventry) and Lucy Hersey (Mansfield).
    23 Asa Parker, Jr., and Hannah Sprague, of Coventry.

1807.

Mar. 5 Stephen Turner (Mansfield) and Naomi Palmer.
April 20 Elisha Streeter (Guilford N.) and Tacy Allen, of Coventry.
Sept. 24 Harry Dow and Sally Sprague, of Coventry.
Oct. 26 Jeremiah Parrish, Esq., and Lydia Manning.
Nov. 26 Milton Clark and Anna S. Dimock, of Coventry.

1808.

Feb. 17 John Eells, Jr., and Eunice Woodworth, of Coventry.
Mar. 31 Phineas Ladd and Huldah Curtis, of Coventry.
Aug. 15 Godfrey Scarborough, Esq. (Suffield), and Eunice Ripley, of Coventry.
Sept. 18 George R. White and Sally Ripley, of Coventry.
Oct. 9 Asa Keach and Elisabeth Cogswell, of Coventry.
Nov. 24 Spencer Woodworth and Amanda Clarke.

1809.

Jan. 1 Charles Woodworth (Columbia) and Desire Badcock.
Feb. 1 Perkins Sharp (Willington) and Anne Swetland, of Coventry.
    15 Selah French and Polly Miner, of Coventry.
    27 Samuel Colman, Jr., and Sally Robertson, of Coventry.

MARRIAGE RECORDS OF FIRST CHURCH

1809.

April 19 Dr. John Howard and Lucy Ripley, of Coventry.
      24 Chester Fuller and Submit Cook, of Coventry.
May 8 Elias Brewster (Columbia) and Lucretia Edgerton.
Oct. 25 Daniel J. Robertson and Harmony Carpenter, of Coventry.
Nov. 4 Christopher Hyde (Franklin) and Hannah Gilbert, of Coventry.
      30 Asa Woodworth and Sally Boyington, of Coventry.
      30 Marcius Boleam (Mansfield) and Eunice Swetland.

1810.

April 2 Harvey Fuller and Betsey Herrelton, of Coventry.
May 28 Erastus Lincoln (Southington) and Lucy Woodworth.
      31 Nathan Lyman and Asenath Sprague, of Coventry.
Nov. 27 Elias Palmer, Jr., and Hannah Sandford, of Coventry.
      29 Horace Russ (Mansfield) and Lucia Brigham, of Coventry.
      29 Amos Richardson and Sally Strong, of Coventry.

1811.

Jan. 24 George Perkins (Hebron) and Lucinda Dimmick, of Coventry.

1815.

Oct. 26 Hezekiah Edgerton 3d and Polly Codman, of Coventry.

1816.

April 10 Samuel Dow 2d and Eliza H. Albro, of Coventry.
Nov. 8 Martin Lyman and Mary Davenport, of Coventry.

1817.

April 9 Whitman Clark (Mansfield) and Phebe Boynton.
Sept. 10 John Little (Columbia) and Submit Lyman.
Dec. 7 John Dresser and Abby Albro, of Coventry.

1818.

Jan. 2 Stephen Morey and Clarissa Shepherd, of Coventry.
      20 Duthan Kingsbury and Anna Greenleaf.
May 21 Harvey Colman (Southampton) and Paulina Colman.
Nov. 5 Luther Robinson (Windham) and Parmelia Herrick.
      5 Stephen B. Pomroy (Norwich, N. Y.) and Sally Dimmick.

1819.

Sept. 12 —— Avery and —— Hebard, of Coventry.
Jan. 4 Lathrop Richardson and —— Hatch, of N. Coventry.
May 6 Col. James White and Lydia Kingsbury, of Coventry.
July 5 Robert Hale (Plainfield) and Maria Bard, of Coventry.
    19 Cyril Case and Laura Burdwin, of N. Coventry.
Nov. 18 William Colman and Lucia Edgerton, of Coventry.
Dec. 8 Samuel Drake (E. Hartford) and Betsey Curtis.
    14 Humphrey White (Hebron) and Wealthy Malbone, of Coventry.
    30 Josiah Fuller, Jr., and Miranda Lyman, of Coventry.

1820.

April 12 Jesse Colman and Jemima Root, of Coventry.
Oct. 15 Bahman Clark (Elba, N. Y.) and Diadama Babcock.

1821.

Mar. 14 Silas Loomis and Esther Case, of N. Coventry.
    21 Royal Manning and Sally Rose, of Coventry.
July 4 Levi Allen (Mansfield) and Maria Brigham.
Dec. 6 Solomon Colman and Nancy Manning.

1822.

Jan. 9 Charles L. Haley (Groton) and Hannah Avery, of Coventry.
Mar. 28 Chauncey Griggs (Tolland) and Harty Dimmick.
Sept. 16 James Alexander and Tryphena Kinne.
    25 Nathaniel P. Perkins (Mansfield) and Lucia Boynton.
Nov. 3 Samuel Davis and Jemima Thompson, of Coventry.

1823.

Oct. 20 Amasa Barrows (Mansfield) and Wealthy Colman, of Coventry.
Nov. 19 Samuel Walker (Willington) and Livina Swetland.
    27 John Spencer and Jerusha Pease, of Coventry.
Dec. 9 John T. Cummings (Mansfield) and Wealthy Dimmick, of Coventry.
    26 John Thomson and Martha Remington, of Coventry.

1824.

Mar. 3 Oliver French and Jane Doan, of Coventry.
May 4 Rufus Brown and Triphena Fuller, of Coventry.

MARRIAGE RECORDS OF FIRST CHURCH

1824.

June 28 Capt. Chauncey Eells and Mary Janes, of Coventry.
Sept. 16 Solomon H. Bissel and Wealthy F. Learned.
Oct. 14 Ralzamon Belknap (Ellington) and Desiah Dimmick.

1825.

Jan. 27 Harry Curtis and Laura Whittemore, of Coventry.
Feb. 9 Rev. Nathaniel Kingsbury (Mount Vernon, N. H.) and Eunice Dow.
Mar. 2 Lucius Evans (Cazenovia, N. Y.) and Mary L. Leech (Mansfield).
    10 Joseph Dorman and Hannah Dow, of Coventry.
June 9 Brewster P. Swift (Mansfield) and Charlotte Maxwell.
July 14 John D. Norton and Harriet Hosmer, of Coventry.
Aug. 11 Bishop Davenport and Eliza Dimmick.
Sept. 1 Col. John Kingsbury (Tolland) and Mary Brigham, of Coventry.
Oct. 26 Capt. Jonathan Gurley and Mary Dunham (Mansfield).
    31 Ashbel Grover and Cynthia Morgan, of Coventry.
Nov. 7 Francis Lathrop and Clarissa Janes.

1826.

Jan. 19 James D. Hosmer (Windham) and Dolly L. Kingsbury.
    25 Sterling Janes and Huldah Loomis, of Coventry.
April 19 Lucius Newcomb (Columbia) and Mary Mead.
June 22 Patrick F. Whitman (Griswold) and Nancy Ladd.
    25 James P. Foster and Eunice Rose, of Coventry.
Nov. 16 Orasmus Story and Elisa Lyman.
    27 George Boynton and Cynthia Whittemore, of Coventry.

1827.

Jan. 9 Hazzard Tinker and Adar Bump (Mansfield).
Sept. 16 Capt. David Robertson (Coventry) and Almira Starkweather (Mansfield).
Oct. 4 Thomas A. Barrows (Mansfield) and Olive R. White, of Coventry.
    14 John H. Price (Providence, R. I.) and Clarissa Davport.

1828.

Jan. 28 Dr. Lockwood Lyon (Wolcott, N. Y.) and Deborah Colman.
Feb. 10 John Crane (Columbia) and Maria Edgerton, of Coventry.
Aug. 31 Ephraim Parker (Vernon) and Abby Ann Wheeler (Columbia).
Nov. 2 Alpheus Cady (Lebanon) and Emmeline Dickinson (Norwich).

1829.

Feb. 17 Joel Lathrop and Ann M. Parish, of Coventry.
Mar. 23 Jonathan W. Fuller (Mansfield) and Cynthia Austin.
Sept. 18 Darius Manley (Troy, Penn.) and Susan Loomis, of Coventry.
Nov. 30 Charles Huntington (Windham) and Nancy B. Strong, of Coventry.

1830.

Feb. 23 Joseph C. Cone (Manchester) and Mary M. Robertson.
May 4 Thomas Rider (Willington) and Cephonia Dunham, of Coventry.
 12 Capt. Chauncey Eells (New Fane, N. Y.) and Diantha Doan.
 26 Austin Dunham and Martha M. Root, of Coventry.
Sept. 20 Norman Tucker (Suffield) and Mary Lyman, of Coventry.
 20 Deacon Lemuel Barrows (Trenton, N. Y.) and Sally Fitch.
Oct. 12 Samuel Wilson (Coventry) and Almira Dow (Columbia).
Nov. 7 Jedediah L. Booth (Western N. Y.) and Abigail P. Barrows (Mansfield).

1831.

Jan. 25 Capt. Edward G. Huntington and Eliza Clark, of Coventry.
Mar. 2 Goodwin Fuller and Hannah Robertson, of Coventry.
June 27 Benjamin Colegrove (Bristol) and Amanda Smith, of Coventry.

MARRIAGE RECORDS OF FIRST CHURCH   265

1831.

Sept. 10 Henry L. Freeman and Sally M. Smith, of Coventry.
Oct. 11 William Woodworth (Coventry) and Mary Ann Knox (Manchester).
Nov. 6 George Jones (Glastonbury) and Elvira J. Goss.
      6 Eleazer Lockwood (Hebron) and Betsey Goss, of Coventry.
     13 Samuel Payson and Clarissa Weeks, of Coventry.
     19 Washington Barrows (Mansfield) and Sara Ann Root, of Coventry.
     29 John W. Gager (Tolland) and Susan Ann Brigham.

1832.

Feb. 28 William Avery (Windham) and Rhoda E. Avery, of Coventry.
April 1 Larenzo Frizelle and Laura Ladd, of Coventry.
     15 Guy C. Robertson (Bolton) and Julia Ann Lewis, of Coventry.
     26 Col. Samuel West (Columbia) and Lucy Manning, of Coventry.
May 2 John W. Boynton and Eunice Stanley, of Coventry.
     27 Seymour Davenport and Fidelia Grover, of Coventry.
July 4 Chauncey Ripley and Lucretia E. Fitch, of Coventry.
Aug. 8 Hiram Payson and Philina Fuller, of Coventry.
     23 Sherman J. Parker and Fanny P. Dow, of Coventry.
Sept. 12 Jared Cady (Ashford) and Mary Eells, of Coventry.
Oct. 10 Newton Fitch and Jane C. Bidwell, of Coventry.
Nov. 29 John H. Preston (Ashford) and Fanny Manning.

1833.

July 30 William Brace and Elisabeth C. Chatfield, Hartford.
Sept. 24 Jesse W. Hatch and Caroline R. Eells, of Coventry.
Dec. 11 Simeon Woodworth (Mansfield) and Lucy A. Dorman.

1834.

Aug. 20 George C. Weston and Abbe Augusta Flack, of Coventry.
Sept. 14 Harvey Tarbox (Coventry) and Sarah S. Jones (Hebron).
Nov. 6 Lewis A. Dimock and Celinda A. Gardner, of Coventry.

1834.

Dec. 9 Richmond C. Lovett (Tolland) and Eliza R. Brigham, of Coventry.

1835.

June 25 Dr. William H. Rockwell (Hartford) and Mrs. Maria F. Chapin, of Coventry.
Aug. 24 Benoni H. Austin (West Greenwich) and Laura Eells, of Coventry.
Sept. 30 L. Perkins Rose and Ann R. Manning, of Coventry.
Oct. 1 William M. Champin (Montville) and Emily Ripley, of Coventry.
    5 George H. Talcott (Huron, N. Y.) and Lucretia Colman, of Coventry.
Nov. 19 Barnabas Hinkley (Rochester, N. Y.), and Olive Ripley, of Coventry.

1836.

Feb. 20 Adrastus Hall (Coventry) and Lucretia Walton (Willimantic).
Aug. 22 Edwin D. Tucker and Abby J. Eells, of Coventry.
Sept. 1 George G. Gilbert and Augusta Russ, of Coventry.
    11 Allen M. Perkins and Julia A. Robertson, of Coventry.
Oct. 16 Benjamin Sisson and Mary B. Eldridge (Hartford).

1837.

Jan. 1 Jesse Tifft, Jr. (Hartford), and Almira Robinson, of Coventry.
April 10 Albert Newcomb (Tolland) and Eunice S. Brigham, of Coventry.
May 8 Spalding Cutler (Mansfield) and Fanny Albro, of Coventry.
June 22 Samuel A. Wadsworth (Hampton) and Jane E. S. Ormsby.
Nov. 22 Charles Gleason and Hannah Tucker (Pomfret).

1838.

Jan. 1 Albert Earl Swift (E. Windsor) and Saphina Cordelia Marsh, of Coventry.
April 1 Nelson Wilson (Ashford) and Emily Topliff, of Coventry.
May 9 Horatio Billings (Somers) and Mary Ripley, of Coventry.

MARRIAGE RECORDS OF FIRST CHURCH

1838.

May 20 William A. Perkins (Hebron) and Eliza Boynton, of Coventry.
June 18 Simon Mens (New York) and Mary F. Lyman, of Coventry.
Aug. 30 Loring Winchester (S. Mansfield) and Amelia Bidwell, of Coventry.
Sept. 24 Thomas Dunham (Mansfield) and Eunice Morey, of Coventry.
Nov. 20 Leander Storrs (Mansfield) and Mary Abby Edgerton, of Coventry.

1839.

Feb. 5 Timothy Colman, Jr. (Coventry), and Lora Hunt, of Stafford.
Mar. 6 Freeman Rindge (Cortlandville, N. Y.) and Olive R. Barrows, of Coventry.
     27 Leonard G. Dunham and Lucy Baxter, of Mansfield.
May 8 Dr. Timothy Dimock and Miss Laura Farnam Booth, of Coventry.
June 30 Dr. Asa W. Fuller (Warwick, R. I.) and Nancy A. Collins, of Columbia.
Oct. 28 Major Richard H. Rose and Mary A. Dimock, of Coventry.

1840.

Feb. 11 Turner F. Upton and Sophronia Bugbee, of Willimantic.
Mar. 3 Waterman C. Woodworth and Ann A. Packard, of Coventry.
     15 Jesse Woodworth and Almira Whittemore, of Coventry.
April 12 Samuel P. Webster and Mary A. Lewis, of Tolland.
May 3 David M. Buell and Louisa Robertson, of Coventry.
Sept. 15 E. Grant Root and Susan Gardner, of Coventry.
Nov. 25 Edward H. Dow and Henrietta E. Lyman, of Coventry.

1841.

Mar. 16 Reuben Barrows (Norwich) and Lydia Edgerton, of Coventry.
     28 George Tracy and Maria L. Cummings, of Coventry.

1841.

April 20 Barzilla Swift (Mansfield) and Martha Gardner, of Coventry.
Sept. 12 Horace Robertson and Laura Woodworth, of Coventry.
Oct. 11 Orrin W. Gardner (Mansfield) and Clarissa L. Dunham, of Coventry.
Nov. 1 George Gurley (Rockland, N. Y.) and Sophia Dimock, of Coventry.
      30 Stanley White (Andover) and Ann R. Rose, of Coventry.

1842.

Sept. 14 Willard Sprague and Laura Colman, of Coventry.
Oct. 20 Orramel Post and Rachael Watrous, of Coventry.

1843.

Mar. 22 James W. Root and Lucretia Edgerton, of Coventry.
     22 George R. Hurlburt and Lucy Ann Edgerton, of Coventry.
May 17 James Stanley and Almira C. White, of Coventry.
    31 Ralph Crittenden and Susan J. Robertson.
Nov. 30 Daniel B. Simpson and Mary D. Fitch, of Coventry.
Dec. 5 Merrill Humphrey (Norfolk) and Maria C. Mason, of Coventry.

PASTORS OF THE FIRST CHURCH IN COVENTRY ORDAINED.

Oct. 18, 1714,	Joseph Meacham,	to 1752
Jan. 7, 1759,	Oliver Noble,	to 1763
June 29, 1763,	Joseph Huntington, D.D.,	to 1794
Oct. 28, 1795,	Abiel Abbot,	to 1811
Sept. 20, 1815,	Chauncey Booth,	to 1844

Records of Deaths and Baptisms, Second Church, in North Parish, called North Coventry, from 1801 to 1843.

DEATHS.

1801.

2 children, Alexander Abbott.
Benjamin Case.
Benjamin Buell.
Joseph Hunt's child.
Israel Fowler's wife.
Widow Dorcas Hibbard.
Mrs. Badger, wife of Daniel Badger.
Wife of William Burns.

1802.

Peter Brewster,	94 years
Stephen Hunt's child.	
Wife and child of Eleazer Loomis.	
Wife of Josiah Brown.	
Wife of Peter Buell.	
Wife of Mathew Bissel.	
Benjamin Lamb.	
Widow King,	84 years
Charles Marlburn's child.	
Amos Richardson,	74 years
Wife of Medad Loomis.	
Widow Sarah Porter,	91 years
Widow Parker,	90 years
Eleazer Kingsbury's child.	
Elijah Wright,	72 years

1803.

Elisabeth Wheeler,	73 years
Thomas Brown,	71 years

1804.

Widow Wright,	71 years
Elijah Morley's child.	
Norman Barnard's child.	
Widow Paulk's daughter,	24 years
John Ladd,	66 years
Wife of William Wilson,	73 years
Selah Hibbard's child,	9 years
Widow Badger,	82 years

1805.

Widow Priscilla Kingsbury,	84 years
Wife of Nathaniel Dexter,	47 years
Israel Fowler,	69 years
Stephen Chapel,	72 years
Elijah Morley's child,	1 day
Margaret Loomis,	84 years
Sarah Thompson,	64 years
Child of Aaron Green.	
Henry Davis,	7— years

1806.

Widow Sarah Porter,	93 years
Wife of Daniel Loomis,	64 years
Gad Hunt,	56 years
Daniel Badger,	64 years
Joseph Porter,	21 years
Guer (a black woman),	72 years
Benjamin Carpenter,	50 years
Ransfard Smith's child.	
Samuel Burdwin's child,	4 years
Wife of Noah Porter,	36 years
Roswell Prior's child,	6 years

1807.

Nersa Lillie,	16 years
Samuel White,	46 years
Wife of Benjamin Carpenter,	49 years
Joseph Norton's child.	
Selah Brown's child,	2 years
Elijah Hunt's child.	
Widow Submit Cook,	34 years
Elijah Hunt's wife,	24 years

DEATHS FROM SECOND CHURCH RECORDS

1807.

John Ripley,	19 years
Stephen Turner,	61 years
Amos Avery's child,	1 year
Aaron French,	51 years
Elijah Hunt,	24 years
Ira Lillie's child.	
Mary, wife of Enoch Badger.	
John Thompson,	72 years
Sarah Root,	86 years
William Porter's child.	
William Wentworth's son,	4 years
Grandchild of Thomas Davenport.	
Child of Lydia Simons.	
Titus Baker's child.	
Widow House,	80 years
David Loomis.	

1808.

Child of Ariel Loomis,	7 months
Child of Ariel Case,	21 months
Wife of Samuel Ladd,	82 years
Child of Billy Woodward,	17 months
Samuel Long, Jr.,	52 years
Dr. Ebenezer Hunt,	42 years
Widow Elisabeth Woodward,	84 years
Widow Hunt,	82 years
Oliver Pierce,	71 years
Aaron Dart's child,	1 year
Moses Woodward's wife,	59 years
Mr. Kinney's child,	1 year
Leonard White,	20 years
Anna Sweetland,	22 years
Nabby Tarbox,	20 years
Ralph Carpenter's child,	6 years
Mr. Young's child.	
Samuel Loomis's child.	

1809.

Widow Mary Pierce,	72 years

1810.

Ebenezer Turner,	16 years
Guer (man of color),	30 years

1810.

Lydia Tarbox,	24 years
Samuel Long,	83 years
John Taylor,	49 years
Abigail Russell,	21 years
Irene Avery,	17 years
Lovicy Cooke,	23 years
Lydia Avery,	22 years
Erastus Kingsbury,	17 years
Pamela Cooke,	19 years
William Russell's child.	
Anna Lyman,	64 years
Elijah Porter's child,	6 years
Luther King,	33 years

1811.

Eleazer Pomeroy, Esq.,	58 years
Ichabod Jewett,	46 years
Harriet Jewett,	24 years
Irene Rose,	37 years
Isaiah Porter,	71 years
Samuel Porter,	69 years
Aimy Bissell,	46 years
Lois Lillie,	29 years
Widow Lillie,	88 years

1812.

George Bissell's child.	
Ariel Loomis's children,	1 and 3 years
Wife of Mr. Scripture,	36 years
Child of Mr. Scripture.	
Josiah Long,	82 years
Ephraim T. Woodruff's child,	7 weeks
Eleazer Pomeroy's child.	

1813.

Sally Chamberlain,	16 years
Kiman (man of color).	
Infant babe of Capt. Young.	

1814.

Fanny Rose,	13 years
Mary Sweetland,	24 years
Wife of Moses Badger,	67 years
Justus Richardson,	76 years

1815.

Wife of Titus Baker	49 years
Wife of Joseph Kingsbury,	53 years
Widow Jedediah Porter,	57 years
Wife of Shubael Brewster,	48 years
Hannah Baker,	70 years
Wife of Jonathan Porter,	78 years
Dan Loomis,	19 years
George Bissell's child.	
Old Mr. Kinney,	106 years

1816.

Samuel Ladd,	88 years
Wife of Joseph Barnard,	72 years
Child of Calvin Tracy,	8 years
Eleazer Pomeroy's child.	

1817

Luther Loomis's child.

1818.

Wife of Capt. Eliphaz Hunt,	78 years
Widow Esther Lyman,	86—8 years
Mrs. Hatch,	31 years
James I. Jewett,	8 years
Infant child of Eleazer Loomis.	
Rosannah Pomp,	23 years
Ebenezer Porter's child,	7 years
Walter Tilden's child,	3 years
Infant child of C. Edwards.	
Widow Miriam Brewster,	90 years
Infant child of Samuel Baxter.	

1819

Deacon Jonathan Porter,	81 years
Mrs. Esther Bingham,	71 years
Infant child of Amasa Loomis.	
Infant child of Eleazer Loomis.	
Mrs. Meriba Fortune (colored).	
Nathan Dexter,	62 years
Capt. William Wilson,	90 years
Infant child of Nathaniel Root, Jr.	
Mrs. Esther Carpenter,	68 years

1819.

Olive Porter,	22 years
Mrs. Mehitable Huntington,	87 years
Joshua Tilden,	6 years

1820.

Mrs. Sybil Andrus,	90 years
Capt. Eliphaz Hunt,	81 years
Elisha Loomis,	72 years
Infant child of Samuel Baxter.	
Infant child of Demeric (colored).	
Infant child of Daniel Smith.	
Mrs. Lydia Tarbox,	64 years
Lucy Wheeler,	72 years
Infant child of Rev. G. A. Calhoun.	
Eliphilet Carpenter,	73 years
Edwin M. Turner.	
Infant son of Capt. John Turner.	

1821.

Sanford Bissel,	24 years
Infant child of Eleazer Loomis 2d.	
Ebenezer Hamlin,	84 years
I. Clark, of Newburg, New York,	47 years
Lydia Hibbard,	60 years
Infant child of Daniel Root.	
Infant child of Ebenezer Porter.	
Infant child of Capt. Daniel W. Badger.	
Mrs. Anna King,	70 years
Oct. 7, Daniel Root,	28 years
Wife of Capt. Thomas Davenport.	
Mrs. Martha Badger,	36 years
Roswell Prior,	63 years
Mrs. H. Morley,	58 years

1822.

Major S. Case,	58 years
Betsey Wright,	34 years
William Burns,	62 years
Capt. Thomas Davenport,	74 years
Mrs. Submit Porter,	74 years
Mrs. Electa Fenton,	27 years
Infant child of Eleazer Loomis 2d.	

DEATHS FROM SECOND CHURCH RECORDS

1822

Mrs. A. Russell,	75 years
Miss Molly Woodward,	68 years
John Russell,	61 years
Levi Sweetland,	53 years
Roswell King.	

1823.

Infant child of Eli Case.	
Child of Samuel Baxter,	2 years
Mrs. Polly Loomis,	56 years
Matthew Bissell,	93 years
Jacob Brewster,	80 years
Mrs. Deborah Root,	79 years
Mrs. Freelove Kingsbury,	52 years
Samuel Burdwin,	44 years
Infant child of Mr. Topliff.	
Horatio Palmer,	36 years
Aug. 11, Amos Avery,	87 years
Child of Harvey Wright	2 years
Martha C. Kingsbury,	65 years
Infant child of Horatio Avery.	
John Russell,	86 years
Cyrus Brown,	11 years
Ira Lillie,	42 years
Gideon Edwards, Jr.,	18 years

1824.

Mrs. Bridget Torrey,	71 years
Fortune Pomp (colored).	
Olive Frink,	23 years
Mrs. Jerusha Richardson,	62 years
Aurelia Leonard,	21 years
Child of Ebenezer Hamlin,	2 years
Moses Badger,	75 years
Child of Amos Turner,	7 years

1825.

Dan Hatch,	67 years
Infant child of Alonso Loomis.	
Gideon Edwards,	46 years
Richard Jenkinson (a transient person),	42 years
Mrs. Ellis Wheatley,	51 years
Infant child of Jasper Gilbert.	

1826.

Mrs. Abigail Kingsbury,	56 years
Mrs. Roxana Hibbard,	29 years
Miss Lois Crocker,	79 years
Ephraim Kingsbury, Esq.,	86 years
Mrs. Zerviah Woodward,	71 years
Urial Andrus,	31 years
Child of Fenton.	
Deacon Joseph Talcott,	70 years
Infant child of Harvey Wright.	
Widow Fox,	56 years
Infant child of Lemuel Waldo.	
Infant child of Silas Loomis.	
Wife of Samuel Waldo,	36 years
Talcott Flint,	62 years
Gurdeon Jeffers,	28 years
Joseph Barnard,	72 years
Infant child of Israel Loomis.	

1827.

Infant child of Roxanna Edwards.	
Infant child of Alvan Kingsbury.	
Eliakim Jones.	
Infant child of Endotia Burns.	
Mrs. Lucy Frink.	
Billy Wintworth,	62 years
Infant child of Mr. Burton.	
Widow Sarah Fields,	91 years
Daniel Woodward,	34 years

1828.

Mary Edgerton,	2 years
Infant child of Porter (mulatto).	
April, Joseph Kingsbury,	75 years
Widow Phebe Kingsbury,	86 years
Nathaniel Woodward,	76 years
Sherburn King,	35 years
Widow Esther Howard,	78 years
Infant child of Deacon I. Loomis.	
Infant child of Samuel Dunham.	
Henry Waldo,	67 years

DEATHS FROM SECOND CHURCH RECORDS

1828.

Widow Irene Badger,		79 years
Widow Eunice Tilden,		80 years
Benjamin F. Keach.		

1829.

	Henrietta Brigham,		23 years
July	13	Widow Elisabeth Hunt,	82 years
		Simon Aaron (Indian),	37 years
April	15	Azel Goodwin,	59 years
May	29	William Arnold,	45 years
June	8	Silas Loomis,	33 years
July	28	Widow Hannah Waldo,	65 years
	29	Uriel Loomis,	21 years
Aug.	24	Israel Loomis,	50 years
Oct.	31	Deacon Jesse Cook,	69 years

1830.

Feb.	5	Widow Prudence Ladd,	91 years
		Widow Carpenter,	85 years
	22	Nathaniel Palmer,	85 years
Mar.	18	Josiah Brown,	73 years
	23	Infant child of Judge Hall, of Ellington.	
		Widow Abigail Parker,	77 years
May		George A. Stone,	21 years
July	17	William Carpenter,	63 years
	20	Abner Porter,	42 years
Nov.	1	Rebecca Parkis,	58 years
Dec.	25	Eunice Lillie,	74 years

1831.

Jan.	7	Infant child of Ezra Isham.	
	21	Abel Porter,	75 years
		Infant child of Mr. Reynolds.	
Mar.	31	Persis Avery,	68 years
April	21	Lucy Carpenter,	13 years
	26	Lavinia Avery,	43 years
		Infant child of Ezra Isham.	
		Bachus Kingsbury,	24 years
		Ebenezer Porter,	51 years
		Child of Otis Buckminster.	

1832.

Mar. 1	Infant child of L. Brewster.	
	Child of Mr. Flint,	5 years
14	Widow Anne Long,	79 years
June 9	Col. Elisha Edgerton,	78 years
10	Samuel Lillie,	78 years
Nov. 14	Eleazer Pomroy Talcott,	23 years
Dec. 27	Jabez Avery, Jr.,	38 years

1833.

Feb. 10	Widow Caner,	83 years
	Infant child of Mr. Mitchell.	
Mar. 6	Minon Jewell (non resident),	52 years
24	Mrs. Prudence Hamblin,	43 years
June 26	Eli N. Case,	39 years
Sept. 21	Susan A. Tourtellotte,	15 years
Nov. 14	Widow Anne Hunt,	74 years
Dec. 23	Infant child of Mr. Malona.	

1834.

Jan. 25	Mrs. Sarah Loomis,	52 years
Mar. 25	Jenny Courts,	78 years
April 14	Infant child of Luther Abbot.	
May 5	Chester Root,	13 years
June 4	Norman Avery,	45 years
10	Infant child of Mr. Flint.	
Oct. 18	Widow Prudence Flint,	70 years
Dec. 1	E. Evans, of Manchester,	70 years
13	Child of Mr. Flint,	2 years
29	Widow Priscilla Cook,	70 years
	Mrs. Lavinia Avery,	69 years
	Simon Stone.	
31	Lydia Tourtelotte,	32 years

1835.

Jan. 1	Mrs. Candace Root,	71 years
29	Cynthia Turner,	62 years
Feb. 25	Mr. Bronson, of Vernon,	69 years
Mar. 13	Gad Hunt,	62 years
	Infant child of Francis Porter.	
Feb. 6	Infant child of Jeduthan Hubbard.	

DEATHS FROM SECOND CHURCH RECORDS

1835.

Mar. 15	Eleazer Loomis,	58 years
May 1	Ephraim Andrus,	75 years
July 3	David Loomis,	70 years
Oct. 21	Delia Brewster,	85 years
26	Rufus Parsons, of Ellington,	69 years
Nov. 19	Widow Eunice Edgerton,	81 years
	Infant child of Trumball Tracy.	
	Wife of Salmon Loomis.	

1836.

Jan.	Infant child of Miss Maynard.	
Sept. 30	Stephen Hunt,	70 years
	Stephen Morey's child,	2 years
	Two children of Mr. Blanchard.	
	Daniel Courts,	74 years
	Infant child of Mr. James Stone.	

1837.

Jan. 29	Miss Molly Porter,	91 years
	Mr. Jonathan Tarbox,	82 years
Feb.	Ebenezer Tilden,	58 years
Mar. 20	Mary Hamlin,	93 years
29	Noah L. Porter,	21 years
Nov. 27	Mary Augusta Hyde,	5 years
Dec.	Mr. Ballon,	81 years
Dec. 27	Widow Mehitable Styles,	94 years

1838.

Feb. 1	Widow Molly Brown,	64 years
Mar. 17	Widow Triphena Porter,	84 years
April 9	Joshua Frink,	61 years
27	Oliver W. Sweetland,	20 years
	Mrs. Wade.	
July 29	Esther Hibbard,	75 years
Aug. 1	Cornelia Case,	8 years
3	Capt. Joseph Rose,	63 years
Nov. 5	George Bissell,	74 years
10	Catherine Porter,	54 years
Dec. 8	Anna Turner,	90 years
28	John Francis Porter,	2 years

1839.

Jan.	9 Amelia Root,	59 years
	25 Sarah A. Barrows,	25 years
Feb.	28 Elijah Wright,	80 years
June	8 P. F. Whitman,	36 years
Aug.	22 Martha Slayter,	63 years
	30 Child of Mr. Merich,	4 years
Sept.	3 Child of Mr. Justen,	2 years
	18 James C. Eldridge,	11 years
Oct.	14 Lucy Robertson,	36 years
	Infant child of Warren Robertson.	
	Infant child of Lemuel Waldo.	

1840.

Jan.	2 Widow Abigail Dexter,	84 years
	23 Widow Mary Case,	46 years
	27 Child of Erastus Blanchard.	
	27 Mrs. Beallon,	74 years
	30 Amasa Loomis,	67 years
Mar.	18 Widow Phebe Prior,	74 years
Sept.	21 Capt. Nathaniel Root,	83 years
Dec.	25 Col. Noah Porter,	71 years

1841.

Jan.	5 Walter Loomis,	60 years
	26 Capt. Gad Page,	76 years
Feb.	2 Elisabeth Jane Waterman,	5 years
	11 Widow Lydia Loomis,	59 years
	14 Child of Salmon Loomis.	
Mar.	2 Two children of Mr. Baxter.	
	19 Widow Priscilla Pomroy,	85 years
	27 Samuel Cooper,	65 years
April	8 Infant child of Marcus Lillie.	
May	Mary L. Loomis.	
Aug.	20 Dan Loomis,	83 years
	31 Child of Gurdon Porter,	2 years
Sept.	20 Dr. Daniel Avery,	80 years
Oct.	18 Widow Sarah Fuller,	90 years
Dec.	4 Martin Kimpton,	41 years
	Child of Libni Hall.	
	27 Widow Silence Palmer,	83 years

BAPTISMS FROM SECOND CHURCH RECORDS

1842.

Jan.	8 Joseph Grey,	38 years
	11 Widow Ruth Sweetland,	77 years
	12 Infant child of Simon Stone.	
	13 Benjamin Waterman,	42 years
Mar.	23 Infant child of Dorias Higginbotham.	
April	4 Oliver Long,	58 years
	10 Hervey W. Daniels,	25 years
	16 Widow Lois Bissel,	72 years
May	30 Infant child of Marcus Lillie.	
June	5 James Thompson,	78 years
	26 Samuel Dunham,	55 years
Aug.	24 Orrin Stone,	23 years
Sept.	30 Duthan Lillie,	56 years
Dec.	10 Mrs. Grant.	
	18 Neria, wife of Z. Loomis, Jr.,	31 years
	30 Zelstes Porter.	

BAPTISMS.

1819.

Children.	Parents.
Milo Loomis,	Amasa Loomis
Nabby Joanna Tarbox,	Benjamin Tarbox
Martha Lois House.	
Nov. 7, Barbara Leonard.	
Hannah Avery,	Josiah Brown
Daniel Loomis, Jr.,	Daniel Loomis
Simon Gager,	Amos Gager
Martha Ransom,	Cogswell
Rebeccah Parker,	Amos Cogswell
Elisabeth M. Phillips.	
Thankful Pinny,	Lemuel Pinny
Henry H. Corrin.	
Laura Chamberlain,	Widow Achsah Chamberlain
Emily Hatch,	Dan Hatch
Jenny Courts.	

1819.

Children.	Parents.
Lucina Needham,	Frederick Needham
Olive Needham,	Frederick Needham
Edna Needham,	Frederick Needham
Laura W.,	Frederick Needham
Mary Anne Sweetland,	Levi Sweetland, Jr.
Olive W. Sweetland,	Levi Sweetland, Jr.
Daniel Loomis 2d,	Daniel Loomis, Jr.
Juliatta Loomis,	Daniel Loomis, Jr.
Marshal N. Loomis,	Eleazer Loomis
Elmira Leonard,	Abial Leonard
Emmeline Leonard,	Abial Leonard
Sally Root.	
Chauncey Hibbard,	Selah Hibbard
Munroe Hibbard,	Selah Hibbard
Lydia Maria Ransom,	Widow Martha Ransom
Amasa Ransom,	Widow Martha Ransom

1820.

Children.	Parents.
Betsey Keach,	Amos Cogswell
Jerusha Edwards,	Erastus Edwards
Prudence Morley,	Elijah Morley
Anna Lillie.	
Sybil Andrus,	Ephraim Andrus
Asenath Andrus,	Ephraim Andrus
Mary Wilson.	
Endotia Edwards,	Gideon Edwards
Edwin M. Turner,	John Turner
George Barnard,	Norman Barnard
Adaline Turner,	John Turner
Martha Turner,	John Turner
John Hart Turner,	John Turner
Calista Turner,	John Turner
Cynthia Loomis,	Dea Selah Loomis
Lydia Maria Avery,	Duthan Avery
Josiah Brown Avery,	Duthan Avery
Anna Edgerton Avery,	Duthan Avery
Warren Rose.	
Susan Root,	Nathaniel Root, Jr.
Kingsbury Root,	Nathaniel Root, Jr.

BAPTISMS FROM SECOND CHURCH RECORDS

1820.

Children.	Parents.
Cordelia Root,	Nathaniel Root, Jr.
Oliver T. Loomis,	Walter Loomis
Sarah Ann Hunt,	Eliphaz Hunt
Alexander Pomroy,	Eleazer Pomroy
Eleazer Pomroy,	Eleazer Pomroy
George Pomroy,	Eleazer Pomroy
Daniel Pomroy,	Eleazer Pomroy
Henry W. Hutchinson,	Deacon Willard Hutchinson
Dwight Needham,	Frederick Needham
Oliver W. Brown,	Selah Brown
Cornelia P. Tarbox,	Benjamin Tarbox
Emily Root,	Nathaniel Root, Jr.
Chester H. Root,	Daniel Root
Janette Lillie,	Ira Lillie
Julia Ann Parkis,	Lyman Parkis
Ebenezer Kingsbury,	Ward Kingsbury

1821.

Children.	Parents.
Joseph S. Ransom,	Joseph Ransom
Stephen Ransom,	Joseph Ransom
Luther Gager,	Simon Gager
Eliza House.	
Emily Root,	Nathaniel Root, Jr.
Nathaniel Root 2d,	Nathaniel Root, Jr.
Rufus B. Chamberlain,	Widow Achsah Chamberlain
Cornelia Turner,	John Turner
Urial Andrus,	Widow Laura Andrus
Royal G. Andrus,	Widow Laura Andrus
Walter S. W. Andrus,	Widow Laura Andrus
Sophronia Goff,	Esquire Goff
Mary Case.	
Sophia Evans.	
Harriet S. Case,	Eli Case
Calisto A. Case,	Eli Case
Daniel Pomroy,	Eleazer Pomroy
Elisabeth H. Gilbert,	Jasper Gilbert
Levi P. Sweetland,	Levi Sweetland
Henry K. Sweetland,	Levi Sweetland
Harriet E. Sweetland,	Levi Sweetland

1821.

Children.	Parents.
George Wodward,	Daniel Woodward
George W. Calhoun,	G. A. Calhoun
Jabez K. Kingsbury,	Jabez Kingsbury
Lydia E. Hibbard,	Selah Hibbard, Jr.
Edwin P. Chamberlain,	Rufus Chamberlain
Lemuel S. Loomis,	Lemuel Loomis
Charles Loomis,	Lemuel Loomis
Henry Loomis,	Lemuel Loomis
Orin H. Loomis,	Lemuel Loomis
James H. Loomis,	Lemuel Loomis
Nancy M. Loomis,	Lemuel Loomis
Henry Brewster,	Shubael Brewster
Julia A. Brewster,	Shubael Brewster
Mary L. Kingsbury,	Harvey Kingsbury
Elisabeth W. Kingsbury,	Harvey Kingsbury
Catherine Loomis.	
Edwin F. Brewster,	Silas Brewster
Ruth Hibbard,	Selah Hibbard, Jr.
Roxana Hibbard,	Selah Hibbard, Jr.
Augustus Kingsbury,	William Kingsbury
Mary Kingsbury,	Daniel Loomis
Erastus A. Kingsbury,	Augustus Kingsbury
Harriet Kingsbury,	Augustus Kingsbury
Mary Kingsbury,	Augustus Kingsbury
Elizabeth Talcott,	Chester Talcott
Mary Talcott,	Chester Talcott
Mary E. Parker,	Lyman Parker
Charles Parker,	Lyman Parker
Olive Brown,	Selah Brown.
Cyrus Brown,	Selah Brown
Mary C. Brown,	Selah Brown
Julia C. Keach,	Asa Keach
Benjamin F. Keach,	Asa Keach
Jason C. Keach,	Asa Keach
Francis Porter,	William Porter
Eunice Porter,	William Porter
Jonathan C. Porter,	William Porter
Harriet N. Kingsbury,	Jabez Kingsbury

BAPTISMS FROM SECOND CHURCH RECORDS

1821.

Children	Parents.
Mary R. Hutchinson,	Deacon Willard Hutchinson
Gurdon Edgerton, Jr.,	Gurdon Edgerton
Cynthia Edgerton,	Gurdon Edgerton
Francis W. Edgerton,	Gurdon Edgerton
David T. Calhoun,	G. A. Calhoun
Mary H. Loomis.	
Clarissa Chesborough.	
Jane Avery,	Horatio Avery
Francis Avery,	Horatio Avery
Aurelia Talcott,	Erastus Talcott
Edwin Talcott,	Erastus Talcott
Mary A. Case,	Eli Case
Eleazer Loomis 2d,	Daniel Loomis
Charles Kingsbury,	William Kingsbury
Pamela Porter,	Noah Porter
Roxana W. Kingsbury.	Alvan Kingsbury
Cynthia Edgerton,	Noah Porter
Faith Porter,	Noah Porter
Amina W. Porter,	Noah Porter
Noah Porter, Jr.,	Noah Porter
Marshall N. Loomis,	Eleazer Loomis 2d
Philo Porter,	Noah Porter

1829.

Augustus Brewster,	Silas Brewster
Olive Maria Brewster,	Silas Brewster
Emily L. Richardson,	Lathrop Richardson
Fillilia Loomis,	Samuel Loomis

1830.

—— Ransome,	Joseph Ransome
Ruth Francis Hunt,	Dr. Eleazer Hunt
Theodore Gaylord Chamberlain,	Rufus Chamberlain
Olive Porter Edgerton,	Gurdon Edgerton

1831.

Joseph Kingsbury,	Alvan Kingsbury
Harriet A. Gilbert,	Jasper Gilbert

1832.

Mary Dunham.
Electa Prior.

1832.

Children.	Parents.
Harriet Chesborough.	
Trimble Tracy.	
Ephraim C. Thomson.	
Samuel Dunham,	James Dunham
Mary Ann Dunham,	James Dunham
Elisabeth Dunham,	James Dunham
Eliza Dunham,	James Dunham
Lydia Ann Arnold,	Widow Arnold
Stephen Payne.	
Edward Brewster,	Lester Brewster
Harriet Talcott,	Erastus Talcott
Silas Lawrence Loomis,	Widow Esther Loomis
Charles Fayette Loomis,	Widow Esther Loomis
Emma L. Loomis,	Widow Esther Loomis

1833.

Nancy Watson Lincoln,	George Lincoln
Joseph Rose Gilbert,	Jasper Gilbert
Ruth Maria Kingsbury,	Alvan Kingsbury

1834.

Joseph Talcott,	Chester Talcott
Mary Elisabeth Talcott,	Joseph A. Talcott
Eliza Jeduthan Hubbard,	Jeduthan Hubbard

1835.

Eliza Lavinia Kingsbury,	Ephraim Kingsbury
John Newton Underwood,	M. Underwood
Mary A. B. Sweet,	Otis Sweet
Francis A. Case,	Widow Mary Case
Danford N. Case,	Widow Mary Case
Marshall L. Chapin,	——Zena Loomis, Jr.
Eunice S. Hunt,	Clark Hunt
Francis A. Bingham,	Horace Bingham
Mary A. Chapman,	Reuben A. Chapman

1836.

Seley Abbott,	Luther Abbott
Mary F. Chamberlain,	R. B. Chamberlain
Cornelia N. Hubbard,	Jonathan Hubbard
Alba N. P. Loomis,	Albermarle Loomis
John F. Porter,	Francis Porter

1837.

Children.	Parents.
Emma Buell.	
Henry Talcott,	Erastus Talcott
Harriet S. Prior,	Prosper Prior
Cornelia M. Hunt,	Clark Hunt
William P. Loomis,	George Loomis
Francis E. Loomis,	Francis Loomis
Lucius A. French,	Oliver French
Emily C. Gilbert,	Edward Gilbert
Edward C. Gilbert,	Edward Gilbert

1838.

Eunice C. Sweet,	Otis Sweet
George A. Lillie,	Mandus Lillie
Maria Talcott,	Chester Talcott
Molly B. Prior,	Prosper Prior
Oliver Loomis,	George Loomis
Lois Cove Bissell,	George Bissell, Jr.

1839.

July, Albermarle E. P. Loomis,	Albermarle Loomis
Aug., Francis L. Brewster,	Lester Brewster
Ellen L. M. Chamberlain,	R. B. Chamberlain
Sept., William C. Hunt,	William C. Hunt
Mary S. Gould,	Joseph Gould
Martha V. Gould,	Joseph Gould

1840.

July, Jane B. Sweet,	Otis Sweet
Nov., Harriet B. Chapman,	R. Chapman

1841.

Sarah R. Chamberlin,	R. B. Chamberlin
Catharine A. Porter,	Francis Porter
Nov., Anna E. French,	Eleazer French
July, Harriet N. Wells,	Benjamin Wells
John N. Wells,	Benjamin Wells
William A. Wells,	Benjamin Wells

1842.

Aug. 22, Orin Stone,	James Stone
Henry W. Porter,	Francis Porter

1842.

Children.	Parents.
Emmeline F. Hunt,	Lucius Hunt
Lydia M. Peck,	John Peck
Nathaniel H. Loomis,	Albermarle Loomis
Charlotte F. Hunt,	Clark Hunt

1843.

Harriet A. Cutler,	Zenas Loomis, Jr.

INDEX

INDEX

NOTE.—A number thus (3) denotes the separate mentions of the name, calling a General Heading and the repetitions under it One.

ABBEY, 1, 126, 172. Abbot, 1, 126 (2), 167, 208 (3), 258, 268, 278. Abbott, 269, 286. Abel, 157, 255. Acley, 142, 162. Adams, 1, 143 (3), 211, 251. Addams, 152, 158, 257, 258, 259, 260. Albro, 136, 218 (2), 236, 238, 239, 241, 247 (2), 261 (2), 266. Alcott, 203, 252. Aldin, 170. Alexander, 2, 126, 262. Alles, 135. Allin or Allen, 2, 126, 135, 136, 169, 172, 235, 236, 251, 253, 260, 262. Alsworth or Alworth, 241, 259. Ames, 206, 222 (2), 223. Andrews (v. Andrus), 2, 127, 129, 133, 140, 158, 256, 274, 276, 279, 282 (2), 283 (3). Andrus or Andrews, 126. Anthony, 256. Antisel, 3, 126, 172. Antizzal, 220, 250. Antram, 126. Archer, 131, 159. Armstrong, 3, 127, 211, 212, 213. Arnold, 3, 167, 172, 217, 250, 251, 254, 277, 286. Aspenwall, 138. Atherton, 3, 126, 252. Austen, 126, 141, 247. Austin, 238, 242, 245 (2), 247, 264, 266. Avery or Avary, 3, 126, 127, 143, 156, 214, 262 (2), 265 (2), 271, 272 (2), 275 (2), 277 (2), 278 (3), 280, 282 (3), 285 (2).

BACON, 4, 232, 234, 242, 250. Babcock or Badcock, 4 sq., 127 (2), 134 (2), 135 (2), 144, 150 (2), 155 (2), 158, 159, 161, 163, 165, 167, 172, 173, 200, 201, 202 (2), 203, 209 (2), 217, 220 (2), 221 (3), 222, 224 (2), 225 (2), 226 (2), 227, 229, 230 (3), 231 (2), 232 (2), 233, 234, 235, 236, 237, 239, 240, 241 (2), 242 (3), 243, 246 (4), 247, 248, 249, 250, 251, 252 (4), 254 (3), 255 (3), 256 (5), 257 (2), 258, 260, 262. Badger, 8, 128, 133, 134, 155, 173, 252, 269, 270 (2), 271, 272, 274 (2), 275, 277. Bailey, 154, 259. Baker, 245, 271, 273 (2). Balcomb, 210 (2). Baldwin, 8, 128, 129, 136, 140, 173. Ballon, 279. Balum, 128. Banks, 160. Bard, 262. Barker, 9, 128, 143, 173. Barnabee, 156. Barnard, 9, 128, 142, 149, 174, 270, 273, 276, 282. Baron, 256. Barrows, 127, 128, 216, 217, 255, 262, 263, 264 (2), 265, 267 (2), 280. Barstow, 9. Basset, 219. Baxter, 139, 257, 267, 273, 274, 275, 280. Beallon, 280. Belding, 10, 136. Belknap, 10, 129, 215, 218, 263. Benit or Bennit, 10, 129. Bentley, 174. Benton, 10, 129, 149, 170, 171. Bestor (Bester), 10, 129. Bidwell, 140, 155, 170, 214, 244, 265, 267. Bill, 10, 129, 249. Billings, 129, 266. Bingham, 129, 131, 132, 171, 240, 250, 273, 286. Birge, 129. BIRTHS, 1. Bishop, 133, 135, 136, 165. Bissel, Bissell, 11, 129, 134, 140 (3), 146, 173, 263, 269, 272 (2), 273, 274, 275, 279, 281, 287. Blackman, 11, 130, 158, 174, 239, 256 (2). Blanchard, 279, 280. Blish, 130. Bliss, 165. Bliven, 217, 245. Boleam, 261. Bols or Bowles, 12,

291

130. Booth, Boothe, 11, 130, 137, 174, 202, 211 (2), 212, 213 (2), 215 (2), 216 (2), 225, 238, 247, 248, 258, 264, 267, 268. Boyington, 261. Boynton, 12, 130, 137, 140, 151, 155, 156 (2), 167, 174, 200, 201 (2), 202, 203, 204 (2), 210, 211, 213 (2), 216 (2), 217, 223 (2), 224, 226, 229, 231 (3), 232, 234, 235, 236 (2), 238, 242, 244, 248, 250, 251 (3), 252, 256, 258, 261, 262, 263, 265, 267. Brace, 130, 217, 265. Brale, 214. Breed, 13. Brenson, 126. Brewster, 152 (v. Bruster), 261, 269, 273 (2), 275, 278, 279, 284 (3), 285 (2), 286, 287. Briant, 13, 130. Bridgham, 153. Bridgman, 13, 131, 167, 174, 220. Brigham, 14, 126, 128, 131, 132, 141, 149, 152, 153, 154, 175, 200, 207, 211, 213 (2), 214 (2), 215 (2), 219, 222 (2), 223, 225, 231, 233 (3), 236 (2), 247, 248, 250 (2), 251, 252, 253, 254, 255, 258, 259, 260, 261, 262, 263, 265, 266 (2), 277. Bristor, 151. Brockway, 207. Bronson, 278. Brown, 15, 127, 129, 130, 131, 135 (2), 137 (2), 138, 140, 143, 144, 148, 152, 153, 160, 162, 163, 164, 169, 175, 202, 205, 211 (3), 212, 213, 225 (2), 232, 235, 236 (2), 237, 243, 246 (2), 248, 250, 251, 254, 258, 259, 262, 269 (2), 270, 275, 277, 279, 281, 283, 284 (3). Brunson, 131, 133, 154. Bruster, 133, 164. Buckingham, 253. Buckminster, 277. Buell, 17, 132, 145, 175, 176, 207, 219, 221 (2), 223, 225, 226 (2), 231, 253, 258, 267, 269 (2), 287. Bugbee, 168, 267. Bump, 166, 263. Burdwin, 166, 262, 270, 275. Burnap, 18, 132, 133, 163. Burns, 132, 204, 226 (2), 240, 259, 269, 274, 276. Burt, 127. Burton, 18, 276. Bushnell, 156, 244. Butler, 166. Byington, 234.

CADY or Cadey, 19, 132, 264, 265. Calhoun, 274, 284, 285. Camp, 254. Caner, 277. Card, 237. Carpenter, 19, 130, 132 (2), 133 (2), 135, 137, 142, 147, 148, 157, 160, 166, 176, 201 (2), 202, 211, 214, 220, 222 (2), 223 (2), 224, 225, 228 (3), 233 (2), 236, 239, 240, 241 (2), 242, 243, 245, 246, 250, 253, 254 (3), 256 (2), 258, 259, 261, 270 (2), 271, 273, 274, 277 (3). Cary, 23. Case, 131, 152 (2), 176, 255, 262, 269, 271, 274, 275, 278, 279, 280, 283 (3), 285, 286 (2). Caswell, 255. Chaffee, 133. Chamberlain, 24, 133, 250, 272, 281, 283, 285, 286, 287. Chamberlin, 130, 134, 287. Champin, 266. Champlin, 133. Chapin, 131, 133, 142, 155, 160, 248, 266. Chapman, 163, 286, 287. Chapel, 24. Chappel, Chappell, 133, 134, 218, 233, 243, 244, 256, 270. Charter, 134. Chatfield, 130, 152 (2), 265. Chatman, 134. Chauncey, 263. Cheney, 241. Chesboro, 134, 285. Christie, Christy, 233, 234, 235, 241, 254. Chubbusch, 157. Church, 24, 131. Clap, 251. Clark, 24, 134, 146, 153, 163, 171, 177, 211 (3), 212 (3), 213, 214, 215 (2), 217, 235, 237, 238 (2), 246 (2), 248 (2), 260, 261, 262, 264, 274. Clarke, 260. Clason, 25. Coan, 156. Codman, 261. Cogeshall or Cogshall, 134, 220. Coggeshall, 25. Coggins, 246. Cogswell, 26, 134, 148, 150, 153, 240, 260, 281 (2), 282. Colbourn, 160. Cole, 134. Cole or Cowles, 26. Colegrove, Colgrove, 134, 264. Collins, 27, 250, 267. Colman, Coleman, 27, 128, 135, 136, 139, 142, 152, 153, 156, 165 (3), 169, 177, 200, 201 (3), 202 (2), 203 (2), 205 (3), 206 (2), 207 (4), 208 (6), 209 (2), 210, 212 (2), 213, 215, 216, 220 (2), 222 (3), 223 (2), 225 (3), 226, 227 (3), 228 (2), 229 (2), 230 (2), 231 (2), 232, 234, 235, 237 (4), 238 (3), 239 (2), 240 (2), 241, 242,

INDEX 293

245, 246 (2), 247, 248 (2), 249 (2), 250 (2), 251, 252 (5), 254 (3), 255 (3), 257 (2), 259 (4), 260 (3), 261 (2), 262 (4), 266, 267, 268. Cooly or Cooley, 151, 177. Cone, 135, 241, 264. Cook, Cooke, Coock, 29, 135, 152, 157, 162, 202, 203, 204 (2), 207 (2), 224, 228, 229 (2), 230, 233, 237, 251, 253, 255, 260, 261, 270, 272 (2), 277, 278. Cooper, 280. Coos, 141. Corrin, 281. Courts, 278, 279, 281. Crandall, 30, 135, 237. Crane, 30, 136 (2), 177, 264. Crocker, 30, 136, 159, 166, 177, 178, 276. Crosby, 31, 146. Cowls, 135, 178. Crittenden, 268. Crosman, 258. Cross, 31, 136. Crossman, 31, 136, 167, 202, 203, 204 (2), 205, 219, 229 (2), 240, 242, 246, 253. Cummings, 136, 167, 214, 246, 262, 267. Cummins or Comins, 31. Curtis or Curtice, 32, 33, 133, 135, 136, 159, 160 (2), 178, 208 (3), 209 (2), 214 (2), 215, 216, 226, 231 (2), 232, 233, 235, 236, 237 (2), 239, 242 (2), 246, 248, 254, 260, 262, 263. Curtiss, 207 (2), 218, 220 (2), 222 (4), 223 (2), 225 (2), 228, 229, 249, 251, 255, 257. Cushman, 32, 136, 164, 178, 179, 200, 201, 202, 204, 219, 222 (2), 223 (2), 228, 249, 256, 257. Cutter, 32, 136, 179, 249, 266.

DAGGETT or Doggett, 33. Daggett, 33, 137, 149, 179, 214, 251. Damman or Damon or Daman, 34, 136, 137, 179. Danes or Deans, 137. Daniels, 137, 281. Darbey, 34. Dart, 271. Daues, 130. Davenport, 34, 137, 147, 149, 150, 158, 210, 211 (2), 215, 216, 218, 220, 227, 228, 230, 231, 232, 233 (2), 239 (2), 243, 250, 255 (2), 261, 263 (2), 265, 274 (2). Daves or Davis, 35, 154, 179, 262, 270. Davidson, 258. Deans or Danes, 35, 179 (v. Deans). Dean, 131, 227 (v. Danes or Deans). DEATHS, 172. Delano, 35, 137. Deman (?) 135. Denton, 158. Dewey, 36, 165, 208, 230, 251, 258. Dexter, 36, 137, 146, 270, 273, 280. Dickinson, 132, 137, 264. Dike, 217. Dimick, 37, 129, 136, 143, 234. Dimmick or Dimick, Dimmock or Dimock, 36, 136, 137 (2), 161, 180, 213 (4), 215 (4), 216 (2), 219, 224, 227, 229, 230, 232, 233, 242 (2), 243 (2), 251, 252 (2), 253, 255, 260, 261 (2), 262 (2), 263 (2), 265, 267 (2), 268. Dimoch or Dimock or Dimmick, 37, 137, 139, 142, 144, 147, 170, 217, 218, 231, 234, 246 (2), 247 (2), 259 (2). Doan, 37, 139, 140, 213, 214, 240, 246, 262, 264. Dodge, 128, 141, 157 (2), 166 (2). Doggitt, 142. Dolbear, 138. Dorman, 38, 138, 167, 171, 180, 200, 201, 202, 204, 209 (3), 210 (2), 212, 215, 216, 217 (2), 224, 229, 233, 235, 237 (2), 238 (2), 241, 244, 254 (2), 255, 256, 258 (2), 263, 265. Doubleday, 254. Dow or Dowe, 38, 40, 134, 136, 138 (3), 146, 149, 156, 170 (2), 180, 200 (2), 201 (2), 202 (2), 205 (2), 207, 208, 209 (3), 210 (3), 211, 212 (7), 213 (3), 214, 215, 218, 219, 220, 221, 223 (2), 227 (4), 228, 229, 230, 231, 232 (2), 233, 234 (2), 235 (3), 236 (2), 237 (3), 239, 241, 242, 244, 245, 247 (2), 248, 250, 252 (2), 253, 255 (3), 257, 258, 259 (4), 260, 261, 263 (2), 264, 265, 267. Downer, 253. Dresser, 211, 216, 232, 236, 247, 248, 261. Dummer, 138. Dunham, 130, 138, 141, 158, 163, 209 (2), 213, 214, 215, 217, 231 (2), 242, 244, 247, 248, 249, 263, 264 (2), 267 (2), 268, 276, 281, 285, 286 (4). Duty or Deuty, 36, 137, 180, 200, 209 (2), 231, 232, 237, 239, 240, 251, 258. Dyke, 216.

EANSWORTH, 40. Eaton, 248.
Edgerton, 40, 129, 139, 210, 237, 248, 259, 261 (2), 262, 264, 267 (2), 268 (2), 276, 278, 279, 285 (4). Edwards, 41, 132, 135, 139, 150, 153, 154, 162 (2), 164 (2), 168, 180, 203 (2), 219, 220, 221, 222, 226 (2), 228, 231, 234, 236, 238, 242, 246, 249 (3), 250, 255, 256 (2), 273, 275 (2), 276, 282 (2). Eells, 43, 126, 131, 132, 139, 144, 160, 167, 201, 206, 207, 211, 212, 223 (3), 225, 229, 230, 232, 233, 239, 242, 244, 250, 252 (2), 253, 259, 260, 264, 265 (2), 266 (2). Egerton, Edgerton, 40, 140, 164, 170, 209, 213, 235, 236, 240 (2). Eldridge, 163, 266, 280. Ellington, 277. Ellis, 181. English, 131, 156. Ensworth, 127, 129, 130, 168, 170. Euerdon, 181. Euetts (?), 152. Evans, 138, 254, 257, 263, 278, 283. Everton, 220. Ewiss or Euiss, 181.

FARNAM, 130. Feald, 155. Fellows, 170. Fenton, 250, 274, 276. Field, 152, 160 (2), 204, 205, 206, 229 (2). Fields, 128, 276. Fish, 236. Fisk, 203. Fitch, 43, 128, 137, 139, 140, 145, 155, 156, 159, 161, 181, 200, 202, 203 (2), 204 (2), 205 (2), 206, 207, 208, 210 (3), 212, 213, 214 (2), 217, 224, 225, 227, 229 (2), 230 (5), 232 (2), 233, 237, 238 (2), 239, 241 (2), 243, 246, 247 (2), 249, 250, 251, 252 (2), 253, 257, 259, 264, 265 (2), 268. Flack, 265. Flint, 45, 142, 157, 181, 276, 278 (4). Follet, 233. Fosler, 263. Fowler, 45, 128, 141, 160, 168, 182, 259, 269, 270. Fox, 131, 276. Freedom (?), 128. Freeman, 46, 140, 182, 218 (2), 222, 265. French, 46, 137, 139, 151, 170 (2), 182, 214, 219, 243, 250, 259, 260, 262, 271, 287 (2). Frink, 140, 275, 276, 279. Frizelle, 140, 244, 265. Fuller, 47, 126, 131, 136, 141, 156 (2), 164, 182, 205 (2), 206, 207 (2), 208 (2), 220 (3), 230, 239, 243 (2), 250, 252 (2), 253, 254, 255 (3), 257 (3), 259, 260, 261, 262 (2), 264 (2), 265, 267, 280. Funker, 141.

GAGER, 48, 141, 265, 281, 283. Galpin, 137. Gardner, 138, 141, 160, 165, 214, 216, 238, 240, 241, 265, 267, 268. Gary, 131, 225. Gates, 127, 162, 250. Geer, 48, 141, 206, 226, 249, 252, 254. Gennings, 254. Gera, 151. Giffords, 139. Gilbert, 49, 141 (2), 211, 214, 261, 266, 275, 283, 285, 286, 287 (2). Gillit, 49, 141. Glason, 162. Gleason, 141, 266. Godfrey, 142, 215, 217, 241. Goff, 144, 162, 283. Gone (?), 132. Goodridge, 49. Goodwin, 49, 142, 211, 277. Goss, 148, 265 (2). Gould, 287 (2). Gove, 159, 218, 225. Grandy, 49. Granger, 168. Grant, 132, 156, 158, 233, 238, 241, 257, 281. Graves, 142. Gray, 142. Green, 50, 153, 241, 255, 270. Grey, 281. Greenleaf, 131, 201, 228, 230, 231, 261. Griggs, 142, 163, 262. Griswold, 50, 142, 182. Grover, 50, 126, 137 (2), 138, 140, 142 (2), 143 (2), 182, 183, 203, 205, 209, 213, 217, 218, 219, 220, 221, 222 (2), 226, 227, 228, 231, 232, 233, 235, 237, 238, 240, 243, 244, 246, 248, 250 (2), 251, 258, 263, 265. Guild, 234, 242, 246, 259. Gurley, 53, 133, 143, 228 (2), 229, 230, 251, 253, 255, 256, 257 (3), 258, 263, 268.

HABART, 53. Hale, 53, 143 (2), 146, 161, 184, 201, 202, 203 (2), 204, 205, 206, 211, 219 (2), 223, 225, 226, 228 (2), 229, 232 (3), 238, 239, 251 (2), 252, 254 (2), 255 (2), 258, 259, 262. Haley, 143, 262. Halkins, 160 (v. Hawkins). Hall, 54, 143, 240, 243, 266, 280. Hamblin, 278. Hamilton, 151. Hamlin, 54, 144, 259, 274, 275, 279. Hammond or Hammon, 54, 144, 160, 169, 171, 201, 257. Hanks, 216. Hannum, 252, 253. Hanover, 144. Harris, 55, 139, 143, 144, 215, 218, 250, 254, 256 (2). Hatch, 55, 131, 144 (2), 161 (2), 184, 262, 265, 273, 275, 281. Hawkins or Halkins or Holckins, 55, 138 (2), 144, 147, 160, 184, 200, 201, 202, 203, 204, 219, 220, 221 (3), 222, 224 (2), 226, 249 (2), 250, 251, 252, 254, 255, 256. Hearich, 134, 158. Hearick, 56, 144. Heath, 57, 144. Hebard, 262. Hendee or Hende, 57, 145, 148, 185. Hendey, 58. Herreton, 261. Herrick, 185, 230, 232, 234, 237, 239, 242 (2), 261. Hersey, 260. Hewitt, 145. Hibbard or Hibberd, 58, 61, 129, 145, 152, 167, 185, 269, 270, 274, 276, 279, 282 (2), 284 (3). Higginbotham, 281. Hilliard, 256. Hills, 126. Hiltham, 148. Hinds, 255. Hinsdale, 160. Hindsel, 159, 160. Hinkley, 145, 266. Hinston, 127. Hitchcock, 147. Hockings or Holckins or Hockins, 58, 161. Holbrook, 145, 237. Holcomb, 138. Hollister, 132, 145. Holman, 145. Holmes, 145. Hoskings, 157. Hosmer, 145, 155, 213, 263. Holt, 207, 244. House, 58, 130, 143, 146, 147, 185, 205, 206, 207, 228, 229, 243, 254, 271, 281, 283. Howard, 59, 144, 146, 185, 204 (2), 205 (2), 206, 207, 208 (3), 212, 228, 230, 232, 233, 235, 245 (2), 254, 255, 261, 276. Hoxie, 150, 162. Hubbard, 59, 146, 278, 286 (2). Huett, 228. Humphrey, 268. Hunt, 59, 134, 135, 142, 146, 147, 154, 157, 170, 186, 253, 258, 267, 269 (2), 270 (3), 271 (3), 273, 274, 277, 278 (2), 279, 283, 285, 286, 287 (2), 288 (2). Huntington, 60, 146, 200, 201, 202, 203, 204, 206, 207, 212 (2), 214, 216, 217, 220, 223, 224, 228, 229 (4), 233 (2), 236, 238, 241 (2), 246, 247, 255, 257, 260, 264 (2), 268, 274. Hurlburt, 268. Hutchinson, 61, 135 (2), 147, 153, 186, 206 (2), 229, 236, 257, 283, 284. Hutherson, 156. Hyde, 147, 261, 279.

INDIANS, 170, 225, 277. Ingraham, 131, 162. Irish, 147. Isham, 61, 186, 213, 239, 277 (2).

JACSON, Jackson, 61, 145. James, 147. Janes, 61, 128, 136, 139, 144, 147, 151, 159, 186, 208, 215 (2), 216 (2), 217 (2), 218, 219, 220 (2), 221 (2), 222, 223, 224, 227 (2), 228 (2), 229 (2), 230, 231 (2), 233 (2), 241 (2), 242, 243 (2), 245 (2), 247, 249 (2), 251, 252 (3), 257 (2), 263 (3). Jeffers, 276. Jeffray, 171. Jenkinson, 275. Jewell, 245, 278. Jewett, 63, 147, 259, 272 (2), 273. Johnson, 63, 252, 253, 254. Jones, Johnes, 63, 129, 145, 147, 148, 151, 157, 166, 186, 207, 208 (3), 209 (3), 210 (2), 230, 233, 242, 250, 257, 265 (2), 276. Judd, 65, 148, 187, 203, 219, 220 (2), 227, 231, 234, 235, 240, 244 (3), 251, 254. Justen, 280.

KAUGHLEY, 148. Keach, 66, 148, 187, 260, 277, 284 (3). Keeny, 148, 256. Kellogg, 149. Kendal, 66. Kendrick, 66. Kenne, 217. Kenney, 163. Kidder, 67, 149, 258. Kilbourne, 247. Killain, 166. Killeen, 132, 150. Kimpton, 71, 134, 143, 150, 280. Kindrick, 187, 218, 250. King, 67, 149, 157, 238, 253, 269, 272, 274, 275, 276. Kingsbury, 67, 128, 132, 144, 145, 147, 149 (5), 155, 156, 157 (3), 160, 161, 165, 187, 209, 216 (2), 217, 230 (2), 235, 237, 238, 239, 245, 247 (3), 251, 252, 253, 257, 262, 263 (3), 269, 270, 272, 273, 275 (2), 276 (5), 277, 283,

284 (7), 285 (3), 286 (3). Kingsley, 250, 251, 258. Kinne or Keeney, 71, 126, 245, 249, 262. Kinney, 128, 271, 273. Knap, 150. Knight, 127, 150. Knox, 171, 265.

LAD or Ladd, 71, 126, 132, 133, 138, 140, 150 (2), 151, 157, 169, 188, 200, 219, 223, 224 (2), 233 (3), 234, 252, 256, 258, 260, 263, 265, 270, 271, 273, 277. Lamb, 73, 131, 150, 155, 188, 269. Lamphear, 73, 128, 150, 151, 188, 258. Lanflear, 213. Larrabe, Larabe, Larrabee, 73, 142, 147, 150, 151, 188, 218, 219, 221, 223, 224, 249, 254. Lathrop, 74, 131, 151, 159, 189, 245 (2), 263, 264. Laus (?), 135. Lawrence, 74, 254. Lea, 189. Leach, 165, 189. Learned, 129, 263. Lee, 74, 151, 160. Leech, 189, 263. Leonard, 75, 275, 280, 282 (2). Lewes or Luis, Lewis, 75, 159, 265, 267. Lilly or Lilley or Lillie, 75, 150, 151, 152, 270, 271, 272 (2), 275, 277, 278, 280, 281, 282, 283, 287. Lincoln, 234, 241, 261, 286. Little, 261. Lockwood, 151, 265. London, 151. Long, 75, 127, 133, 148 (2), 151, 153, 161, 165, 189, 271, 272 (2), 278, 281. Loomes or Loomis, 77, 126, 127 (2), 129, 134, 144, 145 (2), 146, 147, 148 (3), 149, 152, 153 (2), 154 (2), 155, 158 (3), 161, 165 (2), 166, 171, 189, 211, 212, 214, 215, 216, 217, 218, 235, 236, 237, 238, 242, 243, 245 (2), 246, 251, 253, 258 (2), 260, 262, 263, 264, 269 (2), 270 (2), 271 (2), 272, 273 (5), 274 (3), 275, 276 (4), 277 (3), 278, 279 (3), 280 (6), 281, (3), 282 (3), 283, 284 (8), 285 (3), 286 (5), 287 (4), 288 (2). Lord, 79, 152, 215, 216, 219, 244, 250, 255, 258. Lorge (?), 151. Lovett, 152, 266. Lucas, 152. Lyman or Liman, 79, 132, 136, 138, 141, 147, 148 (2), 153, 154, 158, 164, 167, 168, 169, 189, 206 (2), 208 (2), 209 (4), 210 (2), 213, 216 (2), 217, 220, 235, 237, 239, 248, 249, 250 (2), 258, 259, 261 (3), 262, 263, 264, 267 (2), 272, 273. Lyon, 153, 244, 250, 264.

MAINARD, 137. Malbone, 80, 153, 190, 256, 262. Malona, 278. Malone, 240. Man, Mann, 141, 153. Manly or Manley, 81, 142, 153, 154, 200, 202, 203 (2), 204 (2), 205 (2), 206, 214 (2), 219, 221, 224, 226, 227 (2), 229, 230, 231, 249, 253 (3), 255. Manning, 81, 135, 153, 158, 161, 169, 202, 203 (2), 204, 205, 206, 209, 211, 215 (2), 217, 234, 235, 239, 245, 247, 251, 260, 262 (2), 264, 265 (2), 266. Mansfield, 164. 249, 262 (3). Maraugh (v. Meraugh), 82, 132, 165, 218, 219 (2), 225, 249. Mark, 255. Marlburn, 269. MARRIAGES, 126. Marsh, 82, 153, 155, 159, 161, 165, 266. Marshall, 168. Mason, 153, 214, 217 (2), 240, 243, 246, 268. Matheson, 248. Mathewson, 129 (2), 136, 140, 151, 153, 166, 169, 171. Maxwell, 154, 165, 213, 263. May, 151, 152. Mayhew, 253. Maynard, 279. McDowell, 240. McKee, 165. McLean, 171, 257. Meacham, Meachem, Meecham, Mecham, 82, 135, 161, 165, 190, 227, 268. Mead, 82, 154 (2), 161, 190, 222 (3), 229, 232, 239, 243 (2), 244, 249, 257, 259, 263. Mens, 154, 267. Meraugh (v. Maraugh), 127, 139, 155, 190. Merich, 280. Merrill, 164. Merryfield, 252. Metcalf, 152, 154, 167. Millenton, Millinton, 83, 138, 141, 145, 190. Miller, 83, 142, 154. Milton, 207. Miner, 260. Minor, 83. Mitchell, 145, 157, 278. Moody, 164. More, 154, 213. Morey, 83, 139, 164, 232, 234, 235, 240, 246 (2), 261, 267, 279. Morgan, 83, 154, 217 (3), 218, 242, 246, 263. Morley — (2), 274, 282.

INDEX

Morse, 146. Mudge, 245. Murch, 190. Murdock, 83, 148, 154, 190, 256, 258. Murphy, 216 (2), 244. Murray, 235, 253.

NEEDHAM, 211, 282 (4), 283. Neely, 154. Neff, 137, 240, 243. Negroes, 170, 224 (3), 225, 226, 227, 228, 230, 235, 238, 244, 251, 258, 270, 271, 272, 273, 274, 275, 276. Newcomb, 154, 263, 266. Nichols, Nicholls, 83, 154. Noble, 84, 154, 268. Norris, 153. North, 190. North Coventry, 269. Northrop, 155. Norton, 155, 209, 258, 260, 263, 270.

OAKS, 223. O'Brien, 170. Ormsby, 84, 168, 266. Owen, 250.

PACKARD, 267. Page, 84, 155, 168, 190, 280. Pallon, 170. Palmer or Pallmer, 85, 132, 133, 138, 152, 154, 155, 162, 167, 170, 191, 201 (3), 202, 203 (4), 204 (2), 207, 211, 222 (4), 224, 228, 229, 230, 231, 237, 238, 239, 245, 247, 249, 250, 256, 257, 259, 260, 261, 275, 277. Parker, 86, 133 (2), 138, 140, 150, 152, 154, 160, 161 (2), 163, 164, 169, 171 (2), 191, 206, 221, 222, 224 (2), 225, 227, 230, 231 (2), 235 (2), 239, 241 (2), 243 (2), 245, 247 (2), 250 (2), 251, 253, 255, 256, 257, 259, 260, 264, 265, 269, 277, 281, 284 (2). Parkis, 277, 283. Parrish, Parish, 151, 216, 260, 264. Parsons, 279. Partee, 287. Patten, 139. Paulk, 270. Payn or Payne, 88, 156, 286. Payson, 156, 265 (2). Pease, 163, 262. Peck, 89, 156 (2), 244, 288. Peckham, 218. Pelham, 223, 224. Perkins, 89, 156, 161, 202, 240, 253 (2), 256, 257, 261, 262, 266, 267. Perry, 146, 156, 259. Pers, 165. Petty or Pity, 90. Phelps, 89, 146, 149, 156, 159,

191, 249, 258. Phillips, 89, 157, 238, 240, 247, 258 (2), 281. Pierce, 219, 220, 271 (2). Pik, 89. Pingey, 191. Pingree, 254. Pingrey, 89, 157. Pinny, 281. Pomeroy, 272 (2), 273. Pomroy, 90, 146, 157, 191, 251, 258, 261, 280, 283 (5). Pool, 90, 157. Porter, 91, 133, 135, 139 (2), 141, 142, 146, 149 (2), 151, 152, 153, 157, 158, 168, 192, 200, 201, 226 (2), 227, 228, 229, 237, 240, 243, 248, 249, 253 (2), 257, 271, 273 (3), 277 (3), 285 (5), 286, 287. Post, 214, 244, 245 (2), 269, 270 (3), 272 (3), 273, 274 (3), 278, 279 (5), 280 (2), 281, 284 (3). Potwine, 192. Powell, 93. Preston, 93, 127, 158, 227, 232, 250, 265. Price, 93, 158, 191, 263. Prince, 256. Prior, 158, 270, 274, 280, 285, 287. Puffer, 259.

RANSOM, 282 (2), 283 (2), 285. Ranson, 133. Redington, 150. Reed, 94, 158. Remington, 166, 262. Renalls, 94, 193. Reynolds, 207, 253, 277. Rice, 258. Richards, 158. Richardson or Ritchardson, 94, 95, 131, 147 (2), 150, 157, 159, 165, 171, 193, 202, 211, 212, 213 (2), 214 (2), 215 (2), 216, 235, 236 (2), 258, 259, 260, 261, 262, 269, 272, 275, 285. Rider, 158, 264. Riley, 152. Rindge, 227, 267. Ripley, 96, 129, 133, 145, 146, 158, 159, 193, 201, 203, 204, 205 (2), 206, 207, 211, 213 (2), 219 (2), 221, 222, 225, 230, 231, 234, 235, 238, 244, 247, 251 (2), 252 (2), 254, 259, 260 (2), 261, 265, 266 (3), 271. Roberson or Robenson, 193. Robert, Roberts, 210 (2), 212, 242, 245, 246, 247, 248, 250, 251. Robertson, Roberson, 97, 132, 135, 141, 147, 148, 153, 156, 159, 160 (2), 163 (3), 193, 202, 203, 205, 206 (3), 219, 220 (2), 221 (5), 224, 225 (3), 226, 227, 228 (2), 229, 230, 231 (2), 233

298

INDEX

(3), 234, 236 (4), 238, 239, 240 (3), 242 (2), 243, 244, 245, 246, 247, 248, 250, 251 (3), 253, 254 (3), 255 (2), 256, 257 (2), 258 (3), 259 (3), 260 (3), 261, 263, 264 (2), 265, 266, 267, 268 (2), 280 (2). Robinson, Robenson or Robison, 96, 166, 193, 200, 201, 203, 204, 205, 208, 212, 224, 225, 226, 235, 237, 240, 241, 244 (3), 247, 249, 252 (2), 256, 257, 261, 266. Rockwell, 98, 160, 193, 266. Rodgers, Rogers, 140, 259. Rollo, 147, 252. Root, 98, 128, 135, 136, 137, 139 (3), 140, 146, 160, 194, 200 (3), 201 (4), 202 (4), 203 (2), 204 (2), 206 (3), 208, 210, 217, 219 (3), 220 (3), 221 (3), 222 (2), 223 (4), 224 (2), 225 (3), 226 (2), 228, 229, 235 (2), 236, 238, 239, 243, 247, 249, 250 (2), 252 (4), 255, 256 (3), 259, 262, 264, 265, 267, 268, 271, 273, 274 (2), 275, 278 (2), 282 (3), 283 (4). Rose, 102, 138, 139, 140, 141 (2), 144, 152, 153, 160, 161 (3), 166, 167, 169, 194, 200, 201 (4), 202, 203 (2), 204, 205 (3), 206 (2), 208, 209 (2), 210 (3), 216, 217, 218 (2), 221 (4), 224 (3), 225, 226 (3), 227 (2), 228 (2), 230, 232 (5), 233 (2), 235, 238, 239, 240, 241, 242, 243, 245, 246, 249 (4), 250, 251 (4), 253, 254 (2), 255 (2), 256, 257 (2), 258 (3), 262, 263, 266, 267, 268, 272 (2), 279, 282. Roswell, 161, 246. Rowler, 103. Rudd, 237, 254. Russ, 141, 261, 266. Russell, 195, 242, 256, 272 (2), 275 (3). Rust, 103, 144 (2), 149 (2), 150, 159, 161, 162, 166, 168, 170, 195, 200 (2), 221 (2), 222, 223, 232, 236, 241, 253, 259.

Sabins, 162, 196. Sage, 162. Safford, 132. Sanford, 211, 230, 231, 237, 240, 241, 243, 254, 259, 261. Sargent, 196. Sarl, Sarls, 134, 139, 162, 196. Sarle or Searle, 105. Sarels, 131. Sawyer, 130 (2), 131,
147, 157, 250. Scarborough, 260. Scholts, 162. Scot, 221. Scott, 106, 141, 162, 163. Scovill, 257. Scribner, 106, 149. Scripture, 106, 162, 196, 255, 272 (2). Seagrave, 107. Searl or Sarl or Searle, 196, 219, 249, 250. Schaffer, 142. Sergeant, 221. Seilheimer, 241. Shailler, 142. Sharp, 260. Shaw, 107, 140, 162, 258. Sheffield, 146. Shepard, Sheperd, Shepherd, 107, 150, 162, 196, 200, 201, 244, 246, 261. Sherman, 256. Shipman, 144. Sillamer, 241. Simon, Simonds, Simons, 107, 132, 196, 235, 236, 245, 253, 271. Simpson, 163, 243, 268. Sims, 150. Sisson, 163, 266. Skinner, 108, 155, 157, 163, 196, 225, 239, 252. Slack, 134, 169. Slater, Slatter, 162. Slayter, 280. Slocum, 236. Smith, 108, 133, 134, 140, 163, 196, 242, 264, 265, 270, 274. Snow, 246. Southward, 109. Southworth, 249. Spaffard, 240. Spalding, 247. Spencer, Spensor, 150, 163, 262. Spicer, 163. Sprague, 109, 154, 163, 164, 167, 196, 207, 236, 239 (2), 241 (2), 245 (2), 246, 247, 249, 254, 260 (4), 268. Stack, 109. Standly, 126. Stanley, 109, 130, 164, 197, 220, 223, 227, 229, 238 (2), 251 (2), 258, 265, 268. Star, 110, 164. Starkweather, 159, 164, 240, 263. Stebbins, 141, 147, 164. Stedman, 110, 134, 164, 235. Stiles, 110, 146, 159. Stocking, 259. Stone, 169, 277, 278, 279, 281 (2), 287. Story, 164, 263. Storrs, 164, 267. Stow, 155, 250. Stowell, 164. Streeter, 260. Strong, 110, 127 (2), 139, 143, 146, 147, 155 (2), 161, 164 (2), 165 (2), 197, 200, 201, 202, 203, 205, 216 (2), 218, 219, 220, 221, 222, 223, 225 (2), 226, 228, 234, 238, 245, 251, 254, 258, 261, 264. Styles, 279. Suthworth, 144. Sweatland, 198, 208. Sweet, 286.

INDEX 299

287 (2). Sweetland, Swetland, 113, 129, 145, 147, 152, 159, 161, 163, 165, 168, 230, 245, 247, 253, 258, 260 (2), 261, 262, 271, 272, 275, 279, 281, 282 (2), 283 (3). Swift, 165, 263, 266, 268. Symonds, 250.

TALCOTT, 113, 135, 161, 163, 165, 198, 218, 257, 266, 276, 278, 284 (2), 285 (2), 286 (3), 287 (2). Tarbox, 128, 166, 265, 271, 272, 274, 279, 281, 283. Taylor, 166, 198, 200, 201, 204, 205, 218, 219, 224, 225, 249, 254, 255, 272. Terrill, 115, 148, 166 (2), 198. Terry, 151. Thankful, 223. Thayer, 115, 166. Thomas, 142, 239. Thompson or Thomson, 115, 133, 134, 139, 142, 143, 147, 159, 166, 169, 198, 233, 234, 249, 258, 259, 262 (2), 270, 271, 281. Thrall, 257. Throop, 159. Thurell, 250. Tickner or Ticknor, 148, 169, 245. Tiffany, 116. Tifft, 166, 266. Tilden, 116, 130, 131, 138, 145, 150, 166, 169, 198, 227, 255, 273, 274, 277, 279. Tinchnee, 243. Tinker, 166, 263. Topliff, 153, 166, 170, 214, 231, 240, 241, 242 (2), 243, 244, 247, 266, 275. Torrey, 275. Tourtelotte. 278 (2). Townsend, 116, 167, 198. Tracy, 165, 167, 252, 267, 273, 279, 285. Trapp, 116, 138, 147, 153, 167, 198, 204 (2), 245, 257, 259. Trowbridge, 117, 167. Tryon, 167. Tucker, 141, 167, 241, 244, 264, 266 (2). Tupper, 117. Turner, 117, 127, 131, 132, 153, 157, 167, 198, 200, 204 (2), 205, 206, 207 (2), 219 (2), 220, 221 (2), 222, 223, 224 (3), 226 (4), 227, 228, 230 (2), 231, 232 (3), 234, 235, 237, 240, 249, 251 (3), 252, 254, 255 (4), 256 (2), 257 (5), 258, 260, 271 (2), 274 (2), 275, 278, 279, 282 (5), 283. Tyler, 118. Tyrrel, 253.

ULTEY, 144. Underwood, 286. Upham, 130. Upton, 168, 267. Usher, 155. Utley, 118, 162, 238.

VAN BUREN, 163. Vibbert, 168. Vinton, 168, 242. Vorra, 118, 168, 199. Vorry, 236.

WADE, 279. Wadsworth, 118, 168, 266. Waldo, 118, 168, 233, 234, 276 (3), 277, 280. Walker. 168, 262. Wallbridge, 119, 154, 168, 254. Waldo, 233, 234. Walton, 143, 266. Ward, 199. Warner, 160. Warren, 246, 247 (2). Washburn, 119. Waterman, 168, 280, 281. Waters, 119, 159 (2), 168. Watrous, 217, 268. Webster, 119, 148, 151, 199, 223. Weld, 128. Wells, 132, 255, 287. Weller, 120. Wentworth, 150, 199, 218, 232, 249, 271. West, 120, 137, 164, 169, 265. Welch, 254. Weston, 120, 169, 265. Whaley, 120, 164. Wheatley, 275. Wheeler, 169, 264, 269, 274. Wheet, 137. Wheldin, 120, 169. White, 120, 128, 148, 149, 161, 169, 209, 210, 211, 212 (3), 213 (2), 214 (3), 215 (2), 216, 219, 222, 223, 227 (4), 229, 231, 234 (2), 239, 242 (2), 244 (3), 245, 249, 250, 253, 258 (2), 260 (2), 262 (2), 263, 268 (2), 270, 271. Whiting, 169. Whitman, 169, 244, 248, 263 (2), 280. Whittemore, Whitmore, 121, 130, 139, 161, 171, 214, 244, 245, 257, 263, 267. Williams, 121, 127, 147, 168, 169, 212, 237, 238, 252, 253. Willips, 243. Willow, 139. Willson, or Wilson, 121, 170, 199, 264, 266, 270, 273, 282. Winchester, 122, 170, 216, 218, 248, 267. Wintworth, 122, 170, 226, 276. Wise, 123. Wittemore, 136. Wood, 123, 170. Woodruff, 170, 240, 272. Woodward, Wooduard, 123, 127 (3), 146, 148, 149, 150, 153, 167, 170, 199, 207, 244, 271 (3), 275, 276 (3), 284. Woodworth, 124, 159, 171, 202 (2), 206, 207 (2), 211 (2), 212 (2), 215, 216, 228, 231, 235, 236, 239, 241, 244, 246, 248, 252, 256, 258, 260 (3), 261 (2), 265, 267 (2), 268. Woolcott, 124, 170. Wordsworth, 135. Wordworth, 204, 205 (2) (v. Woodworth). Worry, 228. Wright, 124, 131, 132, 137, 142, 143, 149, 152, 167, 171, 199, 230, 234, 238, 239 (2), 248, 250, 255, 269, 270, 274, 276, 280. Writer, 131.

YEOMANS, 171. Yongs, 156. Yound, 133. Young, 171, 259, 271.

SUPPLEMENTARY INDEX

ADDITIONAL AND CORRECTED REFERENCES

Arnold, 127.
Badcock or Babcock, 253.
Baldwin, 259.
Bissell, for 173 read 174.
Booth, for 137 read 138.
Bruster, 133, 164.
Buell, for 219 read 220.
Caner, for 277 read 278.
Case, for 176 read 177.
Chamberlain, 236, 284.
Chapman, 256.
Clark, 237.
Colman, 264.
Cook, 226.
Cowls, for 178 read 177.
Crane, for 177 read 178.
For Cutter read Cutler.
Dimock or Dimmick, 138, 250.
Dorman, 219.
Dow, 243 (3), 254.
Drake, 262.
Dunham, for 138 read 139. Add 259.
Edgerton, 129, 136, 240 (2).
Edwards, 257.
Eells, 263.
English, for 136 read 137. Add 256.
Fitch, 258.
Flint, for 157 read 158.
Foster, 140.
Fowler, 140.
French, 140, 171.
Gilbert, erase 214.
Grant, for 156 read 157.
Grover, for 233 read 234. Add 254.
Guild, 259.
Hall, 277.
Hazelton, 206.
Hearick, 261.
Hitchcock, for 147 read 148.
Jones, 152, 163.

Keeney, 163.
Kingsbury, 244, 261.
Loomis, 168.
Lyman, for 233 read 234.
Manley, 264.
Morgan, 143.
Morley, add 270 (?).
Palmer, 280.
Erase Partee.
Phillips, 243.
Pomp, 273.
Porter, 269, 270, 272 (3), 274 (3), 278, 279 (5), 280 (2), 281, 284 (3).
Post, erase 269, 270 (3), 272 (3), 273, 274 (3), 278, 279 (5), 280 (2), 281, 284 (3).
Price, for 191 read 192.
Richardson, 234.
Root, 280.
Rose, 234.
Erase Schaffer.
Simon, 143.
Skinner, 253.
Sprague, for 196 read 197. Add 261.
Strong, for 147 read 148. Erase 203.
Talcott, 114, 285.
Tilden, 254.
Erase Tinchnee.
Trapp, 254.
Turner, for 198 read 199. Add 253.
Tuttle, 249.
Utley, 118.
Webster, 267.
Weeks, 156, 265.
Welch, 131.
For Willips, line 5, page 243, read Phillips.
Woolcott, for 170 read 171.
Wright, for 137 read 138. Add 275.
Young, 272.

www.ingramcontent.com/pod-product-compliance
Lightning Source LLC
Chambersburg PA
CBHW032051220426
43664CB00008B/948